About Island Press

Island Press, a non-profit organization, publishes, markets, and distributes the most advanced thinking on the conservation of our natural resources—books about soil, land, water, wildlife, and hazardous and toxic wastes. These books are practical tools used by public officials, business and industry leaders, natural resource managers, and concerned citizens working to solve both local and global resource problems.

Founded in 1978, Island Press reorganized in 1984 to meet the increasing demand for substantive books on all resource-related issues. Island Press publishes and distributes under its own imprint and offers these services to other non-profit organizations.

Support for Island Press is provided by Apple Computers, Inc., Mary Reynolds Babcock Foundation, Geraldine R. Dodge Foundation, The Charles Engelhard Foundation, The Ford Foundation, Glen Eagles Foundation, The George Gund Foundation, William and Flora Hewlett Foundation, The Joyce Foundation, The John D. and Catherine T. MacArthur Foundation, The Andrew W. Mellon Foundation, The Joyce Mertz-Gilmore Foundation, The New-Land Foundation, The J. N. Pew, Jr. Charitable Trust, Alida Rockefeller, The Rockefeller Brothers Fund, The Florence and John Schumann Foundation, The Tides Foundation, and individual donors.

About the Institute for Local Self-Reliance

The Institute for Local Self-Reliance (ILSR) is a non-profit research and educational organization, providing technical information and assistance to city and state governments, citizen and neighborhood organizations, and industry.

Since 1974, ILSR has been fostering self-reliant communities by investigating examples of closed-loop manufacturing, materials policy, materials recovery, energy efficiency, and small-scale production. It teaches cities to consider solid waste and the by-products of any one process as the feedstock for another. The Institute stresses a formula that stimulates local employment, provides skills training, and adds to the local tax base.

ILSR presents a vision of self-reliant cities and provides the hard numbers to bring that vision into reality. By providing the tools and information to solve problems in ways that are both economically sound and environmentally sustainable, ILSR seeks to support an active citizenry, which is the foundation of a strong democracy.

Beyond 40 Percent: Record-Setting Recycling and Composting Programs is part of an ongoing series of technical reports prepared by ILSR staff. For more information on ILSR philosophy and practice, write:

Institute for Local Self-Reliance
2425 18th Street, NW
Washington, D.C. 20009
Phone (202) 232-4108
Fax (202) 332-0463

Beyond 40 Percent

Record-Setting Recycling and Composting Programs

Beyond 40 Percent

Record–Setting Recycling and Composting Programs

**Brenda Platt, Christine Doherty,
Anne Claire Broughton, and David Morris**

With Introduction by Neil N. Seldman

INSTITUTE FOR LOCAL SELF-RELIANCE

ISLAND PRESS

Washington, D.C. □ Covelo, California

Library of Congress Cataloging-in-Publication Data

Beyond 40 percent: record-setting recycling and composting programs
    by Brenda Platt ... [et al.].
            p. cm.
        "August 1990."
        Includes index.
        ISBN 1-55963-073-6
        1. Recycling (Waste, etc.) — United States — Case studies.
2. Compost plants — United States — Case Studies. I. Platt, Brenda.
II. Title: Beyond forty percent.
TD794.5.B48 1991
636.72'82'0973 —dc20   90-19181
                                                                              CIP

Printed on recycled, acid-free paper

Manufactured in the United States of America
10 9 8 7 6 5 4 3 2 1

Contents

Case Studies

Index

List of Tables

List of Charts

Abbreviations

ARC	—	Association of Retarded Children
BB	—	buy-back
BSSI	—	Babylon Source Separation, Inc.
BFI	—	Browning Ferris Industries
BY	—	backyard
CCRF	—	Camden County Recycling Facility
C&D	—	Construction and Demolition
CMCMUA	—	Cape May County Municipal Utilities Authority
CS	—	curbside
cu. yd.	—	cubic yard
DANC	—	Development Authority of the North County
DEP	—	Department of Environmental Protection
DO	—	drop-off
DPW	—	Department of Public Works
EAP	—	Environmental Allowance Program
ERC	—	Empire Returns Corporation
fax	—	facsimile
HDPE	—	high density polyethylene
ILSR	—	Institute for Local Self-Reliance
IPC	—	intermediate processing center
lb.	—	pound
LDPE	—	low density polyethylene
MSW	—	municipal solid waste
NA	—	not available
O&M	—	operating and maintenance
ORCA	—	Original Recycling Cooperative Association
PCBs	—	polychlorinated biphenyls
PET	—	polyethylene terephthalate
Priv.	—	private
Pub.	—	public
PVC	—	polyvinyl chloride
RDF	—	Recycling and Disposal Facility
REI	—	Recycling Enterprises Inc.
RFP	—	request for proposal
SWM	—	solid waste management
TPD	—	tons per day
Twp.	—	Township
Vac.	—	vacuum
WPAR	—	West Patterson Automobile Recyclers
WUTC	—	Washington Utility Transportation Commission

Acknowledgments

This report from the Institute for Local Self-Reliance was made possible by the patience, diligent data-gathering, and hard work of many individuals.

We made dozens of phone calls to state and local recycling coordinators, solid waste professionals, recyclers, and local decision-makers in order to identify communities recovering the highest levels of their solid waste through source-separation recycling and composting programs. The assistance of these individuals was invaluable in getting this project off the ground. Approximately 80 surveys were sent to key contact people in those communities reporting the highest materials recovery levels. We extend our thanks to all who took the time to complete and return the surveys, and who had the patience to bear with us during follow-up inquiries, of which there were many. Without their participation and cooperation, this report would not have been possible.

Although most information for the report came from municipal recycling coordinators and Superintendents of Public Works, we also made calls to local landfills, private refuse haulers, county and state solid waste officials, and local political leaders to fill in our knowledge about various communities' recycling and composting programs. We are grateful to these contacts for their helpful information.

In addition to the contacts listed in the case studies included in this report, people in the following communities provided information on their materials recovery programs: Marin County, California; Longmont, Colorado; East Lyme, Connecticut; Holly, Michigan; Fillmore County, La Crescent, Rice County, and St. Cloud, Minnesota; Monett, Missouri; Logan Township, Mt. Olive, Montclair, North Brunswick, Pine Valley, and Piscataway, New Jersey; Islip and Kingston, New York; Lane County, Oregon; Bellevue, King County, Renton, and Spokane, Washington; and Monroe and Prairie du Sac, Wisconsin. We hope to include them in the next report in our series chronicling the development of materials recovery in this country.

We owe many thanks to the staff at the Institute for Local Self-Reliance. In particular, we benefited from the hard work of Steve DeBroux, Michael Gessner, Ingrid Komar, Renee Nida, Neil Seldman, and Jan Simpson.

We would like to extend special recognition to Deb von Roeder, a volunteer at ILSR, for her significant contribution to this report. Her diligent work addressing miscellaneous questions and issues, modifying text and tables, and reviewing the final report is greatly appreciated.

We thank Jodean Marks, our copy editor, for her meticulous reading of this book. Her intelligent queries and demand for clarity have made this book more accessible to the reader.

In researching and writing *Beyond 40 Percent: Record-Setting Recycling and Composting Programs*, we have had the support of many people. Special thanks go to Daniel DeMocker for his continuing encouragement and care in so many ways.

Finally, we would like to thank numerous individual donors and the following foundations for their ongoing support: The Educational Foundation of America, The Moriah Fund, The C.S. Mott Foundation, The Jessie Smith Noyes Foundation, The Public Welfare Foundation, The Rockefeller Family Fund, The Town Creek Foundation, and The Veatch Program of the North Shore Unitarian Universalist Society. We extend special thanks to the Prudential Foundation for supporting our research with a grant to document the best recycling and composting programs in New Jersey.

How to Use This Study

This book addresses the question of how to achieve very high levels of materials recovery through the collection of source-separated materials. Other ILSR publications present information on initiatives to reduce waste at the source, mechanical processing of mixed waste to recover non-source-separated materials, and how to plan for maximum recovery.[1] ILSR's report *Salvaging the Future: Waste-Based Production* (1989) addresses the important parallel issue of the potential for scrap markets.

The raw information gathered by ILSR can be found in the **Case Studies**, pages 73-260. The **Tables** extract the most important information from these studies and present it in a comparative format. (See pages 67-70 for data definitions and the methodology used for making comparisons.) The **Charts** extract information from the Tables (and from the case studies only occasionally) and present it visually, to provide a basis for drawing some tentative conclusions. Each level of extraction distills the data into more easily accessible and readable form, but also makes the resulting conclusions more suspect. We urge the reader to jump back and forth between charts, tables, and case studies.

The case studies provide comprehensive in-depth information about each community. By and large, case study data are provided to us by recycling coordinators and other local officials, who may have estimated the data or relied on other sources, such as private haulers. Berlin Township, for instance, measures waste disposed in cubic yards since there are no weighing scales at the local landfill. The Township uses the State conversion factor to calculate approximate tonnage disposed. In other cases, ILSR staff have estimated tonnage recovered. For Hamburg, which does not keep records of the amount of yard waste composted, we have converted volume amounts based on truckloads into tons. For five communities located in states with beverage container deposit legislation, we have estimated the tonnage recovered through this legislation and have included it under waste generated and materials recovered.

In brief: The case studies give a context for each program, and the nuts and bolts of program operations. The tables provide comparative data, and the charts visually present information to help us form some tentative conclusions.

We don't want the reader to lose the forest for the trees. Therefore the **Observations** section highlights what we believe to be our most important findings. But we also don't want to lose the trees for the forest. The charts and our interpretation of them should be seen simply as entryways to the more in-depth material contained in the tables and especially in the case studies.

---

[1] These publications include *Indiana's Alternatives to Solid Waste Disposal* (1990), *Taking Recycling Seriously: A Primer for Atlantic County, New Jersey* (1989), and *Directory of Waste Utilization Technologies in Europe and the United States* (1989).

The tables list all 17 communities by recovery rate. Those that have recovered the highest percentage of their waste are listed first. (See Table 2.) Many of the charts present data on a smaller sample — those communities which are relevant to the subject matter of the chart and for which the relevant data are available.

This book documents, not a sample, but rather the vast majority of all communities that have achieved high levels of materials recovery. Yet so many program elements (e.g., mandatory versus voluntary, curbside versus drop-off collection, number of materials targeted) vary significantly across communities that any conclusions made in this report should be considered informed judgments only. For example, mandatory programs tend to have higher participation and recovery rates than voluntary ones. However, voluntary programs that incorporate economic incentives have also achieved high participation and recovery rates. Containers provided to households for storage and set-out of recyclable materials can increase participation and materials recovery levels. Yet an inappropriately sized container could actually burden the collection program. In the south section of Seattle, residents receive a 60- or 90-gallon container in which they can commingle all their recyclable materials (mixed paper, glass, metals). Provision of a 5-gallon container might have limited the amount of materials collected.

Introduction

Before the turn of the century, the nature of local and regional economies made recycling and composting relatively easy. Milk bottles were returned locally to be washed and refilled. Organic food and plant wastes were used on nearby gardens or farms. Quilts, rags, and even paper were created from discarded textiles. The old economy had elements of a two-way system, a closed loop.

In the late twentieth century, economic trends undermined this cycle and created a one-way material flow from producer to consumer, ending up at the garbage dump. Consumption has soared. Reusing materials has become much more difficult. The producer is separated, sometimes by thousands of miles, from the ultimate consumer. Products are much more complex. Product packaging that once consisted only of paper may now include a combination of plastics, paper, and even metal. Plastic packages often combine several different resins. Disposable products have become the norm. Even products traditionally considered durable, like cameras and staplers, are now disposable.

In the 1980s, spurred by citizen action against old leaking landfills, new landfills, and profligate waste, the pendulum began to swing back. An unprecedented rise in the cost of waste disposal followed. Communities and businesses turned to the two major alternatives to landfilling: incineration and materials recovery (recycling and composting).

The History of Solid Waste Management in the United States

It is amazing to recall that in 1970, the word "recycling" was not in standard American dictionaries. Today, materials recovery is the law of the land. Materials recovery plans are required in every state of the union. The U.S. Environmental Protection Agency (EPA), in November 1989, reissued its New Source Performance Standards that require a minimum 25 percent materials recovery rate in order to obtain a permit to build a waste incineration facility (grass-roots recyclers argued for significantly higher levels). Currently, the EPA is developing similar guidelines for landfill permitting. For the very first time in federal policy, prevention is the official solid waste policy of the United States. The odyssey of materials recovery in U.S. history is important to understand our current options in solid waste management, and in appreciating the data presented in this book.

After the country experienced two decades of pent-up demand — the depression of the 1930s, when people had little money to spend, and the war years from 1939-1945, when people had money but there were few products to buy — the American people went on a buying spree. New products and new packaging transformed the waste stream from one that was readily handled by open-bodied trucks, which allowed for recycling, to one that needed large compactor trucks to compact the garbage so that the increased volume could be handled. These new trucks also had to tip their loads at transfer stations, where larger, stationary hydraulic systems pressed the garbage yet another time before transportation to landfills.

Recent research shows that the expanded waste stream is mostly the result of new packaging and the transformation of what were once durable goods (razors, beverage containers, and food utensils) into nondurable goods, ready for disposal within minutes of purchase (see Table 1).

Table 1

Products Discarded into the Municipal Solid Waste Stream*

(in millions of tons and by percent)

Products	1970		1988	
	Tons	%	Tons	%
Durable goods	15.1	12.4	24.9	13.9
Nondurable goods	25.5	20.9	50.4	28.1
Containers and packaging	43.5	35.7	56.8	31.6
Other wastes	37.8	31.0	47.5	26.4
Total	121.9	100.0	179.6	100.0

* "Municipal solid waste" is defined here to include residential, commercial, and institutional solid waste.
Source: *Characterization of Municipal Solid Waste in the United States: 1990 Update,* U.S. EPA, June, 1990. (Original source: Franklin Associates, Ltd.)

In addition to the sharp increase of per capita solid waste, the United States had a population explosion after 1945. The country's new families were moving from the city to the suburbs. By 1960, the suburbs had suburbs. This meant that the land traditionally available for new landfill space for cities was no longer available because towns and cities had grown around the older central cities. Solid waste managers thus had more solid waste and fewer places to put it. Further, the discovery that existing landfills were leaking dangerous materials into soil and groundwater and the closure of thousands of unpermitted dumps began the movement to oppose all landfills.

By 1965, the federal government started to take notice. New laws allowed the Department of Health, Education, and Welfare to begin research and technical assistance programs on behalf of local governments, which up to that time had sole responsibility for solid waste management. By 1970, the U.S. EPA was formed and took over an expanded research and development and implementation program. By 1976, EPA had the Resource Conservation and Recovery Act (RCRA) to bolster its authority. The first result was even more pressures on landfills to meet higher sanitary standards. Thus, in 1986, there were 6,000 operating solid waste landfills, less than one-half the landfills operating three years earlier.[1]

The pressure on landfills increased. Industry also was noticing the problem. Keep America Beautiful (KAB) was formed by the nation's largest corporations, which produced the products and packages that made up the waste stream. Without proper disposal methods they could not keep selling products. In the late 1960s, KAB formed the non-profit research group called the National Center for Solid Waste Disposal. This soon was transformed into the National Center for Resource Recovery. Resource recovery meant incineration. Industry had found its answer to the solid waste problem. Despite the early programming of the EPA, which focused on recycling and reduction of waste, industry's approach was soon adopted by the EPA, and in the late 1970s by the Department of Energy (DOE). Together, these agencies, and industry, promoted incineration of waste through a number of commercialization programs (grants, loan guarantees, below-market loans, price supports, energy entitlement grants, guaranteed resale of electricity, reclassification of ash as a nonhazardous waste).

DOE's goal was to build 200 to 250 new waste incineration plants by 1992. These would consume 75 percent of the nation's municipal solid waste and would cost from $11.5 to $21.5 billion. DOE waste incineration commercialization goals are as follows:[2]

Year	1980	1987	1992
Capacity (tons per day)	9,000	160,000	325,000
Capital investment required (billions of $)	$0.45	$5–10	$6–11
Increase		17 fold	36 fold

---

[1]Personal conversation with the EPA November 13, 1990.

[2]Source: Yakowitz, Harvey, *Recent Federal Actions Which Will Affect Prices and Demand for Discarded Fibers,* National Bureau of Standards, October, 1980.

The American public said no. Beginning in the late 1970s and maturing in the 1980s, the citizen-based movement has effectively stopped the EPA/DOE master plan. Since 1985, over one hundred plants have been canceled, more than were ordered in the same period. New orders for waste incineration plants are as follows: [3]

Year	Number of Plants Ordered
1985	42
1986	25
1987	25
1988	22
1989	10 (first 9 months)

In 1987, for the first time, more plant capacity was canceled (35,656 tons per day) than ordered (20,585 tons per day). The decline in waste incineration plant orders has been compared with the decline in nuclear power plant orders.

The movement to stop these plants was based on opposition to the pollution the plants emit, the pollution caused when virgin materials have to be mined and processed to replace those materials destroyed by incineration, and the high economic cost. Whereas the concern over pollution alerted citizens and mobilized citizen organizations, it was the unprecedented rise in the cost of garbage disposal that forced local officials to reconsider incineration. But what was the alternative to incineration? Here the citizens' movement turned to another movement in the United States that had been growing slowly since the late 1960s: the grass-roots recycling movement.

The recycling movement was not a reaction to the landfill crisis, for there was none in the late 1960s when the movement began. Rather, they reacted to the level of waste in our economy and the pollution and the suffering these habits cause worldwide. Through the 1970s the recyclers built strong alliances with industry brokers and mills who wanted the raw materials, and with progressive government officials who realized the cost savings that could be realized through recycling.

In the mid-1980s, it was the joining of the citizens' movement against incineration with the recyclers that has lifted the recycling revolution to its current status. The most dramatic demonstration of how effective this combination of interests can be was in Austin, Texas, in 1987. A mass burn waste incineration plant was under construction there. Yet the combined votes of two environmentalists and two newly elected businessmen on the city council killed the plant. The reasoning: it was better to lose $23 million spent on the plant to date, because over twenty years, the city would save more than $100 million by investing in recycling and composting.

Other dramatic events occurred. In King County, Washington, for example, consultants found that a mass burn plant would take up more space in a landfill than unprocessed waste because of the space

---

[3]*Wall Street Journal*, June 16, 1988, and personal communication with Kidder, Peabody, & Co., New York, November, 1990.

requirements for an ash monofill. From 1985 on, pressure from environmentalists at the grass-roots level forced builders of incinerators to include acid gas scrubbers, fabric filter bag houses, thermal de-NO_x (oxides of nitrogen) systems, and ash monofills, all of which have increased the cost of incineration.

As we enter the 1990s, the effort to maximize recycling and composting continues. The incineration industry, having lost much of its market to well-organized citizens at the local level, are in the middle of an end run around the local decision-making process. Thus, in California, the industry lobbied heavily to allow incineration to be included in the recycling definition in state law. In Ohio, the state was lobbied to allow the use of ash in roadways (as yet untested) to qualify as recycling. In Michigan, the industry pushed through a law that exempts ash from hazardous waste rules. In Connecticut, the state obliged the industry by overriding local zoning boards in order to stifle opposition to siting plants, leaving expensive legal actions as the only option for citizens attempting to oppose heavy-handed tactics. At the federal level, the industry's amendments to the Clean Air Act were presented by Senator Dole, who commented, "This is the green light for incineration." Grass-roots activists worked hard to strip the amendments favorable to incineration from the Clean Air Act.

Most recently, the U.S. DOE proposed a plan to accelerate the permitting of waste incinerators in response to the current Mideast oil crisis. Once again, as in the 1970s, grass-roots groups are demonstrating that recycling saves more energy in industries that use recovered materials than burning waste produces; and at far less the capital and pollution costs.

No matter what new laws and regulations are passed at the state and federal levels, resistance to incineration and promotion of recycling and composting are hale and hearty at the local level. There, citizens' groups have developed techniques for influencing or replacing local officials who are adamant about the need for incineration. Most recently, citizens are demanding that nonincineration planning be undertaken prior to any commitment to incineration. The local level is where the real battleground is. As the outgoing mayor of Lincoln, Nebraska, stated after his defeat, "Garbage is the issue that can unseat an incumbent official."

Is There a Federal Role in Recycling?

There certainly is, but the role is narrower than most people believe. For example, in the mid 1970s, the EPA sponsored panels of consultants that traveled around the country providing expert advice to local officials. Yet, these efforts turned out to be no more than sales pitches for incinerators. In Grand Rapids, Michigan, for example, the local officials won a planning grant from the EPA, but when they wanted to spend the money on materials recovery, they were told that only incineration studies were eligible. Many people fear that the latest round of federally sponsored panels to direct recycling as stated in the

EPA's *Agenda for Action* could lead to another round of ill-informed or misguided "expert advice."

There are two steps the federal government can take that would provide great stimulation for recycling. The first is an executive order from the President to make the already adopted guidelines for procuring products with recycled material content by federal agencies and their contractors mandatory. The guidelines were promulgated by the EPA (ten years after they were required by RCRA) but have yet to be used by federal agencies because they are only voluntary. This one executive order would stimulate demand for recycled paper, roadbed and construction materials, and other commodities.

Second, Congress can create tax credits for manufacturers that use recycled raw materials. For example, under current law, virgin material users get a tax credit called a depletion allowance. This is a perverse incentive, as it makes virgin raw materials cheaper to use than recycled materials. Repealing this allowance is almost impossible, given the political power of the virgin material corporations. Thus, a counterbalancing credit that provides an incentive for automakers, for example, to use secondary paper or plastic to stuff car seats would greatly stimulate markets for recycled materials.

Both the mandatory procurement approach and the tax credit approach are simple. Yet, the signals they give to the market are exactly what the country needs to create demand for recycled products. This process is already working at the state level. For example, in 1990, the state of California passed a law requiring that 50 percent of newsprint used by newspaper publishers must be made from paper with at least 50 percent recycled content by 2000.

The federal government, through the EPA and the Department of Commerce, can act as a clearinghouse of information. This would serve to inform the country, through annual or semiannual reports, on the progress being made in education, recycling, and market development. The EPA provided this service in the early 1970s through its annual reports to Congress.

Why This Book?

Materials recovery was still an afterthought of public policy in the early 1980s. It was primarily viewed as an individual act of conscience rather than a serious foundation for waste management systems. Most cities and towns anticipated no more than 10 percent recovery levels. Faced with vanishing landfills, most chose incineration.

But by the late 1980s, some communities had achieved recycling and composting levels of 25, 35, even 45 percent. For the first time, materials recovery became not a secondary component of solid waste handling systems, but a central element. Still, the incineration industry pushed its ideology in the face of the building factual data base in favor of recycling. The waste incineration industry claimed that 25 percent recycling was the maximum level possible, and therefore 75

Table 2

Record-Setting Recycling and Composting Programs

Ranking Number	Community	Population	Materials Recovery Rate (%, 1989)*
1	Berlin Township, NJ	5,629	57
2	Longmeadow, MA	16,309	49
3	Haddonfield, NJ	12,151	49
4	Perkasie, PA	7,005	43
5	Rodman, NY	850	43
6	Wellesley, MA	26,590	41
7	Lincoln Park, NJ	11,337	41 †
8	West Linn, OR	14,030	40
9	Hamburg, NY	11,000	40
10	Wilton, WI	473	40
11	Seattle, WA	497,000	36 ††
12	Cherry Hill, NJ	73,723	35 ††
13	Upper Township, NJ	10,870	35
14	Babylon, NY	213,234	34 ††
15	Park Ridge, NJ	8,515	34
16	Fennimore, WI	2,430	34 ††
17	Woodbury, NJ	10,450	32 ††

* The ratio of tonnage recycled plus tonnage composted to the tonnage of municipal solid waste generated (residential, commercial, and institutional waste disposed and recovered).
† Based on 1988 data.
†† Residential or commercial recovery levels are at or above 40 percent.

percent of the waste stream must be incinerated.

There was little or no genuine analysis of successful recycling and composting programs to disprove this allegation. Throughout the country, and even within metropolitan areas, individual programs varied dramatically. No standard statistical format existed by which communities could compare themselves with one another, so every community had to travel along the same learning curve as its predecessors.

The Institute for Local Self-Reliance set out to rectify this situation by providing the first in-depth examination of successful recycling and composting programs based on a uniform analytical framework. In *Beyond 25 Percent: Materials Recovery Comes of Age,* we identified the 15 communities with the highest levels of materials recovery (that is, the highest levels of recycling and composting) in the nation. "We have two objectives in distributing this information," we wrote in that volume. "One is to share the experience of the pioneers with those just starting up their programs. The other, and in the long term more important objective, is to encourage communities to refine our methodology and improve their own data gathering."

With this background, this current book presents, in case study format, information on 17 U.S. communities — rural, suburban, and urban, large and small. Table 2 lists these record-setting recycling and composting communities and their overall materials recovery levels.

Confusion and even controversy often surround the definition of "recycling" and "composting." In the analytical methodology we have developed, recycling refers to recovering discarded products and packaging materials for reuse and/or processing into new products. Composting refers to recovering discarded organic materials such as leaves and brush for processing into soil amendment, fertilizer, or mulch. We consider both materials recovery strategies.

These success stories are drawn from communities ranging from rural towns of 500 people to metropolitan areas of almost 500,000 people. This is a representative cross section of the country. The data show that there are solutions to such problems as capitalizing equipment, proximity to markets, education, and incentive programs, no matter how large or small a community is. Indeed, ILSR believes the data show that solutions are transferable to every part of the country, including rural, suburban, and urban communities. Large city managers should not fret that "the problem is too big for us to handle." A small (15,000 to 30,000 population) city's success in implementing and maintaining high materials recovery levels can be translated into big cities (100,000 plus population) one neighborhood at a time, using much the same economic, educational, and technological premises. Similarly, a rural area can take advantage of marketing strategies available to large industrialized cities via cooperative marketing arrangements and the use of back hauls for low-cost transportation.

The data in *Beyond 40 Percent: Record-Setting Recycling and Composting Programs* connect readers with the experience of the cities and towns covered in the book through the case study approach. Readers can contact the public officials who have made recycling work in their community for advice and information.

Lessons to Learn

As we enter the 1990s, communities across the country continue to face tough decisions about how to handle their solid wastes. Preventing waste generation is recognized as the first priority in solving the waste crisis. Implementation of recycling and composting systems is recognized as the second priority. Incineration and landfill disposal are considered last resorts. Yet, controversy continues to rage on how much of the waste stream can be reduced, recycled, and composted.

Citizen and environmental groups oppose incineration and advocate source reduction and materials recovery as the only effective short- and long-term solutions to the solid waste crisis. They call for a new ethic that rejects the throwaway society. They see the misuse of materials and energy resources within the U.S. economy as the root of the solid waste crisis. Materials recovery, not materials destruction, is the objective of grass-roots efforts toward solid waste management in a sustainable economy.

Many industry and government officials, on the other hand, advocate "integrated waste management," a combination of recycling, incineration, and landfill disposal. They see the lack of disposable capacity as the crux of the solid waste crisis. As a result, they tend to promote the siting of large centralized facilities (waste incinerators, landfills, and/or mechanical processing systems for composting mixed refuse). The U.S. EPA, whose *Agenda for Action* emphasizes integrated waste management, has limited its recycling goal for the nation to 25 percent of the municipal solid waste stream. The agency maintains that incineration can complement recycling. The policy of the Governmental Refuse Collection and Disposal Association — an association of solid waste management professionals — states that waste incineration (with energy recovery) "must be used." Industry associations such as the National Solid Wastes Management Association hold similar policies. County governments in Maryland, Connecticut, Florida, New Jersey, Michigan, and elsewhere have plans to burn most of their wastes, thus limiting recycling to only a small fraction.

Recycling opponents argue that curbside source-separation recycling and composting programs are too expensive, that there are no markets for collected materials, and that these strategies can handle only a small portion of the waste stream. A standard tactic of incineration advocates is to claim that recycling is compatible with incineration, and that both strategies are needed to solve the waste crisis.

This book addresses these controversial issues by documenting the operating experiences of communities with the highest materials recovery levels in the country. All are recovering more than 30 percent, and 14 have total, residential, or commercial materials recovery levels at or above 40 percent. All of the programs featured in this report — even the best — can increase their materials recovery levels. Most are actively striving to do so. Consider Lincoln Park, New Jersey. In 1988, the borough reported a 40 percent recovery rate. By 1989 this had increased to 53 percent.[4]

The data presented in this book demonstrate that source-separation recycling and composting systems can be a cost-effective and primary solid waste management option. Several factors contribute to reaching high recovery levels, including mandating recycling, establishing economic incentives, collecting source-separated yard waste for composting, and extending programs beyond the residential sector to the commercial sector. Communities can readily integrate these key features into their programs, thereby increasing recovery rates, extending landfill life, and possibly eliminating the short-term need for additional disposal capacity. For instance, if communities can compost 20 percent of their solid waste streams through source separation of yard wastes alone (as indicated in this book), a mechanical processing facility separating organics from mixed refuse for composting becomes inappropriate as the first strategy of choice. Due to its higher quality, compost from source-separated yard waste is easier to market than compost from mixed refuse. Implementing backyard composting programs offers the added benefit of avoiding collection costs for one of the most significant portions of the waste stream.

We now know that significantly more than 25 percent of the waste stream can be recycled and composted. Communities have reached 40

[4]Lincoln Park 1989 data became available only as this book went to press.

percent levels and beyond. Some, such as Seattle and Cincinnati, have goals of 60 percent. King County, Washington, has a goal of 65 percent. New Jersey recently established the highest statewide materials recovery goal: 60 percent of its total solid waste stream by 1995. Part of that state's new solid waste management policy is to stop encouraging the development of incinerators in most of the state's counties. State policy now stipulates that the 60 percent goal must be met before a waste incinerator can be developed. This policy acknowledges that communities cannot achieve high levels of materials recovery while operating incinerators. Both systems compete for the same materials and the same funds. The experiences of several communities exemplify these difficulties. In Babylon, New York, half of the newspaper collected for recycling in 1989 was burned at the town incinerator to meet the tonnage guaranteed to the plant. Warren County, New Jersey, experienced similar problems in 1988. The Claremont, New Hampshire, waste incinerator has fallen short of its refuse quota largely due to recycling efforts in the 27 towns served by the plant. The plant incurred a $64,000 deficit in the first quarter of 1990.

How much of the waste stream can be reduced, recycled, and composted? Materials recovery levels of 75 percent are well within the realm of possibility for communities that integrate the best features of the best programs. Market development will be essential if collected materials are actually to be utilized. The 1990s are heralding a new era in the way we produce and consume materials. Manufacturers are both redesigning products to be recyclable and retooling their plants to increase scrap-based production. Heinz is introducing a recyclable plastic ketchup bottle. The Postal Service is designing stamps to reduce adhesive contaminant problems in the paper manufacturing process. More than half the newsprint mills in North America are adding deinking capacity. State and federal procurement regulations are spurring industry to supply more paper with recycled content. Labeling to identify products in the marketplace that are made from recycled materials or that can themselves be recycled is being proposed in several states. Bans on unnecessary packaging have surfaced across the country. We have only just begun to tap the wealth of strategies available for maximizing waste reduction and minimizing disposal.

Recycling and composting programs are cost-effective for a number of reasons. First, they are cheaper than competing options, such as waste incineration. Whereas capital costs for waste incineration are about $100,000 per ton per day of installed capacity, the capital costs for the recovery programs detailed here range from about $5,000 to $50,000 per recovered ton per day. The above-mentioned cost for incineration excludes equipment needed for collection and additional capital investment required for disposal of ash residues.

Second, costs incurred for recycling and composting programs are offset by avoiding the costs of collecting these materials as mixed refuse. In many communities, equipment used for collecting refuse is also used for collection of recyclables and yard waste. In some communities, only small capital expenditures are required; in others, no new employees are needed. As communities strive for higher and higher levels of materials recovery, recycling and composting collection systems replace traditional waste collection systems. In general, collection costs may remain about the same. This is especially significant since collection constitutes the major costs of recycling and composting programs. While processing costs may be incurred, disposal costs are avoided.

Third, recycling and composting are cost-effective in a much larger sense than their role in solving the municipal solid waste crisis. They also play a key role in slowing global warming, reducing ozone depletion, and reducing energy consumption and water pollution. Processing recyclables and scrap-based manufacturing can also revitalize depressed economies and help reduce the national trade deficit.

Eleven billion tons of solid waste are generated each year in the United States: 7.6 billion tons of industrial wastes, 2 to 3 billion tons of oil and gas waste, more than 1.4 billion tons of mining waste. While more waste is generated by iron and steel, electric power generation, industrial chemical, plastics, and resin industries than by municipalities — about 300 million tons versus 180 million tons — when we recycle municipal solid waste, less energy is consumed and less waste and pollution are generated in the mining and manufacturing process. Reduced energy consumption translates into reduced combustion and, thus, reduced atmospheric pollution, that is, less greenhouse gases and ozone depletion.

Recycling a ton of steel prevents 200 pounds of air pollutants, 100 pounds of water pollutants, almost three tons of mining waste, and about 25 tons of water use. One ton of remelted aluminum eliminates the need for four tons of bauxite, and almost a ton of petroleum coke and pitch. Burning a ton of paper may generate 1,500 pounds of carbon dioxide. Recycling that paper saves about 17 trees, which absorb 250 pounds of carbon dioxide annually.

The potential energy savings from recycling municipal solid waste are enormous. Utilizing organic waste as a fertilizer product eliminates the use of energy-intensive chemical fertilizers. Substituting scrap aluminum for virgin materials reduces energy consumption by 90 percent. As compared with virgin materials, using scrap steel saves 50 percent of the energy consumed; recycling paper results in a 60 percent savings; and glass can net a 30 percent reduction. The energy generated from burning these materials is but a small fraction of the energy savings realized through recycling. Consider paper. Substituting a ton of scrap paper for virgin paper saves about 10,000 kilowatt-hours (kwh); burning a ton of scrap paper will generate approximately 600 kwh.

If we are to realize the full benefits of recycling in the United States — reduced pollution and reduced consumption of virgin resources and energy — we will have to convert scrap materials into finished goods domestically. Today, a great portion of our scrap materials are shipped abroad. The two largest exports from the Port Authority of New York are scrap paper and scrap steel. When America's cities ship their waste overseas, they deny themselves the benefits of processing abundant, locally available materials. Such cities then function as classic colonies, exporting raw materials and importing finished goods. Processing adds value to materials. It also creates jobs and boosts income for the local economy. Today, these benefits accrue not to the cities that generate the materials, but to the countries that import the waste. Whereas scrap newsprint now has little value, when converted into new newsprint, its value climbs to $600 per ton.

Unaware of the potentially vast volume of materials that can be collected in any given U.S. city or geographic area, those people and agencies involved in economic development have been slow to investigate the opportunities for scrap-based manufacturing. For example, Minnesota's Twin Cities, with 2.2 million people, generate enough scrap material to support a large array of local processing and manufacturing plants. But until cities actually recover their waste, manufacturers will be unlikely to establish plants that use these materials. Dozens of companies that process waste into usable materials established facilities in Pennsylvania and New Jersey after recycling became mandatory in these states. Communities need to collect a significant quantity of scrap materials in order to guarantee a sufficient supply to potential end-users.

Source-separation recycling and composting systems are an important link in our effort for more efficient use of all resources: primary and waste materials, energy, land, air, and water. This book can serve as a valuable resource for communities in designing and implementing such systems, determining their costs, and choosing what strategies are effective in reaching high levels of materials recovery.

Conclusion

The hardest decision to make in recycling is the decision to recycle. After that decision is made, common sense, economics, and entrepreneurialism take over. That is exactly what is happening today throughout the country. Market development, recycling literacy, procurement programs, and economic incentives to haulers and households are all being developed as strategies to meet the recycling policy goals of communities.

Thus, the case studies presented in *Beyond 40 Percent: Record-Setting Recycling and Composting Programs* are a road map for planners, entrepreneurs, and citizen groups that want to replicate and improve upon these successes.

ILSR presents the results of its research with the hope that learning will spread throughout the country. At the same time, we issue a challenge to communities already in the sample of successful programs, to those approaching the 40 percent level, and to those communities that are just beginning the recycling process. We challenge you to do better, to make materials recovery the primary solid waste management approach in your city or town.

— Neil N. Seldman
President, ILSR

Observations

In *Beyond 25 Percent*, we offered several conclusions based on the experience of the 15 communities. These included the following:

- Only those programs with aggressive composting have achieved very high levels of materials recovery.

- For a community to recover a high percentage of its total waste, it must target a variety of materials. Targeting only two or three materials (for example, newspapers, bottles, cans) is insufficient to achieve high levels of recovery.

- Communities with mandatory participation ordinances have significantly higher household participation rates than those with voluntary programs.

- Mandatory participation is a necessary, but not a sufficient, condition for high levels of materials recovery. Economic incentives are also important.

The present study confirms these conclusions, teaches us new lessons, and raises new questions.

Demographics, Location, and Materials Recovery Levels

Tables 3 and 4 provide comparative data on demographics and on total, residential, and commercial waste generation and recovery levels.

Charts A and B provide information on the relationship of community demographics to the percentage of materials recovered. Chart A indicates that almost 80 percent of the 17 communities with the highest levels of materials recovery have populations under 30,000. Although almost 60 percent of these 17 communities are suburban, Chart B shows that rural and urban communities can also achieve high recovery levels.

The reader may be surprised by the proportion of small communities represented in this study. Yet this is fairly representative of national demographics. Many more people live in small cities and towns than in large cities. There are thousands of cities with populations of 5,000 to 30,000, compared to only a few hundred with populations over 100,000.

Large metropolitan areas may consist of one or two relatively large and dense central cities and dozens or even hundreds of smaller, suburban or even rural communities. The reader might find it useful to approach these case studies by thinking of his or her metropolitan area not as a single entity but as hundreds of small cities. Thus the experience of a community like Berlin Township, New Jersey, may be appropriate for a suburban community outside of Los Angeles, or even a Kansas City neighborhood.

The reader may also be surprised by the proportion of New Jersey communities represented — 7 out of 17. Nowhere in the United States have the effects of disappearing landfill capacity been felt more keenly than in New Jersey. By 1985, New Jersey's landfills were full to capacity. Today more than half the State's waste is dumped out of state. Tipping fees for landfilling municipal solid waste (MSW) soared from $1.50 per ton in 1979, to $7.50 per ton in 1984, to $60-$125+ per ton today. Skyrocketing landfill disposal costs combined with implementation of the Statewide Mandatory Source Separation and Recycling Act of 1987 have spurred recycling and composting activities in New Jersey.

Table 3

Total Materials Generated and Recovered, 1989

#	Community	Type	Population	Total Waste Generated (Tons) (a)	% Residential (By Wt.)	Per Capita Residential Waste Generation (lbs/day) (b)	Total Recycled (Tons) (c)	Total Composted (Tons)	Total Recovered (Tons)	% Total Recycled (By Wt.)	% Total Composted (By Wt.)	% Total Recovered (By Wt.) (d)
1	Berlin Twp., NJ	S	5,629	7,778	62	4.7	2,501	1,900	4,401	32	24	57
2	Longmeadow, MA	S	16,309	10,891	87	3.2	1,934	3,424	5,358	18	31	49
3	Haddonfield, NJ	S	12,151 (e)	13,681	90	5.5	2,471	4,207	6,678	18	31	49
4	Perkasie, PA	S	7,005	2,794	80	2.4	831	380	1,211	30	14	43
5	Rodman, NY	R	850	352	99	2.2	114	36	150	32	10	43
6	Wellesley, MA	S	26,590	23,030	NA	NA	3,581	5,831	9,412	16	25	41
7	Lincoln Park, NJ (f)	S	11,337	11,011	63	3.3	3,728	817	4,545	34	7	41
8	West Linn, OR	S	14,030	8,584	NA	3.4	1,940	1,480	3,420	23	17	40
9	Hamburg, NY	S	11,000	6,050	85	2.6	1,360	1,062	2,422	22	18	40
10	Wilton, WI	R	473	226	88	2.3	80	10	90	35	4	40
11	Seattle, WA	LC	497,000	672,024	44	3.2	200,914	42,904	243,818	30	6	36
12	Cherry Hill, NJ	SC	73,723	108,856	47	3.8	29,479	9,046	38,525	27	8	35
13	Upper Twp., NJ	R	10,870	16,474	NA	NA	2,542	3,262	5,804	15	20	35
14	Babylon, NY	LC	213,234	271,750	48	3.4	91,566	1,000	92,566	34	0.4	34
15	Park Ridge, NJ	S	8,515	9,990	68	4.4	2,580	815	3,395	26	8	34
16	Fennimore, WI	R	2,430	1,692	49	1.9	453	125	578	27	7	34
17	Woodbury, NJ	S	10,450	15,829	55	4.6	2,951	2,085	5,035	19	13	32

Key: LC = Large City   R = Rural   S = Suburb   SC = Small City   NA = Not Available

Notes:

(a) Materials disposed and recovered by residential, commercial, and institutional sectors. Bulky waste disposed is included in total waste generation with the following exceptions: Fennimore, Berlin Twp., Wilton, and Longmeadow.   Some bulky waste is included for Perkasie, Hamburg, Seattle, Cherry Hill, Upper Twp., and Park Ridge. See case studies for more detailed information on what is included or excluded from total waste generated.

(b) West Linn's figure is based on total waste generated.   Seattle's figure includes self-haul waste, of which 50% is estimated to be residential.

(c) Includes estimated tonnage recycled through beverage container deposit systems.

(d) Due to rounding figures, Percent Total Recycled plus Percent Total Composted may not appear to equal Percent Total Recovered.

(e) Based on 1988 data.

(f) All figures for Lincoln Park based on 1988.

Table 4

Residential and Commercial Materials Generated and Recovered, 1989

#	Community	Residential Waste Generated (Tons) (a)	Residential Materials Recycled (Tons) (b)	Residential Materials Composted (Tons)	Residential Materials Recovered (Tons)	% Residential Materials Recycled	% Residential Materials Composted	% Residential Materials Recovered (c)	Commercial Waste Generated (Tons) (d)	Commercial Materials Recycled (Tons)	% Commercial Materials Recycled
1	Berlin Twp, NJ	4,841	932	1,835	2,767	19	38	57	2,937	1,569	53
2	Longmeadow, MA	9,467	1,618	2,666	4,284	17	28	45	350	0	0
3	Haddonfield, NJ	12,246	2,128	4,165	6,293	17	34	51	1,435	343	24
4	Perkasie, PA	2,235 (e)	NA	380	NA	NA	17	NA	559	NA	NA
5	Rodman, NY	NA	NA	NA	NA	NA	NA	NA	NA	NA	NA
6	Wellesley, MA	NA	NA	3,238	NA	NA	NA	NA	NA	NA	NA
7	Lincoln Park, NJ (f)	6,911	949	762	1,711	14	11	25	4,100	2,779	68
8	West Linn, OR	NA	1,163	1,480	2,643	NA	NA	NA	NA	282	NA
9	Hamburg, NY (g)	5,155	928	1,062	1,990	18	21	39	565	103	18
10	Wilton, WI	200	70	10	80	35	5	40	26	10	38
11	Seattle, WA (h)	253,925	79,185	31,656	110,841	31	12	44	336,724	117,324	35
12	Cherry Hill, NJ	51,536	7,172	8,847	16,019	14	17	31	57,320	22,307	39
13	Upper Twp, NJ	NA	NA	762	NA	NA	NA	NA	NA	NA	NA
14	Babylon, NY	131,354	9,934	1,000	10,934	8	1	8	133,999	75,235	56
15	Park Ridge, NJ (i)	6,786	1,413	798	2,211	21	12	33	3,204	1,167	36
16	Fennimore, WI	825	282	125	407	34	15	49	867	171	20
17	Woodbury, NJ (j)	8,744	2,160	2,085	4,244	25	24	49	7,085	791	11

Key: NA = Data not available

Notes:

(a) Materials disposed and recovered by single-family and multi-family households and their yards.
(b) Excludes tonnage recovered from beverage container deposit systems as this tonnage cannot be broken down into residential and commercial.
(c) Due to rounding figures, % Residential Materials Recycled plus % Residential Materials Composted may not appear to equal % Residential Materials Recovered.
(d) Materials disposed and recovered by the commercial and institutional sectors (excluding medical wastes). Yard waste composted by landscapers is excluded as this tonnage cannot be broken down into residential and commercial. Non-residential bulky waste such as construction debris and asphalt is included under commercial waste with the exception of Berlin Twp., Longmeadow, Wilton, and Fennimore. In Seattle, Cherry Hill, and Park Ridge, only tonnage of bulky waste recovered is included. For these 7 communities, non-residential bulky waste was neither included in disposal tonnages nor readily available.
(e) Excludes waste generated by condominiums and apartments with more than 4 units, which is collected by private haulers and is not tracked.
(f) All figures based on 1988 data. Waste generated and recycled from condominiums is collected by private haulers and is included under commercial waste.
(g) Residential and commercial tons generated and recovered are based on an estimated 90 percent residential and 10 percent commercial.
(h) Excludes self-hauled materials to recycling, composting, or disposal facilities, since this tonnage cannot be broken down into residential and commercial.
(i) Materials disposed and recovered from 4 schools and the post office are included with residential figures.
(j) Some commercial waste picked up by the City along its residential collection route is included in residential figures.

Chart A
Population and Materials Recovery

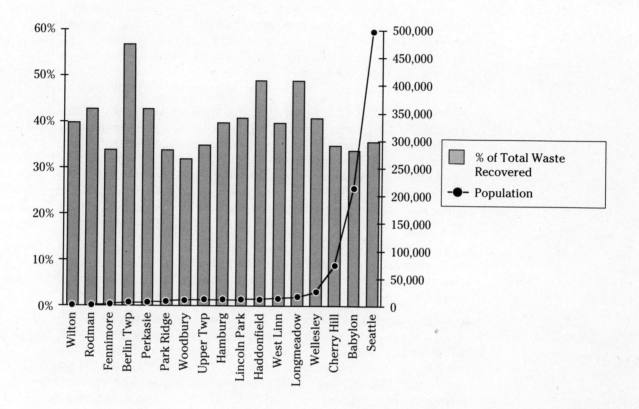

Chart B
Demographics and Recovery Levels:
Rural, Suburban, and Urban Communities

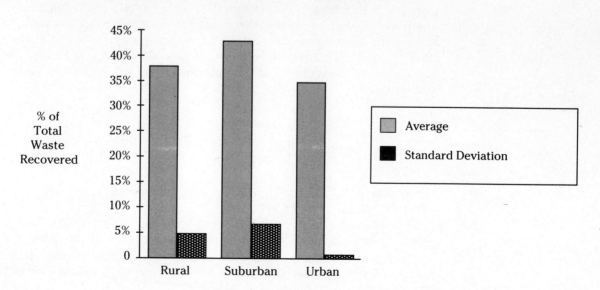

Per Capita Waste Generation

Charts C and D provide information on community size and per capita residential waste generation. The wide variation in per capita residential waste generation shown in Chart C may be attributed to several factors: demographics, source reduction initiatives (such as backyard composting programs or volume-based refuse rates),[1] the amount of yard waste in the residential waste stream, and the exclusion of any materials which may be burned by residents.

Charts C and D indicate that the rural communities of Rodman [5],[2] Fennimore [16], and Wilton [10], which have the smallest populations in this study, generate less per capita waste than suburban or urban communities.[3] However, this may not actually be the case. Residents of Wilton and Fennimore are burning some yard waste. In Rodman, residents reportedly burn some wastepaper in wood burning stoves. They may be burning some of their yard waste as well, since the State of New York allows communities of 20,000 or fewer residents to do so.

The fact that Rodman does not provide curbside collection service for refuse or recyclable materials may contribute both to burning at home and to lower waste generation rates. (Residents haul their own refuse to the Township transfer station or recycling drop-off center.)

The amount of yard waste in the residential waste stream may significantly affect the per capita residential waste generated, especially in suburban communities with many trees and spacious yards. The two suburban communities of Berlin Township [1] and Haddonfield [3] have the highest per capita residential waste generation; they also compost the highest proportions of their residential waste. Both communities have comprehensive yard waste collection programs. In both, yard waste is a large portion of the waste stream.

Source reduction initiatives such as charging residents by volume for the refuse they generate (through per-can or per-bag fees) have reduced per capita residential waste generation in Perkasie [4], West Linn [8], and Seattle [11]. Chart E compares the per capita residential waste generation of these three suburban and urban communities to that of the nine suburban and urban communities without volume-based rates. (See Economic Incentives, pages 39-40, for a more detailed discussion of the effect of volume-based refuse rates on waste generation.)

---

[1]In this report, "refuse" refers to discarded materials that are **not** source-separated for recycling or composting.

[2]Numbers in square brackets, [ ] following mention of a community, represent that community's ranking number among our 17 programs.

[3]Our small sample of communities with populations greater than 70,000 limits our ability to draw conclusions about per capita residential waste generation for large communities.

Chart C
Size of City Compared to Per Capita
Residential Waste Generation

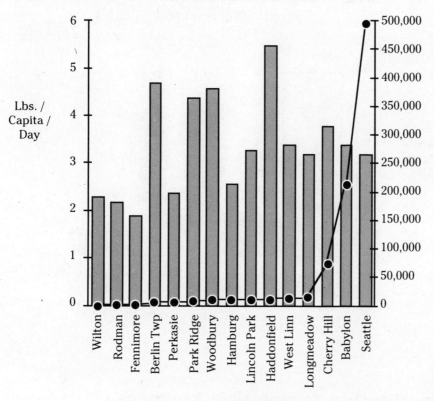

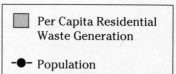

Note: West Linn's figure is based on per capita total waste generation, most of which is residential.

Chart D
Population and Residential
Waste Generation

(pounds per capita per day)

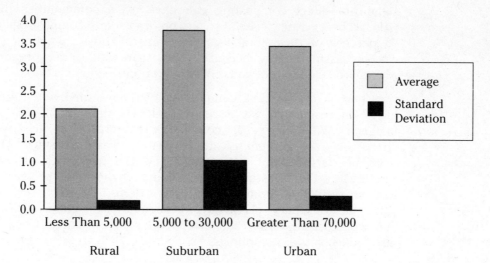

Chart E
The Effect of Volume-Based Refuse Rates
on Per Capita Residential Waste Generation
(excluding rural communities)

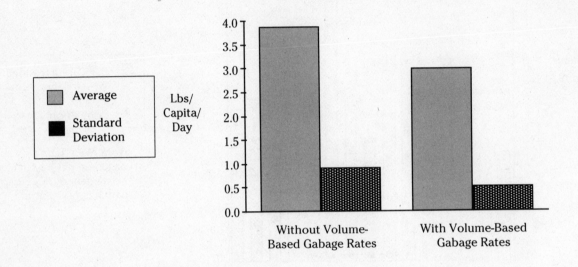

Comprehensive Composting Programs

All 17 communities have some sort of composting program. Some are more comprehensive than others in terms of the number of materials targeted and frequency of collection. Table 5 compares composting program characteristics among the 17 communities. Chart F shows the significant effect composting can have on a community's overall materials recovery rate. The top ten programs are composting, on average, 20 percent of their total waste streams. These composting operations are successful largely because yard waste and other organic materials are source separated and collected at curbside.

Chart G shows that composting can have an even more significant effect on residential waste recovery levels than on overall levels. For instance, Woodbury [17] composts 13 percent of its overall waste stream, but 24 percent of its residential waste stream. The types of materials targeted for composting and the frequency of pick-up affect the level of composting. Three out of the four programs with the highest residential composting levels (Berlin Township [1], Haddonfield [3], and Woodbury [17]) have year-round collection of leaves, brush, and wood waste, and seasonal collection of Christmas trees. Woodbury also collects grass clippings.

Table 5
Composting Program Characteristics

# Community	Type of Compost Program	Materials Collected for Composting	Private/ Public Collection (a)	Pick-up Frequency	Same Day Collection (b)	Set-Out Method	Collection Period (Year-round/ Seasonal)	Collection Method	Private/ Public Compost Site	Composting Operation (c)
1 Berlin Twp., NJ	CS, DO	BR,L,[CT,WW]	Public	Weekly	No	Bag/Loose	Year-round	Scoop/Chipper	Public	Windrow
2 Longmeadow, MA	CS, DO	L,[BR,GC]	Public/Private	Monthly	No	Loose	Seasonal	Dump Truck/Vacuum	Private	Farm (Tilling)
3 Haddonfield, NJ	CS	BR,L,WW,[CT]	Public	Varies	Yes	Varies	Both (d)	Vacuum/Chipper	Public	Windrow
4 Perkasie, PA	CS	[BR,L]	Public	Weekly	No	Loose	Seasonal	Dump Truck/Vacuum	Private	Farm (Windrow)
5 Rodman, NY	BY	[BR,FW,GC,L]	--	--	--	--	--	--	--	--
6 Wellesley, MA	DO, BY	[BR,GC,L,WW]	Public	--	No	--	--	--	Public	Windrow
7 Lincoln Park, NJ	CS, DO	BR,L,[CT]	Public	Varies	No	Bag/Loose	Both (e)	Dump Truck/Vacuum	Public	Windrow
8 West Linn, OR	DO, BY (f)	[BR,CT,GC,L,WW]	Public	--	--	--	Feb-Nov	--	Public	Windrow
9 Hamburg, NY	CS	BR,L	Public	Varies	No	Loose	Both (g)	Vacuum/Chipper	Private	Farms
10 Wilton, WI	CS	BR,GC,L,WW	Public	Weekly	No	Not Loose (h)	Year-round	Dump Truck	Public	Farm (Spread)
11 Seattle, WA	CS, DO, BY	BR,GC,L,WW	Contract	Varies (i)	Yes	Not Loose (h)	Year-round	Packer Truck	Private	Windrow
12 Cherry Hill, NJ	CS	BR,L	Public	Monthly	No	Loose	Seasonal	Loader/Dump Truck	Public	Windrow
13 Upper Twp, NJ	CS	L,[BR,GC]	Public	Weekly	No	Bag/Loose	Both (j)	Vacuum/Packer/Chipper	Public	Windrow
14 Babylon, NY	CS	[L]	Public	Triweekly	No	Bag/Loose	Seasonal	Packer Truck	Public	Windrow
15 Park Ridge, NJ	CS, DO (k)	L,[BR,GC,WW]	Public	Triweekly	No	Loose	Seasonal	Loader/Packer	Private	Windrow
16 Fennimore, WI	CS, DO	BR,GC,L,WW	Public	Monthly	No	Loose	Both (l)	Dump Truck	Public	Windrow
17 Woodbury, NJ	CS	BR,CT,GC,L,WW	Public	Weekly	No	Not Loose	Year-round	Packer/Vac./Chipper	Private	Farms (Windrow)

Key: Materials enclosed in brackets [ ] are those for which set-out or drop-off is voluntary. Participation is mandatory for all other materials.

BY = Backyard	CS = Curbside	DO = Drop-Off	CT = Christmas Trees	FW = Food Waste
GC = Grass Clippings	L = Leaves	WW = Wood Waste	Vac. = Vacuum	
	BR = Brush	-- = Not applicable		

Notes:

(a) "Public" -- city provides service; "Private" -- one or more private haulers provide the service; "Contract" -- city contracts with one or more providers.

(b) Same day as refuse collection.

(c) "Windrow" -- collected organic materials are piled in a row or rows for decomposition. "Farm(s)" -- organic materials are tilled, spread, or windrowed at one or more local farms.

(d) Brush is collected weekly year-round, and leaves are collected 2-3 times in the fall and spring.

(e) Bagged leaves and brush can be brought to drop-off year-round. Brush is collected at curbside on an on-call basis. Brush and leaves are collected at curbside during the spring and fall.

(f) Private hauler will begin on-call curbside collection of yard waste in 1990.

(g) Brush is collected monthly year-round, and leaves 2-3 times in the fall.

(h) "Not Loose" -- materials should be contained in some way, either bagged, bundled, or placed in a reusable container.

(i) Collection is weekly year-round in north section. Collection is biweekly March-Oct. and monthly for the rest of the year in the south section.

(j) Leaves are collected year-round, collection of grass clippings and brush is seasonal.

(k) Brush and grass clippings are collected at drop-off (year round), not curbside.

(l) Brush is collected at curbside monthly, and leaves two times per year. Grass clippings must be hauled by residents to the drop-off.

Chart F
Recycling, Composting, and Total Materials Recovery
(percent by weight of total waste generated)

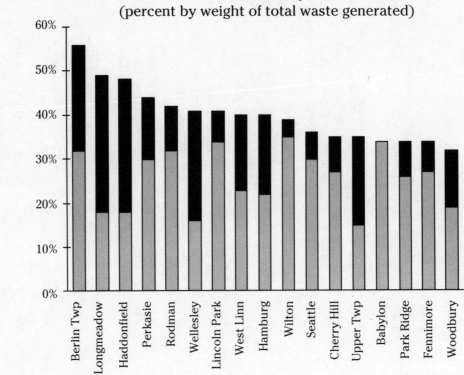

Chart G
Percent of Residential Waste Composted

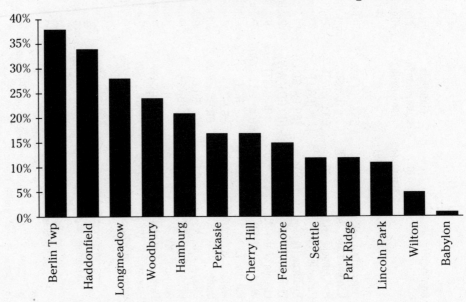

In comparison, Babylon [14] composts less than 1 percent of its waste. The town has two yard waste collection districts: a "sunny" district (that is, the section of Town with fewer trees) and a "shady" district. The yard waste generated by residents in the shady district is disposed, while leaves in the sunny district are collected in the fall for composting. Clearly, Babylon could increase its materials recovery rate by collecting leaves in its shady district for composting, by targeting other yard wastes for collection, and by implementing year-round collection.

Yard waste generated by landscapers — those who engage in the development and decorative planting of gardens and grounds — can be a significant portion of total waste generated. In order to achieve high levels of recovery, communities need to encourage landscapers to compost their waste. Economic incentives for landscapers to bring their yard waste to composting sites have significantly increased recovery rates in Longmeadow [2], Wellesley [6], and Upper Township [13]. Chart H illustrates the effect of composting landscapers' yard waste on overall composting levels for these communities.

Although tipping fees at nearby disposal facilities are moderate ($23 per ton), Longmeadow landscapers can dump their yard waste for free at the 100-acre farm where the Town's collected leaves are tilled into the soil. As a result, Longmeadow diverted an additional 7 percent of its waste from disposal in 1989.

Chart H
The Effect of Composting Landscapers' Yard Waste on Overall Composting Level

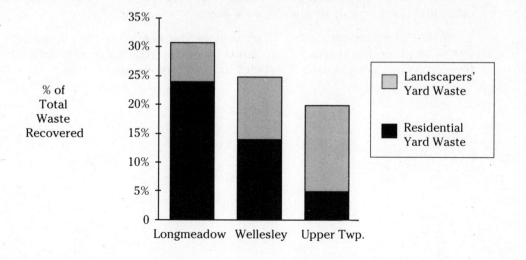

In order to discourage illegal dumping of leaves, Upper Township allows landscapers to drop off their yard waste at the County compost facility at no charge. The tipping fee at the local landfill is $49 per ton. In 1989, landscapers composted 2,500 tons of yard waste — 15 percent of Upper Township's total waste.

The Town of Wellesley charges landscapers lower fees for dumping yard waste at one of its composting sites than at its transfer station. Composting yard waste generated by landscapers alone diverted 14 percent of Wellesley's waste from disposal in 1989. In fact, the Town's overall composting level of 25 percent indicates that, in unusual circumstances, drop-off composting operations can be effective in increasing recovery rates. Wellesley is unusual in that it does not offer curbside collection service for refuse, recyclables, or compostables. This fact, combined with the targeting of several materials (leaves, grass clippings, brush, and other wood waste from both residential and commercial sectors) for composting at two drop-off sites, and the economic incentives for landscapers, is key to Wellesley's composting level.

West Linn [8] too is unusual in that it composts 17 percent of its waste through its drop-off center alone. Although residents in West Linn receive curbside refuse collection, they are charged steep monthly per-can refuse rates for what they set out. As a result, residents tend to bring their yard waste to the drop-off site, where only small fees are charged, or to compost it in their backyards. Since 1984, West Linn has offered 2-hour seminars on how to compost at home, taught four times a year by the faculty of the local community college. It is estimated that 15 to 20 percent of West Linn's yard debris is composted in backyards.

In Rodman, as in Wellesley, the lack of curbside service for refuse and recyclables has encouraged backyard composting. A non-profit environmental group in Rodman, Pure Water for Life, provides volunteer technical assistance to anyone interested in setting up a backyard composting bin. A 1989 survey indicated that 55 percent of Rodman's residents were composting at home, resulting in the recovery of an estimated 11 percent of the Town's waste.

In Wellesley an estimated 39 percent of the residents are composting leaves in their backyards.[4] The Town provides residents with information on composting through articles in local newspapers.

---

[4]Tonnage composted in backyards is not known and is therefore excluded from waste generation and recovery figures.

Mandatory Versus Voluntary Participation

Mandatory materials recovery programs are necessary to reach high participation rates and, in turn, high levels of recovery. Following establishment of Haddonfield's [3] mandatory ordinance, for example, the number of households setting out newspapers each week increased 53 percent, while the set-out rate for glass increased 153 percent.

Voluntary recycling programs, if accompanied by sufficient public education and infrastructure development, can achieve respectable levels. But even with incentives like variable can rates and weekly pickup (see pages 32, 34, 39, and 40), only mandatory programs achieve very high levels.

In gathering data for *Beyond 25 Percent: Materials Recovery Comes of Age*, we initially examined more than 60 community programs. Of the 45 programs dropped from consideration because they did not achieve a 25 percent materials recovery level, 80 percent were voluntary. Of the 15 communities included, 60 percent had mandatory recycling programs. This volume documents 17 communities, all with recovery levels above 30 percent and 14 with either overall, residential, or commercial recovery levels above 40 percent; 13 of these — almost 80 percent — have mandatory residential recycling programs. Residents are required to segregate designated materials for recycling and to set them out at curbside or deliver them to a drop-off site.

Among our 17 communities, those with mandatory participation ordinances have slightly higher household participation rates than those without. Participation rates for the 13 mandatory recycling programs average 90 percent (plus or minus 10 percent); for the four voluntary programs they average 75 percent (plus or minus 14 percent). Chart I compares the participation rates of mandatory programs to those of voluntary programs in our sample. Chart J combines data in *Beyond 25 Percent* with data in this volume in order to compare participation rates between mandatory and voluntary programs for a larger sample. The average participation rate for the 17 mandatory programs is 90 percent. For the seven voluntary programs it is 54 percent.

Nine of the 13 mandatory programs documented in this report have some type of enforcement system. For most of these, enforcement consists of not picking up refuse that contains materials designated for recovery. At least six of the mandatory programs may assess fines for noncompliance. Enforcement appears to contribute to higher participation rates. Babylon has no enforcement program; its 63 percent participation rate is the lowest of the mandatory recycling programs.

Note that the voluntary programs with the highest participation rates — Wellesley [6], Seattle [11], and West Linn [8] — provide residents with strong incentives to recycle. In Wellesley, residents are not served with curbside collection for refuse or recyclables. The conveniently located drop-off center is designed to encourage recycling. In Seattle and West Linn, volume-based rates for refuse collection increase participation in recycling/composting programs.

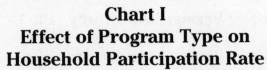

Chart I
Effect of Program Type on
Household Participation Rate

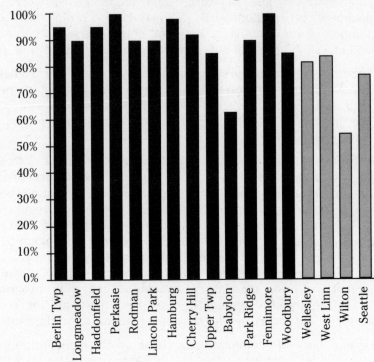

- ■ Mandatory Programs
- ■ Voluntary Programs

Chart J
Average Household Participation Rates
for Mandatory and Voluntary Programs

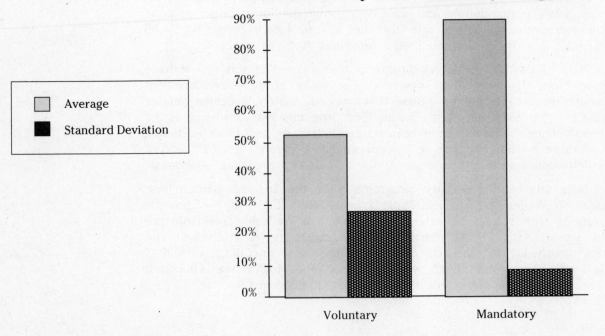

- ■ Average
- ■ Standard Deviation

Requiring businesses to recycle certain materials has contributed to high commercial waste recovery rates. Thirteen of the 17 communities require businesses to recycle at least one designated material. Commercial waste recovery levels for these 13 communities ranged from 11 to 68 percent in 1989. In comparison, Longmeadow [2], with no commercial waste recycling requirements, reported no commercial waste recycling. The other three programs that do not require businesses to recycle — Wellesley [6], Seattle [11], and West Linn [8] — have established economic incentives for businesses — or for private haulers serving businesses — to recycle.

Besides ordinances designating certain materials for mandatory recycling, other legislation can be effective in increasing recovery rates. The New Jersey Statewide Mandatory Source Separation and Recycling Act of 1987, which prohibits landfilling of leaves, spurred Berlin Township to implement an aggressive yard waste collection program. All seven of the New Jersey communities evaluated collect leaves for composting at least during the fall season.

When Cherry Hill [12] contracts with private companies to repair roads, the contract stipulates that the torn asphalt must be pulverized and used as a bottom layer on the same street. This process, called Pulverization Stabilization Layover, resulted in 19,413 tons of asphalt (18 percent of total waste) being recycled in 1989.

Targeting Commercial Materials for Recovery

If a community wants to recover a high percentage of its waste, it must designate a wide range of materials for recovery and secure the participation of those sectors of the community that generate the most waste.

Charts K and L show that communities with larger populations tend to generate more commercial waste[5] than residential waste. Commercial waste for 11 communities with populations under 30,000 averages 25 percent (plus or minus 16 percent) of the total waste stream. In comparison, commercial waste for the three communities with populations greater than 70,000 averages 54 percent (plus or minus 2 percent). In Seattle [11], for instance, commercial waste is 56 percent of the total generated. Even in smaller towns — Berlin Township [1], Lincoln Park [7], Fennimore [16], Woodbury [17] — commercial waste can be a large portion of the total waste generated.

---

[5]Commercial waste refers to non-residential waste. In this study, commercial waste includes waste generated by businesses and institutions (such as government buildings and schools). Where possible, we have also included non-residential bulky waste such as construction debris and asphalt with commercial waste. See Data Definitions and Methodology, pages 59-62, footnote (d) in Table 4, and case studies for more information on what is included or excluded from commercial waste generated.

Chart K
Average Proportions of Waste Generated by Residential and Commercial Sectors in Larger and Smaller Cities

(percent by weight of total waste generated)

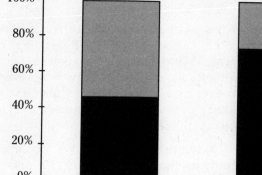
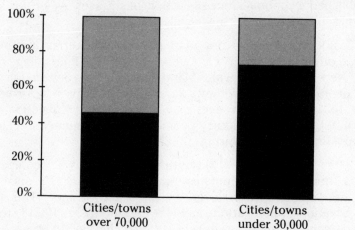

Chart L
Contribution of Commercial Sector to Waste Generation and Recovery

(percent by weight)

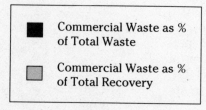

Note: Longmeadow reported no commercial waste recovery.

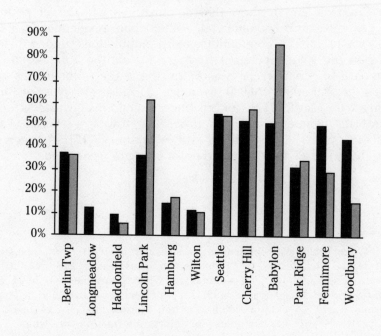

By comparing commercial materials recovery as a percentage of total recovery to commercial waste as a percentage of total waste generated, Chart L indicates which communities are successfully recovering materials from both their residential and their commercial sectors — Seattle [11], Berlin Township [1], Haddonfield [3], Hamburg [9], Wilton [10], and Park Ridge [15]. Likewise, it indicates which communities can improve either their commercial or their residential recovery efforts — Longmeadow [2], Lincoln Park [7], Babylon [14], Fennimore [16], and Woodbury [17].

Chart M shows residential and commercial waste recovery levels for those communities for which this information is available. Most of these communities target both the residential and the commercial waste sectors for materials recovery. The chart indicates which of these two sectors receives the most attention in terms of materials recovery activities, and which sectors need more attention. For instance, like Chart L, Chart M indicates that Longmeadow [2], Lincoln Park [7], Babylon [14], Fennimore [16], and Woodbury [17] can improve either their commercial or their residential waste recovery efforts.

Babylon alone among our 17 communities recovers less than 10 percent of its residential waste stream. Babylon's high commercial waste recovery level is responsible for its inclusion in this book. And, as we shall see below, the vast majority of commercial waste recovered in Babylon is construction debris.

Chart M
Commercial and Residential
Recovery Levels

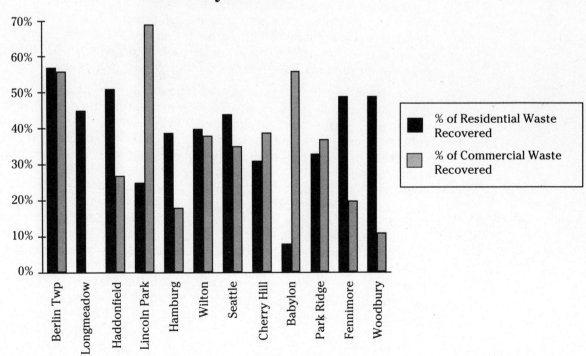

Fennimore [16], on the other hand, has a successful residential recovery program, but could improve its commercial materials recovery activities. Although the City generates more commercial waste than residential waste, its residential recovery rate is 49 percent while its commercial recovery rate is only 20 percent. In order to increase its commercial recovery rate, Fennimore may need to (1) implement measures to recover more high-grade or mixed paper (in 1989, less than 1 percent of the commercial waste stream was diverted through mixed paper recycling), (2) explore recovery of other large components of the commercial waste stream such as food waste, (3) implement a per-bag fee or variable can rate for the commercial sector (residents in Fennimore must purchase special clear plastic bags for their refuse, but receive recycling containers free), and (4) step up enforcement and public education.

Woodbury [17] also has a successful residential recycling program. Forty-nine percent of the waste hauled by the City (mostly residential) is recovered. In contrast, only 11 percent of the waste hauled by private contractors is recovered (mostly commercial and bulky wastes). Yet commercial waste makes up 45 percent of the total generated.

Communities that structure their recycling and composting programs to recover only residential materials will generally fail to maximize overall recovery levels. Commercial waste recovery strategies often differ from strategies for recovering residential waste. Whereas residential waste collection is typically designed and directly operated by local government, commercial waste collection is often carried out by the private sector. Even so, local government initiatives can encourage materials recovery without getting involved in the physical collection.

Sixteen of the 17 communities directly encourage or provide for commercial waste recovery through a variety of strategies: establishing economic incentives for businesses or private haulers serving businesses, providing convenient curbside service, allowing private haulers or businesses to deliver materials to public drop-off sites, and mandating that businesses recover certain designated materials.

In 1989, Seattle [11] recovered about 36 percent of its waste; 60 percent of the amount recovered (22 percent of the total waste) was commercial waste recycled by the private sector. The two companies collecting mixed commercial waste in Seattle offer reduced rates for collection of source-separated materials — typically a 45 percent price reduction. The City gives them an incentive to do this by excluding collection of commercial recyclables from the tax that the companies must pay on refuse collection revenues. The high transfer station tipping fee of $62 per ton for commercial customers provides another incentive for private haulers to recycle. The City plans to continue to work with private haulers to influence the setting of commercial sector rates that encourage waste reduction and recycling. Over the next 5 years, the City will require companies providing mixed waste collection to offer recycling collection service to all commercial customers, with enough unit choices to fit the needs of small and large customers.

Seattle's City office recycling program has also contributed to its commercial waste recovery level. A non-profit organization under contract with the city picks up paper and corrugated cardboard weekly from City offices.

In New Jersey, skyrocketing landfill disposal costs, combined with the Statewide Mandatory Source Separation and Recycling Act's requirements that businesses and households recycle designated materials, have spurred increased recycling by the private sector. Consider Lincoln Park [7], New Jersey, where waste generated from the commercial sector and from multi-family dwellings is collected by private haulers. The Borough reports the highest commercial/private sector recycling rate of the 17 communities in our study — 68 percent. The tipping fee at the local transfer station was also the highest — $123 per ton. The Borough requires businesses to recycle glass, aluminum, high-grade paper, newspaper, and corrugated cardboard. Although some businesses self-haul recyclable materials to the Borough drop-off center, most contract out with private haulers for collection.

Berlin Township [1], New Jersey, successfully targets its commercial waste stream for recovery. See Charts L and M. Commercial waste makes up 38 percent of the total waste generated and 37 percent of the materials recovered. In 1989, Berlin Township recycled 53 percent of its commercial waste, representing 20 percent of its total waste. The Township collects recyclables on a weekly basis from approximately 200 of its 280 institutional and business establishments (schools, offices, bars, restaurants, gas stations, and stores). This collection service is offered at no extra charge, thus creating an incentive for businesses to recycle. In addition, businesses may bring their recyclable materials to the drop-off site at the public works yard.

In Haddonfield [3], commercial waste makes up 10 percent of the total generated and 6 percent of the materials recovered. By targeting its commercial sector, even though it represents a relatively small portion of the total waste generated, Haddonfield diverted an additional 3 percent of its waste stream from disposal in 1989. Haddonfield provides curbside collection of recyclables for all but two of its 270 businesses.

The case studies provide more detailed information on each community's commercial waste recovery activities.

Targeting a Wide Range of Materials for Recovery

In order to achieve high recovery levels, communities must designate a wide range of materials for recovery. Table 6 lists the types of materials collected for recovery. Berlin Township [1] has the highest residential recovery level and also targets the widest range of materials for collection at curbside. Babylon [14], on the other hand, targets few materials from its residential sector for recovery (newspaper, metal cans, and glass). Its residential recovery rate is only 8 percent.

Charts N and O provide a breakdown of residential materials recycled as a percentage of total residential waste generated, and in pounds per capita per year, respectively. We present the residential data both ways for two reasons. First, we are able to include four more communities in Chart O than in Chart N. Second, percentages alone may be misleading since they depend on other components of the waste stream. For instance, Chart O shows that Haddonfield [3] recycles about 350 pounds of residential waste per capita per year — a figure surpassed only by Woodbury [17]. Yet in Chart N, where this amount is divided by the per capita residential waste generation of 2,016 pounds per year — the highest among our communities — the percentage of residential waste recycled appears relatively low. The high proportion of yard waste in Haddonfield's waste stream largely accounts for this high per capita generation figure.

Wastepaper from the Residential Sector

Paper, the largest component of the waste stream, also accounts for the largest portion of residential recycling. Seattle [11] and Fennimore [16] have the highest residential wastepaper recovery levels, diverting 24 percent and 22 percent of their residential waste, respectively, through wastepaper recovery alone. Both cities target a wide array of wastepaper grades. Seattle collects newspaper, corrugated cardboard, magazines, junk mail, coupons, flyers, wrapping paper, used envelopes, cereal boxes, checks, old bills, old papers, phone books, paper tubes, paper egg cartons, and brochures. In fact, the only types of paper not collected in Seattle are those contaminated with other materials such as wax coated milk cartons, juice packs with aluminum and/or plastic, used paper plates and towels, or wet paper and paperboard. In contrast, recovered wastepaper accounts for less than 10 percent of residential waste in Lincoln Park [7], Wilton [10], Cherry Hill [12], and Babylon [14]. Lincoln Park and Babylon provide curbside collection for newspaper only. In Cherry Hill and Wilton, newspaper, corrugated cardboard, and magazines are collected.

The five communities with the highest per capita recovery of residential wastepaper (Longmeadow [2], Haddonfield [3], Seattle [11], Park Ridge [15], and Woodbury [17]) all target at least newspaper, corrugated cardboard, junk mail, magazines, and high-grade office paper. Four of the five also target paperboard such as cereal boxes. Communities recycling fewer grades of wastepaper can increase recovery rates

Chart N
Residential Materials Recycled

(percent by weight of residential waste generated)

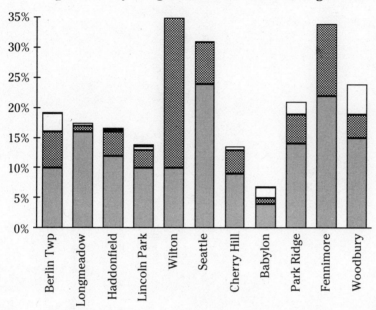

Notes: Containers recovered through deposit legislation are excluded. This affects Longmeadow and Babylon.

Woodbury figures include some commercial materials. Ferrous cans are included with scrap metal for Woodbury.

Chart O
Residential Materials Recycled

(pounds per capita per year)

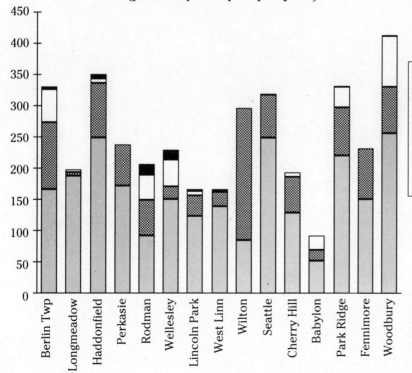

Notes: Beverage containers recovered through deposit legislation are excluded. This affects Longmeadow, Rodman, Wellesley, West Linn, and Babylon.

Perkasie, Rodman, Wellesley and Woodbury figures include some commercial materials. Ferrous cans are included with scrap metal for Woodbury.

Table 6
Materials Collected for Recovery

#	Community	Materials Collected at Curbside or Alley: Residential (a)	Materials Collected at Curbside or Alley: Commercial (b)	Materials Privately Collected (c)	Materials Collected at Drop Off, Buy-Back, or Through Bottle Bill (d)
1	Berlin Twp, NJ (e)	A,B,BR,C,F,G,L,M,N,O,P,S,T,[CT,W,WW]	A,C,F,G,N,P,S	B,H,M	A,B,C,F,G,H,L,M,N,O,P,S,T,[BR,W,WW]
2	Longmeadow, MA	C,H,L,M,N	--	[BR,GC,L]	[A,F,G,P,S,W]
3	Haddonfield, NJ	A,BR,CT,F,G,H,L,M,N,WW,[C,O,W]	C,H,[A,F,G,M,N]	C,H,[FW]	P
4	Perkasie, PA (f)	A,C,G,M,N,[BR,L]	[A,C,G,M,N]	[C]	A,C,G,N,P
5	Rodman, NY (g)	--	--	--	A,B,C,F,G,M,N,P,[H,O,S,T,W,X]
6	Wellesley, MA	--	--	[BR,GC,L]	[A,B,BR,C,F,G,GC,H,L,M,N,O,P,S,W,WW,X]
7	Lincoln Park, NJ	BR,L,N	--	--	A,BR,G,L,N,[B,C,CT,H,M,O,P,S,T,W]
8	West Linn, OR	[A,C,F,G,M,N,O,W]	[C,H]	[C]	[A,BR,C,CT,F,G,GC,H,L,M,N,O,P,WW]
9	Hamburg, NY	A,BR,C,F,G,L,N,P,[O,W]	A,C,F,G,N,P,[O]	[A,C,G]	A,G,P
10	Wilton, WI	BR,GC,L,WW,[A,C,F,G,M,N,P]	[C]	[A,C,F,G,H,M,N,P]	--
11	Seattle, WA	BR,GC,L,WW,[A,C,F,G,M,N,P]	--	--	BR,GR,L,[A,B,C,F,G,H,M,N,O,P,S,W,WW,X]
12	Cherry Hill, NJ	A,BR,C,F,G,L,M,N,[S,T,W]	C,H,[A,F,G]	C,H,O,[CD,FW,M,T,WW]	O
13	Upper Twp, NJ	A,C,F,G,H,L,M,N,P,[BR,GC,W,WW]	A,C,F,G,H,M,N,[P]	C,H,M,O,[FW,S]	A,F,G,H,M,N
14	Babylon, NY	A,F,G,N,[L,W]	--	[C,CD,H,M]	A,F,G,N,[B,C,O,P,S,T,W,X]
15	Park Ridge, NJ (h)	A,C,CT,F,G,H,L,M,N,P,W	C,[A,F,G,H,M,N,P]	C,[FW,O]	A,C,F,G,H,M,N,P,WW,[B,BR,GC,O,S,W]
16	Fennimore, WI	A,BR,C,F,G,L,M,N,P,WW,[W]	A,BR,C,F,G,H,L,M,N,P,WW	C,[FW]	BR,GC,L,WW
17	Woodbury, NJ	A,BR,C,CT,F,G,GC,H,L,M,N,P,W,WW	A,C,F,G,H,M,P	C,[FW]	A,C,F,G,M,N,O

Key: Materials enclosed in square brackets [ ] are those for which set-out or drop-off is voluntary. Participation is mandatory for all other materials.

A = Aluminum	B = Batteries	BR = Brush	C = Corrugated Cardboard	CD = Construction Debris
CT = Christmas Trees	F = Ferrous Cans	FW = Food Waste	G = Glass	GC = Grass Clippings
H = High-Grade Paper	L = Leaves	M = Mixed Paper	N = Newspapers	O = Oil
P = Plastics	S = Scrap Metal	T = Tires	W = White Goods, Appliances, or Furniture	
WW = Wood Waste	X = Other	-- = Not applicable		

Notes:

(a) Materials that public or private haulers will pick up from households.

(b) Materials that public or private haulers operating under the municipal curbside program will pick up from businesses served.

(c) Materials from the commercial sector being privately recycled or composted by businesses or private haulers.

(d) Materials that residents may take to another collection point.

(e) Businesses must choose 3 of the materials mandated for residents to recycle; the 10 listed above are those most often chosen.

(f) Junk mail is not mandated, but magazines are.

(g) Magazines are not mandated, but paperboard is.

(h) Businesses, commercial establishments, and government buildings are required to separate 1 of 6 specified materials. Most choose to recycle corrugated cardboard.

by targeting some of these additional grades. Even Berlin Township [1], which may have the highest residential recovery rate in the country, can increase its rate by targeting junk mail, high-grade office paper, magazines, and other mixed paper in addition to the newspaper, corrugated cardboard, and paperboard boxes it currently collects from the residential sector.

Aluminum, Glass, Plastics, and Ferrous Cans from the Residential Sector

Charts N and O also indicate that targeting glass, aluminum, plastics, and ferrous cans for recycling can significantly increase the percentage of residential waste recovered and, of course, the amount of materials recovered per capita. Here again, targeting a wide range of materials increases recovery. Wilton [10] is the most successful at this. In addition to glass, tin, and aluminum, the Village targets a variety of plastic containers (milk jugs, HDPE and PET beverage containers, shampoo and detergent bottles) and a variety of film plastics (bread wrappers, saran wrap, shopping bags, and milk bags). Plastics made up 21 percent by weight of the residential recyclables Wilton collected in 1989. Berlin Township [1] also targets a wide range of recyclables including metal and bi-metal cans, and HDPE and PET plastics (beverage, shampoo, and detergent containers). Fennimore [16] targets a variety of HDPE and PET plastics (beverage, shampoo, detergent, and even motor oil containers) in addition to glass, tin, and aluminum. Charts N and O also indicate that Lincoln Park [7], Cherry Hill [12], and Babylon [14] can increase their recovery rates by targeting additional materials for residential collection.

Other Materials from the Residential Sector

Scrap metals (white goods, appliances, non-ferrous scrap, and other large pieces of metal such as aluminum furniture or doors) are another component of the residential waste stream that has significantly increased recycling levels in communities collecting these materials for recovery. In Berlin Township [1], white goods, appliances, and other scrap metal are collected from households on a weekly basis. These materials alone accounted for 16 percent of the residential recyclables collected in 1989. Rodman [5], Hamburg [9], Babylon [14], and Park Ridge [15] have all increased their residential recycling rates 2 to 5 percent by targeting scrap metals.

Targeting even small components of the residential waste stream such as tires, batteries, books, and motor oil has helped raise recovery levels in Rodman [5], Wellesley [6], Haddonfield [3], and Lincoln Park [7]. Rodman recovered 2 percent of its waste stream through recovery of oil, car batteries, tires, and books at its drop-off center. In Wellesley, motor oil, batteries, books, eyeglasses, clothing, and other reusable items accounted for 7 percent of all recyclables collected at the drop-off center.

Wastepaper from the Commercial Sector

Chart P, which provides a breakdown of commercial materials recycled, shows that paper may be as critical to high levels of commercial recycling as it is to high levels of residential recycling.   In 1989, corrugated cardboard recycling alone diverted 38 percent of Wilton's [10] commercial waste and 34 percent of Lincoln Park's [7].   Collecting other paper, such as newspaper and high-grade office paper, for recycling has raised commercial recovery rates in Berlin Township [1], Lincoln Park [7], Seattle [11], and Park Ridge [15].

Lincoln Park's recycling law requires businesses to recycle high-grade paper and newspaper, among other materials.   These two grades of paper alone accounted for 37 percent of recyclables collected from the commercial sector and 25 percent of total commercial waste generated in 1988.

Recovery of newspaper, corrugated cardboard, and mixed paper from local businesses in Park Ridge diverted 21 percent of the Borough's commercial waste in 1989.

Seattle diverted 31 percent of its commercial waste by recovering newspaper, corrugated cardboard, and mixed paper including high-grade office and computer paper.   A number of private recyclers in Seattle collect recyclables from businesses.

Chart P
Commercial Materials Recycled
(percent by weight of commercial waste generated)

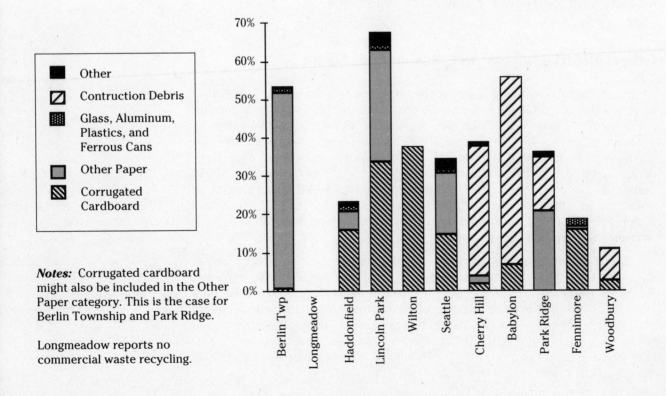

Notes: Corrugated cardboard might also be included in the Other Paper category. This is the case for Berlin Township and Park Ridge.

Longmeadow reports no commercial waste recycling.

Construction Debris

Although many may consider construction debris industrial waste rather than municipal solid waste,[6] it frequently is a solid waste problem at the municipal level. Bulky waste (including white goods, other appliances and furniture, car batteries, tree stumps, tires, asphalt, concrete, and other construction debris) is often handled by the local Department of Public Works, thus burdening local collection and disposal systems. Most bulky waste can be recovered for remanufacturing or reuse. For these reasons, we requested the tonnage of bulky waste from all our communities, and, where possible, have included it in total waste generated.[7]

Recycling construction debris has contributed significantly to commercial waste recovery rates in Babylon [14], Cherry Hill [12], Park Ridge [15], and Woodbury [17]. See Chart P.

In Babylon, concrete alone accounted for 68 percent of materials recovered in 1989 (66,000 tons) and is responsible for the City's 56 percent commercial waste recovery rate. In fact, because Babylon burns half the paper it collects and targets so few materials for recovery, it has only a modest recovery program aside from its concrete recycling efforts.

Cherry Hill recycled 34 percent of its commercial waste (18 percent of total waste) in 1989 by using old torn-up asphalt in new road construction.

Recycling asphalt has also significantly increased commercial recycling rates in Park Ridge (14 percent of commercial waste) and Woodbury (8 percent of commercial waste). As part of Park Ridge's street resurfacing program, any asphalt milled prior to the resurfacing is used for the construction of new road beds.

In Woodbury, 36 percent of the commercial waste stream is bulky waste such as construction debris. Although 21 percent of bulky waste is already being recovered, Woodbury could increase its current 32 percent recovery rate by targeting more bulky wastes for recovery.

The experience of these four communities indicates that construction debris often makes up a significant portion of overall waste generation and that it can readily be recovered.

---

[6]Such as the National Recycling Coalition.

[7]In fact, for four communities, waste disposal tonnage figures included bulky wastes, and breakdowns were not available. Refer to footnote (d) in Table 4 or directly to case studies for more information on whether or not construction debris is included in a community's waste generation figures.

Other Materials from the Commercial Sector

Chart P indicates that even the best programs have room for improvement. For instance, glass, aluminum, plastics, and ferrous cans may represent a significant portion of the commercial waste stream. Yet programs targeting these materials have increased commercial recovery levels only 1 to 2 percent (Berlin Township [1], Haddonfield [3], Lincoln Park [7], Seattle [11], and Fennimore [16]). Improving collection systems and establishing incentives could help increase recovery levels.

Food waste is another significant component of the commercial waste stream typically not targeted for recovery. Where food waste is being recovered, such as by private businesses in Cherry Hill [12], Lincoln Park [7], and Park Ridge [15], commercial recovery rates have increased by 1 to 2 percent. Pilot projects to recover this material for animal feed or through composting will be important for communities striving to maximize recovery rates.

Motor oil and non-ferrous and ferrous scrap metals can also contribute to increased commercial recovery levels. Recovery of these materials alone diverted 2 percent of Lincoln Park's commercial waste from disposal. In Seattle [11], recovery of motor oil and appliances alone diverted 3 percent of commercial waste from disposal.

Other Program Design Considerations

In addition to mandating participation, implementing a composting program, targeting both residential and commercial waste for recovery, and designating a wide range of materials for recovery, communities need to consider other factors in developing materials recovery programs that will play a primary role in solid waste management. These include curbside and/or drop-off service, public or private collection service, pick-up frequency, container types and sizes, economic incentives, and publicity and education.

Table 7 compares recycling program characteristics among the 17 communities. It indicates, for instance, that most provide drop-off and curbside service, most are publicly run and mandatory, most serve at least a portion of their business community, and most offer frequent pick-up of materials.

Pick-up Frequency

Frequent pick-up of materials for recycling or composting increases participation and set-out rates, which, in turn, increase recovery rates. Programs with weekly pick-up have consistently high participation rates, while those with less frequent pick-up tend to have fluctuating participation rates. The average participation rate of the eight curbside

Table 7
Recycling Program Characteristics

#	Community	Type of Program	Total Households	Households Served	Total Businesses	Businesses Served (a)	Mandatory Source Separation	Public/Private Operation (b)	Pick-up Frequency	Same Day Collection (c)	Containers Provided	Segregations Required (d)	Economic Incentives	Participation Rate (%) (e)
1	Berlin Twp, NJ	CS, DO	1,700	1,600	280	200	Yes	Public	Weekly	Yes	Yes	3	Yes	95
2	Longmeadow, MA	CS, DO	5,744	5,744	150	0	Yes	Contract	Weekly (f)	Yes	No	2	No	90
3	Haddonfield, NJ	CS, DO	4,750	4,750	270	268	Yes	Public	Weekly	Yes	Yes	3	Yes	95
4	Perkasie, PA	CS, DO	3,600	3,200	75	12	Yes	Public	Varies (g)	No	Yes	4	Yes	100
5	Rodman, NY	DO	270	270	2	2 (h)	Yes	Public	--	--	--	--	No	90
6	Wellesley, MA	DO	8,500	8,500	1,000	NA	No	Public	--	--	--	--	No	82
7	Lincoln Park, NJ	CS, DO	5,500	4,450	200	0	Yes	Public	Monthly	No	No	1	Yes	85-95
8	West Linn, OR	CS, DO	5,900	5,900	379	379	No	Private	Weekly	Yes	No (i)	3	Yes	84
9	Hamburg, NY	CS	3,350	3,350	110	NA	Yes	Public	Weekly	Yes	No	3	No	98
10	Wilton, WI	CS	200	200	9	5	No	Public	Biweekly	No	No	8	No	50-60
11	Seattle, WA	CS, DO, BB	250,913	147,000	30,000	0	No	Contract	Varies	No	Yes	Varies (j)	Yes	77
12	Cherry Hill, NJ	CS	24,000	18,810	1,009	190	Yes	Contract	Weekly	Yes	Yes	2	Yes	92
13	Upper Twp, NJ	CS, DO	3,800	3,800	260	222	Yes	Public	Weekly	Yes	No	2	No	85
14	Babylon, NY	CS, DO	53,000	50,000	5,800	0	Yes	Contract	Biweekly (k)	No	No	2	No	63
15	Park Ridge, NJ	CS, DO	2,800	2,800	75	5	Yes	Public	Biweekly	No	No	2	No	90
16	Fennimore, WI	CS	850	850	96	96	Yes	Public	Biweekly	No	Yes	5	Yes	100
17	Woodbury, NJ	CS, DO	3,500	3,500	175	NA	Yes	Public	Weekly	No	No	8	Yes	85

Key: CS = Curbside   DO = Drop-Off   BB = Buy-Back   -- = Not applicable

Notes:

(a) Those served by the community's municipal curbside collection program for recyclables. This figure should not be confused with the number of businesses actually recycling. Figures may include institutions such as schools or government buildings.

(b) "Public" -- city provides service; "Contract" -- city contracts with one or more providers; "Private" -- one or more private haulers provide the service.

(c) Same day as refuse collection.

(d) The number of segregations citizens must make when setting out recyclable materials at curbside. Excludes the set-out of appliances, other white goods, tires, car batteries, and motor oil because these materials are not generated by a household on a frequent basis.

(e) The portion of households served that take part in the curbside collection program for recyclable materials. There are several exceptions: Rodman, Wellesley, Lincoln Park, West Linn, Seattle, Park Ridge, and Babylon. See Data Definitions and Methodology. Refer to case studies for an explanation of the specific method of calculation.

(f) Newspaper and mixed paper collected one week, corrugated cardboard and other paperboard the next.

(g) Newspaper and corrugated cardboard collected once a month, aluminum and glass weekly.

(h) Served by drop-off not curbside.

(i) Containers were provided in 1990.

(j) 1 segregation is required in south section; 4 segregations are required in north section.

(k) Commingled collected one week and wastepaper the next.

programs with weekly collection is 91 percent (plus or minus 6 percent). For the seven programs with less frequent pick-up, participation averages 81 percent (plus or minus 18 percent).

The experience of Haddonfield, Seattle, and Park Ridge demonstrates the advantage of more frequent collection of recyclables.

When Haddonfield switched from biweekly to weekly collection of recyclables, set-out rates for glass and newspaper increased 150 percent.

In Seattle, the north section of the City is served with weekly collection of recyclables, while the south section receives only monthly collection. The participation rate is 90 percent in the north section, and 67 percent in the south section. The amount of recyclables collected per participating household per year is 18 percent greater in the north than in the south.[8]

Park Ridge initially offered curbside collection of newspaper once per month and of commingled recyclables twice per month. In 1990, in response to requests from citizens, paper collection was increased to twice per month. The amount of paper recycled has increased as a consequence. For the first 5 months of 1989, an average of 148,000 pounds of paper per month was collected. The monthly average for the same months in 1990 is 171,000 pounds — a 16 percent increase.

As mentioned earlier, programs with year-round collection of yard waste generally have higher composting levels than those with only seasonal collection.

Container Types and Sizes

Providing containers to households for storage and set-out of recyclable materials can increase participation rates as well as recovery levels. Participation rates for the six communities that provide containers for curbside collection of recyclables average 93 percent (plus or minus 9 percent). For the nine that do not provide containers, participation averages 82 percent (plus or minus 14 percent). Babylon, which has the lowest participation rate of all the mandatory programs in this study, may be hampering its program by requiring residents to purchase special 20-gallon buckets for $4 each.

When choosing a container size to provide to residents, communities should take two factors into consideration: (1) containers should be large enough to accommodate substantial program growth, and (2) commingling many recyclable materials will necessitate larger containers than the commingling just a few materials.

---

[8]In addition to pick-up frequency, socio-economic factors may contribute to these differences. The north section has many more affluent pockets that the south section.

Many curbside recycling programs provide a 5- or 6-gallon container to residents for setting out commingled glass bottles and metal cans. However, as communities increase the materials targeted for collection, step up enforcement and publicity/education programs, and establish economic incentives, the amount of materials recovered increases and larger containers may become necessary.

Berlin Township's experience with different containers provides the most striking example of the importance of size. In February 1988, Rutgers University gave the Township and its citizens 2,000 yellow 20-gallon buckets for a pilot study on plastics collection. Previously, residents had used 5-gallon buckets to store their commingled recyclables (glass, aluminum cans, and other metal cans). During 1986 and 1987, the Township had collected an average of 181 tons of commingled food and beverage containers. In 1988, the Township collected 27 tons of plastics, but the overall tonnage of commingled recyclables increased to 296 tons. In other words, the amount of commingled recyclables, excluding plastics, increased 49 percent with the distribution of the larger buckets.

Berlin Township had tried several different storage containers before deciding to stay with the 20-gallon buckets. In 1984, the Township received 100 blue rectangular recycling boxes for demonstration purposes. The boxes, which were distributed to residents, were popular for storing record albums, and disappeared quickly. The collection crew has found that, overall, the 20-gallon buckets are sturdier than the square boxes or the 5-gallon buckets and easier to empty. Residents find the 5-gallon buckets convenient for short-term storage of recyclable materials before they dump these into the 20-gallon container left outside, or for storage of extra materials that do not fit in the 20-gallon containers.

Chart Q provides information on container size/capacity available per week for storing and setting out glass and plastic bottles and metal cans plotted against the amount of these materials collected from each household served by curbside collection. The chart includes only those communities that provide containers at no extra charge.[9] On a weekly basis, Berlin Township provides its residents with the largest container capacity for storing commingled glass, plastic (PET and HDPE including detergent and shampoo bottles), and metal cans; it has the highest recovery rate per household. In comparison, Perkasie provides its residents with the smallest container (a 5-gallon bucket) and is recovering the lowest amount of the six programs. Perkasie does not include tin cans or plastics in its collection program. The Borough could increase its recycling level by targeting these additional materials and providing greater storage capacity. Fennimore, which targets tin cans and PET and HDPE plastic bottles, and which provides larger containers, collects 60 percent more recyclables (excluding paper) per household than Perkasie.

---

[9]Cherry Hill, which provides 6-gallon containers, is excluded from Chart Q because tonnages for residential waste recycled include some commercial materials.

Chart Q
Size of Storage Container Provided
and Recovery Levels for
Glass, Plastic, and Metal

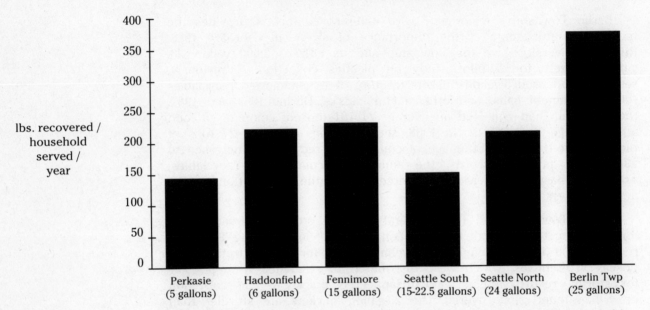

Notes: Container sizes, in gallons per week, refers to the size of containers provided for setting out and storing commingled glass, plastic, tin, and aluminum. The capacity given for Seattle South includes that provided for wastepaper.

In Seattle, the two different curbside collection programs for recyclables, one that serves the City's north section and another that serves the City's south section, exemplify the effect set-out method, pick-up frequency, and other factors can have on participation rates and recovery levels. Households signed up for the monthly curbside pick-up program in the south section receive either a 60- or a 90-gallon container in which to commingle all their recyclables (wastepaper and food and beverage containers). In the north section, served with weekly collection, residents receive 3 stacking containers of 12 gallons each (36 gallons total). One stacking container holds food and beverage containers, another holds mixed wastepaper, and a third holds newspaper. Although their containers are larger, residents in the south actually have less storage capacity on a weekly basis than those in the north (15 to 22.5 gallons versus 36 gallons). The north program collects 18 percent more recyclables per household served than the south program. Furthermore, materials collected in the south section go to a processing center that uses a combination of conveyors, trommels, disc screens, magnetic separation, air classification, hand picking, and baling to sort and recover the commingled materials. In comparison, the partially separated recyclables collected in the north in compartmentalized trucks, go to a facility that is used primarily for baling. The level of contamination of recyclables in the south is almost five times that of the north. This further enhances the greater recovery levels achieved in the north as compared to the south.

Providing containers to businesses and institutions (such as schools and government buildings) may also encourage participation from this sector. Berlin Township, Upper Township, and Fennimore all provide containers to businesses for storage and set-out of recyclable materials. Berlin Township provides 55-gallon containers for storage of glass to bars and restaurants. Other businesses may request a 20-gallon container for storage of glass, aluminum and tin cans, and plastic HDPE and PET containers. Upper Township has supplied 460 20-gallon containers to large generators of recyclable materials, such as campgrounds, bars, and restaurants. Recycling containers have also been placed on Upper Township's boardwalks and beaches. In Park Ridge, where schools are served with curbside collection of recyclables, each classroom has clearly labeled recycling boxes for paper. Yellow barrels for cans and other recyclables are placed around the school and in the cafeteria. The cafeterias recycle ferrous cans, plastic containers, and glass containers.

Economic Incentives

Economic incentives such as high tipping fees at disposal facilities, reduced or no tipping fees to haulers who deliver recyclable or compostable loads, volume-based refuse rates, and assessing fines for noncompliance with recycling laws can play a major role in increasing participation in materials recovery programs, thus increasing materials recovery rates and reducing waste disposal.

Tipping Fees

Tipping fees may be one of the most significant factors contributing to commercial waste recycling. Chart R indicates that as tipping fees increase at disposal facilities, commercial recycling rates also increase. Commercial recycling levels may be more sensitive to higher tipping fees than residential recycling levels for two reasons. First, commercial waste is typically handled by the private sector. Higher tipping fees are passed back more quickly to the commercial sector than to the residential sector, where collection costs are often hidden in the tax base. Second, collection costs may represent a greater portion of overall costs for residential waste than for commercial waste, where fewer stops are made per ton collected. Thus, disposal fees make up a greater portion of overall costs for commercial waste than for residential waste.

Lincoln Park [7] has the highest tipping fee of the communities in Chart R and reports the highest commercial recycling level. Longmeadow [2], on the other hand, reports no commercial recycling; the Town has one of the lowest tipping fees in this study, at $23 per ton. Fennimore's [16] commercial recycling level has more to do with the City's recycling initiatives than with tipping fees. The City of Fennimore handles all the waste generated in the City, including commercial waste. There

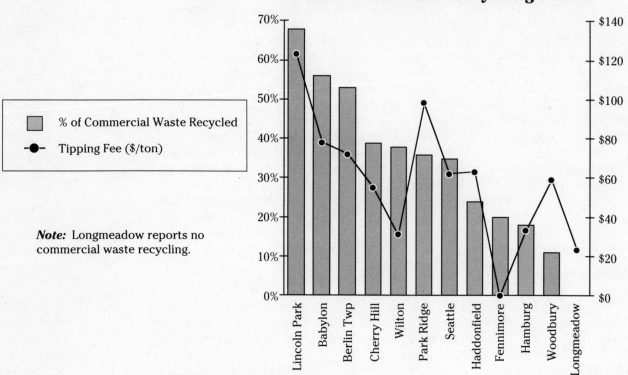

Chart R
Tipping Fees and
Commercial Waste Recycling Levels

Note: Longmeadow reports no commercial waste recycling.

are no tipping fees at the landfill, which is owned by the City. In both Park Ridge [15] and Woodbury [17], commercial recycling levels may be higher than they appear. Private haulers or businesses that recycle may not always report recovered tonnage to their local government agencies. In both these communities, commercial recycling levels represent private sector recycling.

Several communities offer reduced tipping fees to haulers that bring in separated loads of recyclables or yard waste. In Wellesley [6], dumping permits are sold to commercial landscapers for the leaf season, allowing them to dump loads of uncontaminated yard waste at the composting site at a cost lower than the $80 per ton tipping fee at the transfer station. Seattle's [11] two transfer stations accept clean yard waste (grass clippings, leaves, and brush) from residential and commercial customers at a discounted fee. This incentive diverted 2 percent of the City's total waste in 1989. Economic incentives for landscapers to bring their yard waste to composting sites have significantly increased recovery rates in Longmeadow [2], Wellesley [6], and Upper Township [13]. (See page for a more detailed discussion.)

In some communities — Rodman [5], Lincoln Park [7], and Wellesley [6] — businesses or private haulers are allowed to deliver recyclables free of charge to the town drop-off center. In Wellesley, all incoming loads from private haulers are weighed twice — first for a total weight, including recyclable materials, and a second time after these materials have been sorted out. The tonnage bill is based on the weight to be disposed, thus providing an incentive for private haulers using the facility to recycle. As a result, 200 private haulers were attracted to the facility in 1989. In contrast, Longmeadow, which discourages businesses and private haulers from using its drop-off recycling center, reports no commercial waste recycling.

Volume-Based Collection Fees

Three of the 17 communities charge by volume for mixed waste — a direct economic incentive for residents to recover as much as possible and generate as little waste as possible. Seattle [11] and West Linn [8] have variable can rates. Perkasie [4] has per-bag fees.

In Seattle, less than 30 percent of the tonnage recovered was attributable to the publicly sponsored residential curbside collection program, which began in 1988. Prior to this program, the private sector alone recovered almost 25 percent of Seattle's waste. This level of recycling is attributed to the City's variable can rate for mixed refuse, which has been in effect since 1981. By charging by volume for the waste generated, the City provides a strong incentive to its citizens to recycle as much as possible. Almost 40 percent of residential materials recovered were collected at drop-off centers located throughout the City. Thus, even though only 59 percent of the households are served by the residential curbside recycling and composting programs, Seattle still managed to recover 44 percent of its residential waste in 1989.

Seattle offers different rates for four different container sizes available at the household level for non source-separated refuse: a 19-gallon "mini-can" at $10.70 per month; a 32-gallon can at $13.75 per month; a 60-gallon can at $22.75 per month; and the largest container, a 90-gallon can, at $31.75 per month. An analysis published by Seattle's Solid Waste Utility[10] showed that more refuse would have been generated and disposed if the City had not imposed a variable rate structure. In 1986 and 1987, the City increased refuse collection rates. More customers subscribed to fewer cans. Curbside recycling, instituted early in 1988, further influenced the downward shift in subscriptions. The weighted average number of cans subscribed by single-family customers decreased from 3.5 to 1.4 per customer between 1981 and 1988.

Although residents pay no direct fees for participating in Seattle's recycling program, they are charged a nominal fee (less than the charge for refuse collection) for collection of source-separated yard waste for composting. For $2 per month, haulers contracting with the City collect up to 20 cans, bags, or bundles of grass clippings, leaves, and brush. The modest fee reduction has had surprising results. Tonnages during 1989 totalled approximately 95 percent of the tonnage goal for 1998.

---

[10]Lisa Skumatz, *Volume-Based Rates in Solid Waste: Seattle's Experience,* Seattle Solid Waste Utility, Seattle, Washington, February 1989.

Businesses also have an economic incentive to recycle in Seattle. Pick-up of source-separated materials costs 45 percent less than pick-up of mixed waste.

In West Linn, weekly collection of one 32-gallon container of refuse costs $11.30 per month. Two containers cost $22.60 per month. Recyclers are charged $1.50 less per can for pick-up of a 20-gallon mini-can. Participation in the recycling program is free. In addition, starting July 1990, the private hauler providing all curbside service will offer year-round on-call collection of source-separated yard debris for a nominal charge (less than the charge for refuse collection).

In January 1988, the Borough of Perkasie replaced its flat annual fee of $120 per household for refuse collection and disposal with a per-bag fee. All wastes collected and disposed by the Borough must be contained in green 20- or 40-pound plastic bags sold by the Borough. The 20-pound bag sells for 80 cents; 40-pound bags sell for $1.50. A comparison of 1988 municipal solid waste generation with the average generated from 1985 to 1987 shows a source reduction of 26 percent by weight. Perkasie has the lowest per capita residential waste generation among the suburban communities evaluated. While the number of households served by the Borough has increased 23 percent, total waste generated in 1989 has increased only 2 percent over the average amount generated from 1985 to 1987.

Publicity and Education

Virtually all 17 communities inform citizens about their recycling and composting programs. Publicity and education measures take many forms: calendars, flyers, newsletters, school curricula, articles, ads in local newspapers and on radio shows, videos, slide shows, demonstrations and exhibits, posters, utility bill inserts, buttons, and telephone hotlines.

Chart S shows residential recovery levels plotted against costs per household for education and publicity. These costs vary from 1 cent per household in Longmeadow [2] to $2.95 per household in Babylon [14]. Yet Longmeadow recovers 45 percent of its residential waste, whereas Babylon only recovers 8 percent. This indicates that, while education and publicity may be necessary, program design characteristics (such as economic incentives and targeting a large portion of the waste stream for recovery) are more effective in achieving high participation and high recovery rates.

Chart S
Education and Publicity Costs and Level
of Residential Materials Recovered

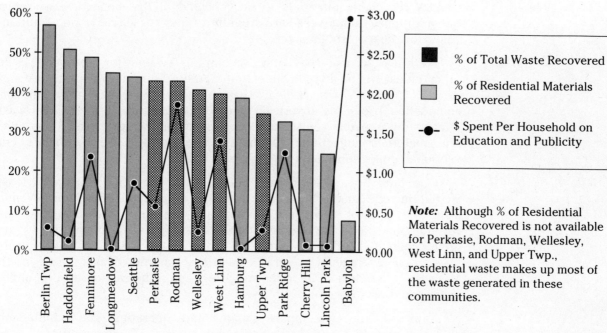

Note: Although % of Residential Materials Recovered is not available for Perkasie, Rodman, Wellesley, West Linn, and Upper Twp., residential waste makes up most of the waste generated in these communities.

The Economics of Recycling and Composting

Evaluating the economics of community materials recovery programs is a challenging task. Although these operations have become much more businesslike in recent years, the lack of reliable and consistent data is still disappointing. Publicly funded programs may underestimate their costs by including large volunteer efforts, while private operations' data are often unavailable for public scrutiny.

There is another difficulty. Traditional refuse handling systems have two components: collection and landfill disposal. Recycling and composting programs have three elements: collection, processing, and marketing. Thus data on recycling/composting collection costs alone underestimate the full costs of these programs. Yet it is also true that currently most recycling/composting programs are viewed as add-ons to conventional waste hauling systems. Most cities continue their conventional refuse pick-up and disposal operations, complete with energy-inefficient and expensive compactor trucks. They collect recoverable materials separately from refuse, and consider their recycling and composting operations as additional expenditures.

When materials recovery programs achieve levels above 50 percent, they are no longer simply add-ons to conventional waste handling systems. At that point recycling/composting costs are offset by the reduced costs of conventional collection.   In Rodman, refuse collection and disposal costs were cut in half after the recycling program began. In Hamburg, recycling is completely integrated into the traditional collection system.   A trailer attached to village waste-hauling vehicles enables recyclable materials to be collected at the same time as refuse. No additional employees are required, and practically no additional collection costs are incurred.

Were we to use the same accounting system for Hamburg as for other cities, we might conclude that Hamburg's recycling costs are near zero.   However, we believe that in the future, as recycling and composting programs divert 60 and 70 percent or more of the waste stream, our current refuse collection systems will give way to recoverable materials collection systems.   Therefore, we use Hamburg's conventional collection costs as its recycling costs.

One final note.   As pointed out above, recycling/composting costs should include marketing costs, but they should also include revenues from the sale of recovered materials.   We have included the sales revenues in our case studies, but for comparative purposes we use gross costs.   In this manner we exclude the effect of higher sales prices, on average, for scrap materials on the coasts than in the Midwest.   Readers can refer to the case studies for the complete economic breakdowns.

Tables 8 to 13 compare capital and operating and maintenance costs of recycling and composting among the 17 communities.   Table 13, Per Ton Costs for Materials Recovery Programs, indicates that per ton costs vary a great deal from one community to another.   Many factors contribute to this variation, including number and types of collection vehicles, high labor costs, household density, materials processing costs, and volume of materials collected.   Although many solid waste professionals contend that beverage container deposit legislation will increase program costs due to loss of materials revenues, net per ton costs shown in Table 13 for the six communities located in states with deposit legislation do not support this argument.

Table 8

Capital Costs for Materials Recovery Programs, in Constant 1989 Dollars (a)

#	Community	Recycling Capital Costs			Composting Capital Costs			Total Capital Costs
		Collection (b)	Processing (c)	Subtotal	Collection (b)	Processing (d)	Subtotal	
1	Berlin Twp, NJ	$90,320	$0	$90,320	$29,041	$12,761	$41,802	$132,122
2	Longmeadow, MA	--	--	--	$544,302	$0	$544,302	$544,302
3	Haddonfield, NJ	$76,152	$0	$76,152	$283,180	$43,152	$326,332	$402,484
4	Perkasie, PA	$20,542	$0	$20,542	NA	NA	NA	NA
5	Rodman, NY	$11,697	$6,800	$18,497	$0	$0	$0	$18,497
6	Wellesley, MA	$0	$60,047	$60,047	$0	$42,003	$42,003	$102,050
7	Lincoln Park, NJ	$6,692	$0	$6,692	$18,432	$18,784	$37,216	$43,908
8	West Linn, OR	$29,332	$8,761	$38,093	$0	$68,045	$68,045	$106,138
9	Hamburg, NY	$69,967	$4,713	$74,680	$32,000	$22,341	$54,341	$129,021
10	Wilton, WI	$300	$0	$300	$0	$0	$0	$300
11	Seattle, WA	--	--	--	--	--	--	--
12	Cherry Hill, NJ	--	--	--	$220,119	$34,952	$255,071	$255,071
13	Upper Twp, NJ	$126,977	$0	$126,977	$138,759	$1,888	$140,647	$267,624
14	Babylon, NY	--	--	--	NA	NA	NA	NA
15	Park Ridge, NJ	$106,822	$0	$106,822	$15,515	$10,371	$25,886	$132,708
16	Fennimore, WI	$77,358	$37,922	$115,280	$3,000	$744	$3,744	$119,024
17	Woodbury, NJ	$144,199	$0	$144,199	$281,902	$39,425	$321,327	$465,526

Key: NA = Data not available   -- = Not applicable

Notes:

(a) Each capital expenditure was converted to constant 1989 dollars using producer price indices.

(b) The capital investment made for equipment used to collect materials for recycling or composting.

(c) The capital investment made for equipment used to process recyclable materials in preparation for marketing to end-users. Processing typically includes sorting, contaminant removal, and crushing or baling.

(d) The capital investment made for equipment used to process -- compost, chip, or mulch -- organic materials. Processing or composting equipment typically includes shredders or chippers and front-end loaders.

Table 9

Annualized Capital Costs for Materials Recovery Programs, in Constant 1989 Dollars

#	Community	Annualized Recycling Capital Costs			Annualized Composting Capital Costs			Total Annualized Capital Costs
		Collection	Processing	Subtotal	Collection	Processing	Subtotal	
1	Berlin Twp, NJ	$14,699	$0	$14,699	$4,726	$2,077	$6,803	$21,502
2	Longmeadow, MA	--	--	--	$88,583	$0	$88,583	$88,583
3	Haddonfield, NJ	$12,393	$0	$12,393	$46,086	$7,023	$53,109	$65,502
4	Perkasie, PA	$3,343	$0	$3,343	NA	NA	NA	NA
5	Rodman, NY	$1,904	$1,107	$3,010	$0	$0	$0	$3,010
6	Wellesley, MA	$0	$9,772	$9,772	$0	$6,836	$6,836	$16,608
7	Lincoln Park, NJ	$1,089	$0	$1,089	$3,000	$3,057	$6,057	$7,146
8	West Linn, OR	$4,774	$1,426	$6,199	$0	$11,074	$11,074	$17,273
9	Hamburg, NY	$11,387	$767	$12,154	$5,208	$3,636	$8,844	$20,998
10	Wilton, WI	$49	$0	$49	$0	$0	$0	$49
11	Seattle, WA	--	--	--	--	--	--	--
12	Cherry Hill, NJ	--	--	--	$35,823	$5,688	$41,512	$41,512
13	Upper Twp, NJ	$20,665	$0	$20,665	$22,582	$307	$22,890	$43,555
14	Babylon, NY	--	--	--	NA	NA	NA	NA
15	Park Ridge, NJ	$17,385	$0	$17,385	$2,525	$1,688	$4,213	$21,598
16	Fennimore, WI	$12,590	$6,172	$18,761	$488	$121	$609	$19,371
17	Woodbury, NJ	$23,468	$0	$23,468	$45,878	$6,416	$52,294	$75,762

Key: NA = Data not available   -- = Not applicable

Note: Capital costs presented in Table 8 have been converted to annual costs by assuming 10 percent interest over a 10-year amortization period.

Table 10

Operating and Maintenance Costs for Materials Recovery Programs, 1989

#	Community	Recycling				Composting				Total O&M Recovery Costs
		Collection	Processing	O&M Costs Other (a)	Subtotal	Collection	Processing	O&M Costs Other (a)	Subtotal	
1	Berlin Twp, NJ	$28,982	$9,360	$4,500	$42,842	$4,185	$864	$0	$5,049	$47,891
2	Longmeadow, MA	$73,340	$0	$45	$73,385	$47,812	$89,733	$0	$137,545	$210,930
3	Haddonfield, NJ	$109,855	$0	$1,000	$110,855	$150,000	$19,425	$0	$169,425	$280,280
4	Perkasie, PA	$37,173	$5,129	$3,229	$45,531	NA	NA	NA	NA	NA
5	Rodman, NY	$200	$3,791	$500	$4,491	$0	$0	$0	$0	$4,491
6	Wellesley, MA	$0	$38,385	$10,668	$49,053	$0	$39,439	$10,668	$50,107	$99,160
7	Lincoln Park, NJ	$57,000	$8,000	$12,800	$77,800	$31,000	$0	$0	$31,000	$108,800
8	West Linn, OR	$112,807	$0	$31,331	$144,138	$0	$30,398	$7,322	$37,720	$181,858
9	Hamburg, NY	$49,183	$33,267	$100	$82,550	NA	NA	NA	NA	NA
10	Wilton, WI	$200	$0	$0	$200	$380	$0	$0	$380	$580
11	Seattle, WA (b)	$2,098,820	$30,835	$82,900	$2,212,555	$2,637,531	$202,477	$131,000	$2,971,008	$5,183,563
12	Cherry Hill, NJ	$300,000	included (c)	$4,000	$304,000	$99,000	$5,000	$0	$104,000	$408,000
13	Upper Twp, NJ	$148,000	$0	$9,400	$157,400	$42,600	$10,608	$0	$53,208	$210,608
14	Babylon, NY (d)	NA	NA	$156,496	NA	NA	NA	NA	NA	NA
15	Park Ridge, NJ	$110,000	$58,000	$13,000	$181,000	$68,000	$25,000	$3,000	$96,000	$277,000
16	Fennimore, WI	$11,400	$18,500	$6,000	$35,900	$1,000	$2,500	$0	$3,500	$39,400
17	Woodbury, NJ	NA	NA	NA	$87,896	NA	NA	NA	$60,701	$148,597

Key:

NA = Data not available   O&M = Operating and Maintenance

Notes:

(a) Refers to operating and maintenance costs other than collection and processing such as education and publicity.

(b) Recycling and composting collection costs represent contract fees paid to private haulers and cover processing. The City does, however, pay for processing materials dropped off at its transfer station.

(c) Collection costs for recycling represent contract fees paid to private hauler and cover processing.

(d) The City does not keep any records of O&M costs for collection and processing; the $156,496 in "Other" column reflects education and publicity costs.

Table 11

Total Costs for Materials Recovery Programs, 1989 (a)

#	Community	Recycling Collection Costs	Recycling Processing Costs	Subtotal	Composting Collection Costs	Composting Processing Costs	Subtotal	Overall Collection Costs	Materials Recovery Processing Costs	Total Gross	Revenues	Total Net Costs
1	Berlin Twp, NJ	$43,681	$9,360	$57,541	$8,911	$2,941	$11,852	$52,592	$12,301	$69,393	$5,159	$64,234
2	Longmeadow, MA	$73,340	$0	$73,385	$136,395	$89,733	$226,128	$209,735	$89,733	$299,513	$31,872	$267,641
3	Haddonfield, NJ	$122,248	$0	$123,248	$196,086	$26,448	$222,534	$318,334	$26,448	$345,782	$4,000	$341,782
4	Perkasie, PA	$40,516	$5,129	$48,874	NA	NA	NA	NA	NA	NA	$10,586	NA
5	Rodman, NY	$2,104	$4,898	$7,502	$0	$0	$0	$2,104	$4,898	$7,502	$1,970	$5,532
6	Wellesley, MA	$0	$48,157	$58,825	$0	$46,275	$56,943	$0	$94,432	$115,768	$75,453	$40,315
7	Lincoln Park, NJ	$58,089	$8,000	$78,889	$34,000	$3,057	$37,057	$92,089	$11,057	$115,946	$7,000	$108,946
8	West Linn, OR	$117,581	$1,426	$150,338	$0	$41,472	$48,794	$117,581	$42,898	$199,132	$37,700	$161,432
9	Hamburg, NY	$60,570	$34,034	$94,704	NA	NA	NA	NA	NA	NA	$12,413	NA
10	Wilton, WI	$249	$0	$249	$380	$0	$380	$629	$0	$629	$0	$629
11	Seattle, WA (b)	$2,098,820	$30,835	$2,212,555	$2,637,531	$202,477	$2,971,008	NA	NA	$5,183,563	$50,000	$5,133,563
12	Cherry Hill, NJ	$300,000	included (c)	$304,000	$134,823	$10,688	$145,512	$434,823	$10,688	$449,512	$0	$449,512
13	Upper Twp, NJ	$168,665	$0	$178,065	$65,182	$10,915	$76,097	$233,847	$10,915	$254,162	$0	$254,162
14	Babylon, NY	NA	NA	NA	NA	NA	NA	NA	NA	NA	$0	NA
15	Park Ridge, NJ	$127,385	$58,000	$198,385	$70,525	$26,688	$100,213	$197,910	$84,688	$298,598	$500	$298,098
16	Fennimore, WI	$23,990	$24,672	$54,662	$1,488	$2,621	$4,109	$25,478	$27,293	$58,771	$6,700	$52,071
17	Woodbury, NJ	NA	NA	$111,364	NA	NA	$112,995	NA	NA	$224,359	$19,106	$205,253

Key: NA = Data not available

Notes:

(a) Total costs are the sum of annualized capital costs plus operating and maintenance costs. Materials Revenues are subtracted from the gross costs for recycling and composting combined to yield a total net cost for each materials recovery program.

(b) Collection costs for recycling and composting represent contract fees paid to private haulers and cover processing. The City does, however, pay for processing materials dropped off at its transfer station.

(c) Collection costs for recycling represent contract fees paid to private hauler and cover processing. Costs listed under Total Processing Costs only represent those for composting.

Table 12

Per Ton Collection Costs for Materials Recovery Programs, 1989 (a)

#	Community	Recycling			Composting			Total Materials Recovery		
		Capital	O&M	Gross	Capital	O&M	Gross	Capital	O&M	Gross
1	Berlin Twp, NJ	$14	$28	$42	$2	$2	$4	$7	$11	$18
2	Longmeadow, MA	--	$48	$48	$33	$18	$51	$21	$29	$50
3	Haddonfield, NJ	$5	$48	$53	$11	$36	$47	$9	$40	$49
4	Perkasie, PA	$4	$45	$49	NA	NA	NA	NA	NA	NA
5	Rodman, NY	$22	$2	$24	--	--	--	$22	$2	$24
6	Wellesley, MA	--	--	--				--	--	--
7	Lincoln Park, NJ	$1	$61	$62	$4	$46	$50	$3	$55	$58
8	West Linn, OR (b)	$5	$122	$127	$0	$0	$0	$5	$122	$127
9	Hamburg, NY	$11	$48	$59	$5	NA	NA	$8	NA	NA
10	Wilton, WI	$1	$3	$4	$0	$38	$38	$1	$6	$7
11	Seattle, WA (c)	--	$52	$52	--	$83	$83	--	$65	$65
12	Cherry Hill, NJ	--	$44	$44	$4	$11	$15	$2	$25	$27
13	Upper Twp, NJ	$9	$64	$73	$30	$56	$86	$14	$62	$76
14	Babylon, NY	--	NA	NA	NA	NA	NA	NA	NA	NA
15	Park Ridge, NJ	$9	$59	$68	$3	$85	$88	$8	$67	$75
16	Fennimore, WI	$28	$25	$53	$4	$8	$12	$23	$21	$44
17	Woodbury, NJ (d)	$11	$41	$52	$22	$29	$51	$16	$35	$51

Key: NA = Data not available   -- = Not applicable   O&M = Operating and maintenance

Notes:

(a) These costs represent annualized capital and operating and maintenance costs incurred for collection of recyclables and compostables on a per ton basis. Annualized capital, O&M costs, and gross costs are not calculated by dividing the total tons recovered into program costs, but by dividing the tons recovered due to the program itself into program costs. For instance, tonnage of beverage containers recovered due to deposit systems are not included, as provided costs do not cover the recovery of this tonnage. See Data Definitions and Methodology, pages 59-62.

(b) Costs reflect those incurred by private hauler for collection and processing of recyclables.

(c) Costs reflect contract fees paid to private haulers for collection and processing.

(d) Operating and maintenance costs reflect total operating and maintenance costs. Most of this is incurred for collection.

Table 13

Per Ton Costs for Materials Recovery Programs, 1989 (a)

#	Community	Recycling			Composting			Total Materials Recovery				
		Capital	O&M	Gross	Capital	O&M	Gross	Capital	O&M	Gross	Revenue	Net
1	Berlin Twp, NJ	$14	$41	$56	$4	$3	$6	$7	$16	$24	$2	$22
2	Longmeadow, MA	--	$48	$48	$26	$40	$66	$18	$43	$60	$6	$54
3	Haddonfield, NJ	$5	$48	$54	$13	$40	$53	$10	$43	$53	$1	$53
4	Perkasie, PA	$4	$55	$59	NA	NA	NA	NA	NA	NA	$13	NA
5	Rodman, NY	$34	$51	$85	$0	$0	$0	$24	$36	$60	$16	$45
6	Wellesley, MA	$3	$16	$19	$1	$9	$10	$2	$11	$13	$8	$5
7	Lincoln Park, NJ	$1	$84	$85	$9	$46	$55	$4	$68	$72	$4	$68
8	West Linn, OR	$7	$156	$163	$7	$25	$33	$7	$76	$83	$16	$67
9	Hamburg, NY	$12	$80	$92	$8	NA	NA	$10	NA	NA	$6	NA
10	Wilton, WI	$1	$3	$3	$0	$38	$38	$1	$6	$7	$0	$7
11	Seattle, WA	--	$49	$49	--	$69	$69	--	$59	$59	$1	$58
12	Cherry Hill, NJ	--	$44	$44	$5	$12	$16	$3	$26	$29	$0	$29
13	Upper Twp, NJ	$9	$69	$78	$30	$70	$100	$14	$69	$83	$0	$83
14	Babylon, NY	--	NA	NA	NA	NA	NA	NA	NA	NA	$0	NA
15	Park Ridge, NJ	$9	$98	$107	$5	$120	$126	$8	$105	$113	$0	$113
16	Fennimore, WI	$41	$79	$121	$5	$28	$33	$34	$68	$102	$12	$90
17	Woodbury, NJ	$11	$41	$52	$25	$29	$54	$18	$35	$53	$5	$48

Key: NA = Data not available   O&M = Operating and maintenance   -- = Not applicable

Note:

(a) These costs represent annualized capital and operating and maintenance costs incurred for recycling, composting, and total materials recovery on a per ton basis. Revenues are subtracted from gross to yield net materials recovery costs. Annualized capital, O&M, gross, and net costs are calculated by dividing the tons recovered due to the program itself into program costs. For instance, tonnage of beverage containers recovered due to deposit systems are not included, as provided costs do not cover the recovery of this tonnage. See Data Definitions and Methodology, pages 59-62.

Chart T, Total Gross Costs Per Ton Recovered, confirms that for those communities with comprehensive curbside programs, collection costs account for most of the total costs.[11] The two programs without curbside collection, Rodman and Wellesley, have zero or low collection costs. Other costs include those incurred for processing, administration, and publicity and education.

Chart T illustrates the wide variation in costs per ton. Wilton [10] and Wellesley [6] report the lowest gross costs per ton recovered — $7 and $13, respectively. Park Ridge [15] and Fennimore [16] report the highest gross costs per ton recovered — $113 and $102, respectively.

In Park Ridge, marketing and hauling fees have contributed to high costs. For instance, in addition to pick-up charges, the Borough has to pay $25 per ton in marketing fees to have its paper recycled. It pays tipping fees to compost its leaves. And its recovery program for grass clippings, which involves transporting them for composting to a town about 80 miles away, has proved costly ($65 per ton). Encouraging backyard composting and siting a small-scale local composting facility might reduce costs in Park Ridge.

Chart T
Total Gross Costs per Ton Recovered

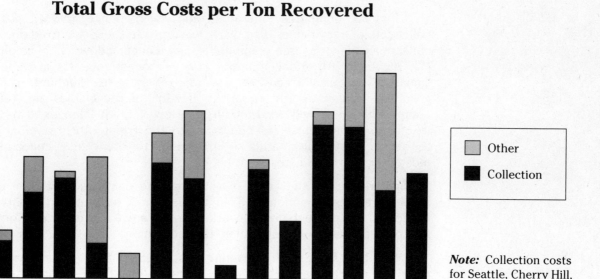

Note: Collection costs for Seattle, Cherry Hill, and Woodbury include some processing costs.

[11]Babylon is the only community of the 17 documented for which no capital or operating and maintenance costs were available, with the exception of its costs for education and publicity.

In Fennimore, processing costs have contributed to high total gross costs. In several communities, processing costs are picked up at the county level. Recyclables from Berlin Township [1], Haddonfield [3], and Upper Township [13] are processed at county facilities. These municipalities pay no tipping fees and receive no materials revenues. In contrast, Fennimore can, at least offset its costs by retaining revenue from the sale of materials.

In Wilton, a rural village of 473 people, volunteer crews collect recyclables. Volunteers are drawn from a list of 40 to 50 regular participants; each crew consists of four or five volunteers. The only paid employee is one worker who is responsible for picking up yard waste and miscellaneous items such as appliances or old furniture. Aside from this worker's wages, the only operating and maintenance costs Wilton incurs for its recovery program are the cost of gasoline and oil for the Village dump truck. Capital equipment consists solely of this dump truck, a trailer and frame rack, a storage building and storage barrels. The building and barrels were donated.

Wellesley's low gross cost can be attributed to the fact that the Town does not provide curbside collection for refuse or recyclable materials. Gross costs for all the other programs except Rodman's [5] include curbside collection costs. When comparing recycling costs to costs for other waste management options, such as waste incineration, which rely on conventional refuse collection systems, it is important to add collection costs to the costs for the non-materials recovery option.

Chart U compares operating and maintenance (O&M) costs for collection of recyclables and yard waste with those incurred for refuse collection. For several communities — Longmeadow [2], Lincoln Park [7], Hamburg [9], and Fennimore [16] — collection costs are about the same for materials recovered as for refuse. In Hamburg, collection costs are almost exactly equal. Collection of recyclables and refuse is completely integrated in Hamburg. However, the longer trip to the landfill to dump refuse, as compared to the trip to the recycling center to deliver recyclables, adds a little more to the refuse collection bill, mostly in extra fuel costs.

In Perkasie [4] the costs of recycling are combined with the cost of regular refuse collection. The breakdown presented in Chart U is based on the percentages of worker hours spent on collection of refuse (46 percent) and of recyclables (54 percent).

West Linn's [8] high recycling costs reflect high labor costs. Not only are hourly wages high, but curbside collection vehicles used for pick-up of recyclables are staffed by two to three workers. The private hauler that picks up refuse and recyclables spent almost $90 on labor alone for every ton recycled in 1989. Refuse collection cost about $86 per ton.

The experience of at least two communities — Cherry Hill [12] and Park Ridge [15] — indicates that contracting out for collection may cost more than collection by local government agencies. Both of these communities contract out with private haulers for residential refuse collection. However, the Borough of Park Ridge provides collection service for recyclables and yard waste. Per ton O&M costs for materials recovery collection are almost 40 percent less than the per ton contract fees paid for refuse collection. In Cherry Hill, although the private contractor collects recyclables, the Township Department of Public Works collects leaves and brush (55 percent of residential materials recovered). Per ton contract fees are $53 for refuse collection and $44 for collection of recyclables. In comparison, O&M costs incurred for yard waste collection are $11 per ton.

Chart V shows the effects of adding landfill disposal costs in Chart T. When we take into account avoided disposal costs, materials recovery costs less than conventional refuse collection and disposal. Fennimore [16] is the exception; since the City owns the landfill, it incurs no per ton disposal fees.

Charts W, X, Y, and Z provide further information on collection costs. Chart W plots per ton collection costs for recyclables, yard waste, and overall materials recovered in order of percent of total waste recovered, highest first. In some cases — Berlin Township [1], Cherry Hill [12], and Fennimore [16] — per ton collection costs are significantly less for composting than for recycling. In other cases, per ton composting costs are about the same as per ton recycling costs or higher.

Chart X plots household density against per ton collection costs for recyclables and yard waste. Household density does not appear to be an important factor except perhaps at very low densities — fewer than 200 households per square mile.

Chart Y compares per ton collection costs for recyclables to tons recycled per year per household served. Although at first glance there may appear to be no direct correlation, note that the community with the highest cost — West Linn [8] — also recovers the lowest tonnage of recyclables per household. Lincoln Park [7], which collects only newspaper at curbside, has one of the highest collection costs. The two programs with higher costs than Lincoln Park are in communities with household densities lower than 200 per square mile. Fennimore [16], Berlin Township [1], and Woodbury [17] have the lowest per ton collection costs (with the exception of Wilton's volunteer-based operation); all three have high household recovery rates.

Chart Z presents similar information for yard waste collection. Again, programs collecting the most yard waste per household have the lowest per ton costs. And again, those with the lowest household densities have the highest costs, except for Seattle [11].

Chart U
O&M Costs for Collection:
**Materials Recovery Versus
Conventional Refuse Collection**

($/ton)

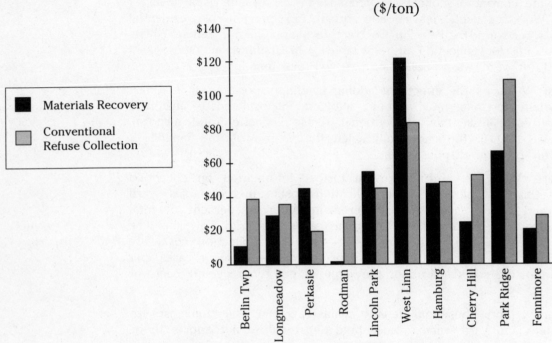

Chart V
O&M Costs, Including Tipping Fees,
**for Materials Recovery Versus Conventional Refuse
Collection and Disposal**

($/ton)

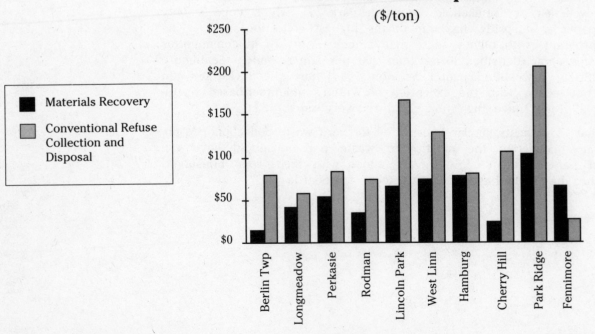

Chart W
Per Ton Collection Costs for Materials Recovery
(O&M and annualized capital costs)

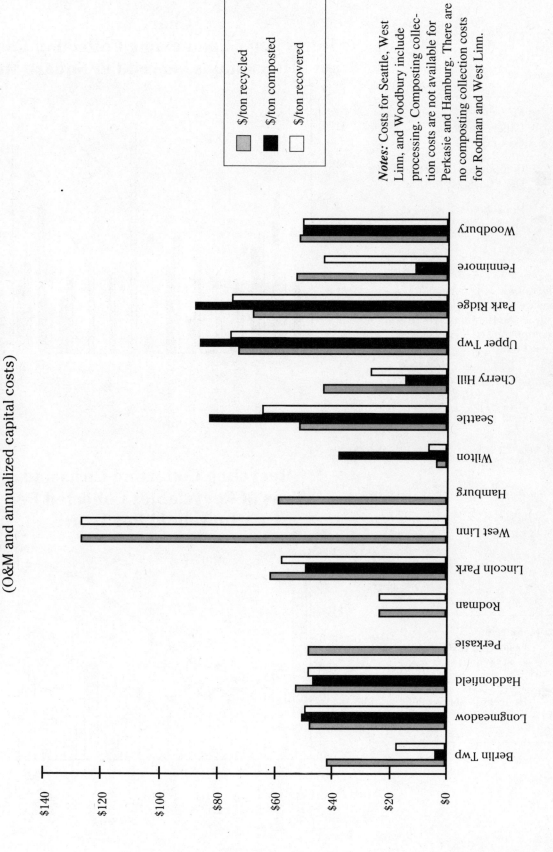

Legend:
- $/ton recycled
- $/ton composted
- $/ton recovered

Notes: Costs for Seattle, West Linn, and Woodbury include processing. Composting collection costs are not available for Perkasie and Hamburg. There are no composting collection costs for Rodman and West Linn.

Chart X
Recycling / Composting Collection Costs and Households Served Per Square Mile

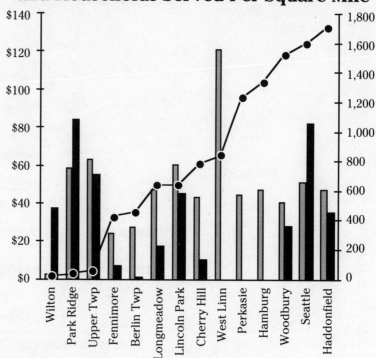

Note: Composting collection costs are not available for Perkasie and Hamburg. There are no composting collection costs for West Linn.

Chart Y
Recycling Collection Costs and Tons of Recyclables Collected Per Household Per Year

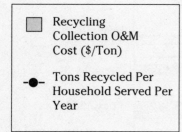

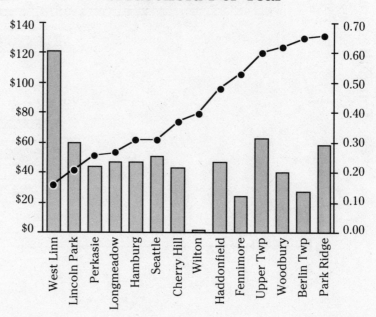

Chart Z
Composting Collection Costs and
Tons of Yard Waste Collected Per
Household Per Year

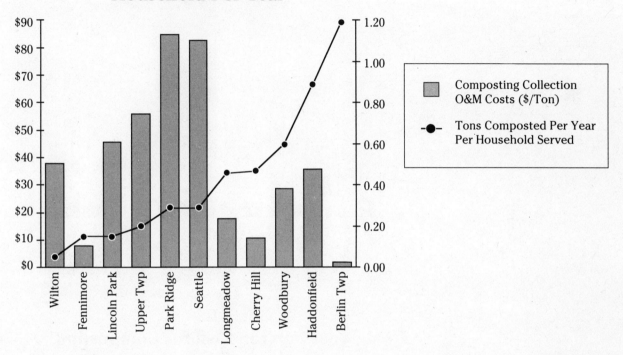

Charts AA and BB indicate that capital costs are a small portion of total costs. Materials recovery programs don't have huge fixed investments. Recycling and composting systems are more flexible than more capital-intensive solid waste management strategies, and better able to respond to near-term changes in their operating environment (e.g., the advent of higher or lower quantities of waste, better processing technologies, changes in the composition of the waste stream, and more rigorous environmental standards). In addition, capital costs are a measure of the amount of debt the community may have to assume and the sensitivity of program costs to changes in interest rates.

The integration of materials recovery collection systems with refuse collection systems is one reason for the low capital investment. In Berlin Township [1], Longmeadow [2], Haddonfield [3], Hamburg [9], Wilton [10], Cherry Hill [12], Park Ridge [15], and Fennimore [16], equipment used for collecting refuse (such as front-end loaders and dump trucks) is also used for collection of recyclables and yard waste, and in some cases for processing these materials as well.

Chart AA
Total Gross Per Ton Cost for Recycling

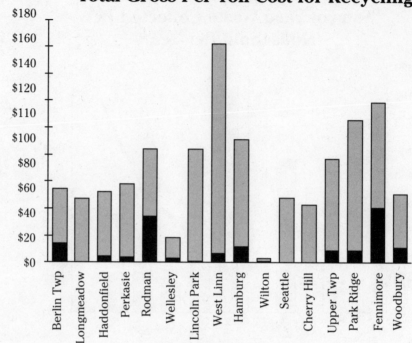

Chart BB
Total Gross Per Ton Cost for Composting

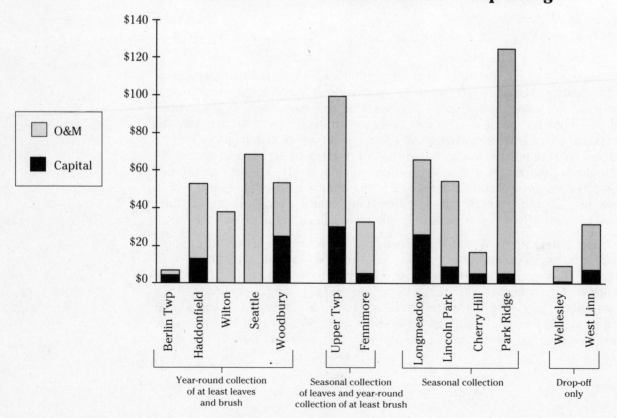

Chart BB indicates that per ton composting costs are lower for drop-off centers, probably because collection costs are avoided. The chart also indicates that per ton costs may be lower for programs with year-round collection of several different types of yard waste than for programs without year-round collection that target only one or two types of yard waste. Tonnage collected can be expected to be higher for programs with year-round collection of several types of yard waste. As tonnage increases, per ton costs would tend to decrease.

Toward Higher Recovery Rates

We look forward to expanding this data base and statistical format over the next few years as communities surpass even 40 percent materials recovery levels and continue to extract ever larger amounts of useful materials from their waste streams. When our first volume *Beyond 25 Percent: Materials Recovery Comes of Age*, was published in May 1989, only 33 percent of the 15 best recycling and composting programs were recovering more than 40 percent of their waste streams. Of the 17 programs in this study, concluded only 1 year later, 60 percent are recovering 40 percent or more. It is the comprehensive nature of the recycling and composting programs that has allowed these communities to achieve such high recovery levels. The following characteristics are typical of these programs:

- **Comprehensive composting programs** (year-round collection of many types of yard waste at curbside and incentives for land-scapers to compost their yard waste)

- **Mandatory participation**

- **Recovery of materials from single- and multi-family households, and from commercial and institutional establishments** (through both curbside and drop-off collection)

- **Targeting a wide range of materials for recovery**

- **Economic incentives for materials recovery** (volume-based refuse rates, reduced tipping fees for recyclable or compostable materials at drop-off sites, and higher tipping fees for disposal of non-source-separated refuse)

- **Weekly pick-up of materials at curbside**

- **Provision of adequate containers for setting out materials at curbside**

- **Education and publicity**

All the programs documented in this report — even the best — can increase their materials recovery levels. Most are actively striving to do so. For instance, Berlin Township, ranked number one in this study, will offer curbside recycling service to its apartment complexes next year. Haddonfield, ranked number three, plans to add HDPE and

PET containers to materials collected at curbside in the fall of 1990. Seattle has the most ambitious goal: to recover 60 percent of its waste stream by 1998. The City is taking new initiatives to increase recovery levels, including multi-material collection programs for City offices and curbside recycling service to apartment buildings. Materials recovery levels of 75 percent are well within the realm of possibility for communities that integrate the best features of the best programs.

As landfills all over the country reach capacity, communities are turning to two major alternatives: incineration and materials recovery. Yet they cannot reach high levels of materials recovery while operating waste incinerators. Both systems compete for the same materials and the same funds.

Babylon's experience exemplifies these difficulties. The Town plans to take several initiatives to increase its materials recovery rate. However, its 750 ton-per-day mass burn waste incinerator will prove a major obstacle. The Town guarantees the plant 225,000 tons per year — 83 percent of its waste stream — for which it pays $78 per ton. In order to meet this tonnage requirement, half of the newspaper collected for recycling in 1989 was burned.

Herein lies one of the most important lessons we can learn from the communities studied in this text: in order to reach high levels of recycling and composting, local officials must implement comprehensive waste reduction and recovery and use disposal as a last resort only.

This study offers voluminous evidence that recycling and composting combined can be the primary solid waste management strategy. Billions of dollars will be spent in this country restructuring our solid waste management systems. The key to success — and to long-term environmental protection and economic stability — will be redirecting investment from materials destruction to materials recovery.

Data Definitions and Methodology

Those comparing this volume to *Beyond 25 Percent: Materials Recovery Comes of Age* will note that we have refined our methodology and data gathering. Capital and operating and maintenance costs are broken down into recycling and composting and into collection and processing. We more clearly distinguish between residential and commercial collection program characteristics. Likewise, recycling collection characteristics are distinguished from composting collection characteristics. We have indicated which materials are mandatory for residents and businesses to recycle and which are voluntary. Our method for calculating the tonnage of beverage containers recovered through deposit legislation has changed. Instead of applying an average statewide percentage of waste diverted to each applicable community's waste stream, we apply an average statewide per capita tonnage of redeemed beverage containers to each applicable community's population.

The following section explains some of the terms we use in this study. All tonnage and cost data are 1989 data and are reported on an annual basis unless noted otherwise.

Annualized Capital Costs — capital costs have been converted to annual costs by assuming 10 percent interest over a 10-year amortization period.

Businesses Served — the number of businesses served by the community's municipal curbside collection program for recyclables, with the exception of Rodman, where Businesses Served refers to the number of businesses served by the drop-off center. This figure should not be confused with the number of businesses actually recycling, which may be greater than the number of businesses served by the municipal program. Businesses served may include institutions such as schools, hospitals, or government buildings.

Collection Capital Costs — the capital investment, in 1989 dollars, made by the community for collection equipment used to collect recyclable or compostable materials. Each capital expenditure was converted to 1989 dollars using producer price indices.

Commercial Waste Generated (Tons) — the tonnage of waste disposed and recovered by the commercial and institutional sectors (excluding medical wastes). The commercial sector includes theaters, retail establishments, hotels, and restaurants. The institutional sector includes hospitals and schools. Non-residential bulky waste such as construction debris and asphalt is included under commercial waste with the exception of Berlin Township, Longmeadow, Wilton, and Fennimore. In Seattle, Cherry Hill, and Park Ridge, only tonnage of bulky waste recovered is included. For these communities, non-residential bulky waste was neither included in disposal tonnages nor readily available.

Composting — recovering discarded organic materials for processing into a soil amendment, fertilizer, and/or mulch.

Mandatory — whether citizens are required to source separate materials for recycling. In several communities, citizens may be required to set out certain materials at curbside for recycling. In others it may simply be illegal for them to set these out with their refuse. Not all materials collected are designated as mandatory. Refer to case studies or to Table 6, Materials Collected for Recovery, for detailed information on which materials residents and businesses are required to recover.

Participation Rate (%) — the portion of households served that take part in the curbside collection program for recyclable materials. There are several exceptions: Rodman, Wellesley, Lincoln Park, West Linn, Seattle, Park Ridge, and Babylon. For Rodman, Wellesley, and Lincoln Park, Participation Rate refers to the portion of the total population that brings recyclable materials to the drop-off center. For West Linn, Participation Rate is based on the portion of single-family households that recycle. For Seattle, it is defined as the sign-up rate — the ratio of the number of households registered for the program to the number of households eligible. For Park Ridge, it is based on participation in both curbside recycling and drop-off recycling. For Babylon, it refers to the portion of total households (not just those served) that take part in the curbside collection program. Refer to the case studies for an explanation of the specific method of calculation.

Per Ton Collection Costs — These costs represent annualized capital and operating and maintenance costs incurred for collection of recyclables and compostables on a per ton basis. Capital, O&M, and gross costs are not calculated by dividing the total tons recovered into program costs, but by dividing the tons recovered *due to the program itself* into program costs. For instance, in Seattle, although about 244,000 tons were recovered in 1989, the costs available from the City only cover the residential curbside collection and the City-operated drop-off collection programs, which recovered 88,041 tons. Therefore, per ton costs are calculated by dividing expenses by 88,041 tons, not by 244,000 tons. To do otherwise would be to underestimate the costs per recovered ton for those communities whose own programs were recovering relatively little but whose private or other programs were recovering a great deal. Bottle bill tonnage was also excluded. Refer to case studies for detailed information on the tonnage recovered that costs cover.

Per Ton Costs for Recycling and Composting — These costs represent annualized capital and operating and maintenance costs incurred for recycling, composting, and total recovery on a per ton basis. Capital, O&M, and gross costs are calculated by dividing the tons recovered *due to the program itself* into program costs. Refer to case studies for detailed information on the tonnage recovered that costs cover. Net cost was calculated by subtracting revenues from the gross cost.

Processing Capital Costs (Recycling) — the capital investment, in 1989 dollars, made by the community for equipment used to process recyclable materials in preparation for marketing to end-users. Processing typically includes sorting, contaminant removal, and crushing or baling. Each capital expenditure was converted to 1989 dollars using producer price indices.

Processing Capital Costs (Composting) — the capital investment, in 1989 dollars, made by the community for equipment used to process — compost, chip, or mulch — organic materials. Processing or composting equipment typically includes shredders or chippers and front-end loaders. Each capital expenditure was converted to 1989 dollars using producer price indices.

Recycling — recovering discarded products and packaging materials for reuse and/or processing into new products.

Residential Waste Generated — the annual tonnage of waste disposed and recovered from single-family and multi-family households and their yards. Perkasie, Lincoln Park, Seattle, and Park Ridge, and Woodbury are exceptions. In Perkasie, the tonnage of waste generated excludes waste generated by condominiums and apartments with more than four units, which is collected by private haulers and is not tracked. In Lincoln Park, the tonnage of waste generated from condominiums cannot be included with residential waste since it is collected by private haulers serving the commercial sector. In Seattle, Residential Waste Generated excludes any residential waste self-hauled to recycling, composting, or disposal facilities, since the tonnage of self-hauled waste includes commercial waste. In Park Ridge, Residential Waste Generated includes waste from four schools and the post office. In Woodbury, Residential Waste Generated includes some commercial waste picked up by the City along its residential collection route.

Segregations Required — the number of segregations citizens must make when setting out recyclable materials at curbside for collection. For instance, in the south section of Seattle, residents commingle all recyclables into one container; this is considered one segregation. In Hamburg, residents are required to put newspapers in one container or bundle; glass, plastic, and metal in another container; and cardboard flattened and placed next to glass and cans. This is considered three segregations. We have excluded the set-out of appliances, other white goods, tires, car batteries, and motor oil from this figure, since households do not generate these materials on a frequent basis. Case studies provide detailed information on how materials should be separated and set out for curbside collection.

Total Waste Generated (Tons) — the tonnage of material disposed and recovered by residential, commercial, and institutional sectors on an annual basis. (Tonnage disposed includes any waste incinerated, as incineration destroys materials and all their embodied energy.) Perkasie and Wellesley are exceptions. In Perkasie, total waste generated excludes commercial waste collected by private haulers, which is not tracked. In Wellesley, total waste generated reflects the waste generated by the residential and commercial population that use its Recycling and Disposal Facility. Note that Residential Tons plus Commercial Tons may not add up to Total Waste Generated due to bottle bill tonnage estimations, tonnage of yard waste composted by landscapers, or tonnage of materials self-hauled (Seattle). These three items cannot be broken down into residential and commercial.

Case Studies

BERLIN TOWNSHIP, NEW JERSEY

Demographics

Jurisdiction: Township of Berlin

Population: 5,629 (1989 estimate based on an annual growth of 0.58 percent between 1980 and 1985; the growth rate is assumed to be the same between 1985 and 1989)

Total Households: 1,700 (1,552 single-family homes, 48 duplexes, and 100 units in large apartment complexes)

Total Businesses: 280

Area: 3.5 square miles

Other: Berlin Township is a residential community in southern Camden County. Located directly across the Delaware River from Philadelphia, the Township is part of the Philadelphia metropolitan area.

Solid Waste Generation and Collection

(Annual Tonnages for 1989)

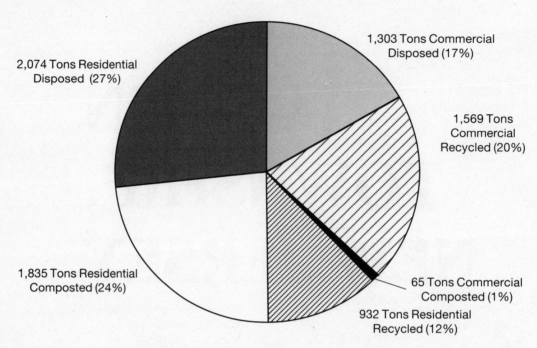

2,074 Tons Residential Disposed (27%)

1,303 Tons Commercial Disposed (17%)

1,569 Tons Commercial Recycled (20%)

65 Tons Commercial Composted (1%)

932 Tons Residential Recycled (12%)

1,835 Tons Residential Composted (24%)

Total Waste Generated: 7,778 tons in 1989 (This figure is based on an estimate for commercial waste generation [see below] and excludes bulky materials disposed, such as construction debris and furniture, but includes bulky waste recovered, such as tires, appliances, and scrap metal.)

Residential Waste Generated: 4,841 tons in 1989 (excluding bulky materials disposed, but including recycled scrap metal, appliances, and tires)

Commercial Waste Generated: 2,937 tons estimated for 1989[1] (1,135 tons estimated disposed, 103 tons recycled by Township, 1,466 tons estimated recycled by private haulers based on 1988 data, and 65 tons composted)

---

[1]Commercial waste is largely handled by private haulers, and figures for tonnage are not available. The tonnage of commercial waste generated has been estimated by using a per capita waste disposal figure of 0.6 tons per year to calculate total residential and commercial waste disposed. (This per capita figure for Berlin Township was developed by the consulting firm O'Brien-Kreitzberg & Associates, Inc.) Tonnage of residential waste disposed, which is known, is subtracted from this total, leaving commercial waste disposed. Total commercial waste generated is then calculated by adding this estimated 1989 tonnage of commercial waste disposed to the sum of 1988 tonnage of commercial waste recovered by private haulers and 1989 tonnage of commercial waste recovered by Township crews.

Bulky Waste Generated:

Tonnage breakdown is unavailable because residential and commercial bulky materials (including furniture and construction debris) bypass the local landfill; however, 169 tons of bulky materials (tires, appliances, and scrap metal) were recycled in 1989.

% By Weight of Total Waste Recovered:

57 percent in 1989 (32.2 percent recycling and 24.4 percent composting)

% By Weight of Residential Waste Recovered:

57 percent in 1989 (19 percent recycling and 38 percent composting)

% By Weight of Commercial Waste Recovered:

56 percent estimated in 1989 (53.4 percent recycling and 2.2 percent composting)

Landfill Tipping Fee:

$12.76 per cubic yard at the Winslow Landfill

Collection of Refuse:

The Department of Public Works (DPW) collects refuse from residents and about 20 small bars, restaurants, and other businesses located in residential areas. According to local ordinance, Berlin Township cannot collect refuse from businesses located in commercial zones, but must collect from businesses located in residential zones, if they request the service from the DPW. The Township cannot charge these businesses for collection. The remainder of the businesses contract with private haulers.

Residential and commercial refuse collected by the Township is disposed at the Winslow Landfill in Winslow, New Jersey. Tires, leaves, brush, tree stumps, and light construction debris were banned from the landfill as of March 1, 1985. Private haulers of commercial and industrial refuse were banned from tipping at the Winslow Landfill in June 1988. Since then, the private haulers servicing businesses have disposed of commercial refuse at a number of different landfills. Tipping fees for this refuse range from $59 to $81 per ton. Berlin Township does not require private haulers to report the tonnage of refuse hauled out of the Township.

Residential waste disposed is reported from the Winslow Landfill in cubic yards. The State conversion factor of 3.3 cubic yards per ton has been used to convert 6,845 cubic yards to tons. In 1989, the Township incurred $79,940 collecting this refuse for disposal.

Future Solid Waste Management Plans:

In 1990, the Township plans to participate in a new countywide household hazardous waste program, and to expand its 2-acre municipal composting site into a 4-acre regional facility. Berlin will offer alley collection of recyclable materials to its two apartment complexes in 1991.

The Berlin Township governing body is in the process of drafting legislation that will require all commercial establishments to submit proof of their recycling program prior to obtaining or renewing a Mercantile License, which is required for every business or industry in the Township.

Materials Recovery

Berlin Township has been developing its recovery program for the past decade. In 1980, the Township began operating both a curbside program for glass and a drop-off center for glass and appliances in the public works yard. Curbside recovery of glass was accomplished by having Town refuse haulers separate glass bottles from the refuse as it was being dumped into the trucks, storing them in burlap bags attached to the trucks. The full bags were left along the road, and the Superintendent of the Public Works Department would return for the loads the same day. In 1982, the first year that tonnages were recorded, the Township collected 237 tons of glass, which were sold to Recycling Enterprises.

In 1981, 6 years before recycling became mandatory throughout the State, Berlin Township adopted its "Garbage, Rubbage, and Refuse" ordinance, requiring residents to separate glass and mixed paper (including newspaper, junk mail, envelopes, and computer paper) for recycling. The curbside collection program, serving 1,600 households, became one of the first in the State to supply buckets to its residents when a local glass manufacturer donated 3,000 5-gallon white buckets for storing glass. A local bank donated stickers for each of the buckets. The glass was color separated on the truck by the collection crew, and then unloaded into a Eager Beaver trailer at the public works yard prior to being sold.

In November 1984, Camden County, in which Berlin is located, appended the County Mandatory Municipal Recycling Plan to its Solid Waste Management (SWM) Plan. The County plan requires that each municipality institute collection programs for the recycling of newspaper, aluminum cans, used oil, and scrap metal. In addition, the Plan mandates that all whole trees, tree trunks, tree stumps, leaves, and branches be disposed at facilities approved by the New Jersey Department of Environmental Protection, or mulched for use as a ground cover. The Plan included construction of an intermediate processing center (IPC) by the Spring of 1986 to expand the recycling of materials and provide for a stable market for glass and non-aluminum cans.

In anticipation of the IPC, the residents of Berlin were informed in 1984 that they could start separating all PET soda bottles for recycling. Participation was voluntary, but, according to Recycling Coordinator Mike McGee, residents were very eager to participate. The Township stockpiled the plastics in the public works yard. After 2 months, however, it was forced to cancel this program due to a lack of markets. Regardless, many of the eager residents continued to put out their soda bottles for recycling.

The IPC, known as the Camden County Recycling Facility (CCRF), began operation in April 1986 and provides markets for glass and all types of metal cans. According to the February 1, 1986 amendments to the county SWM Plan, all county municipalities must include metal food and beverage containers in their curbside recycling programs. The SWM Plan was amended further to streamline the establishment of composting facilities. Berlin Township built its compost site in 1989, and plans to expand it into a 4-acre regional composting facility by the end of 1990.

In February 1988, Rutgers University provided the Township with 2,000 yellow 20-gallon buckets for a pilot study on plastics collection. The round buckets with molded handles, which are used to store plastic, glass, and aluminum and other metal cans, allow residents to store a greater volume of materials than the 5-gallon buckets. During 1986 and 1987, the Township collected an annual average of 181 tons of commingled glass, aluminum, and other metal containers. In 1988, the Township collected 27 tons of plastics, and the overall tonnage of commingled recyclables increased to 296 tons with the distribution of the larger buckets. The plastics were taken to Rutgers University for processing.

Berlin Township had tried several different storage containers before deciding to stay with the 20-gallon buckets donated by Rutgers University. In 1984, the Township received 100 blue rectangular recycling boxes for demonstration purposes. The boxes, which were distributed to residents, were popular for storage of record albums or tools, and disappeared quickly, according to Mike McGee. The collection crew has found that, overall, the 20-gallon buckets are sturdier than the square boxes or the 5-gallon buckets and easiest to empty. Residents find the 5-gallon buckets convenient for short-term storage of recyclable materials before they dump these into the 20-gallon container left outside, or for storage of extra materials that do not fit in the 20-gallon containers.

The Township still runs the drop-off center at its public works yard, which, as of January 1990, is open 7 days a week, 24 hours a day. (Previously, the center was open only Monday through Friday from 6:00 a.m. until 2:30 p.m.) Because the center is not staffed, residents are required to separate all materials into the proper bins themselves. Glass, plastic, aluminum, and ferrous cans are stored in an Eager Beaver trailer on the site. Wastepaper (including newspaper, paperboard, high-grade paper, and corrugated cardboard) is stockpiled in one corner of the yard. Oil delivered in sealed containers can be left at the center, as well as car batteries and tires. Scrap metal and aluminum are stored in 55-gallon drums and bins made from tires, both of which have been recovered from the waste stream. In addition, residents may bring white goods to the facility.

The Township and its recycling coordinator have received several awards for its recycling program. In May 1989, the Township was recognized as having the *Best Recycling Program* in Camden County, and Mike McGee was honored as *Camden County's Recycler of the Year.*

In the same year, the program was recognized as one of the best recycling programs in the State at the New Jersey State Recycling Awards Presentation, and, again, the Coordinator was honored as one of the two top recyclers in the State. In November 1989, Berlin won the *Best Curbside Recycling Program* award from the National Recycling Congress. In February 1990, the Township won the *Highest Recovery Rate* and the *Best Overall Program in a Suburban Community* awards in the *Record Setting Recycling Contest 1989*, sponsored by the Institute for Local Self-Reliance. And most recently, in April 1990, Berlin won the *Source Reduction and Recycling Award* in Renew America's *Searching for Success Contest*.

Curbside Collection

Start-up Date:

September 1980 (mandatory as of June 1981)

Private/Public:

Public

Materials Collected:

Glass and newspaper collection began in 1980. In 1982, aluminum cans were collected with glass. In 1985, ferrous cans were added to the list of commingled materials. Car batteries, scrap metal, corrugated cardboard, and paperboard (including cereal boxes, but not milk cartons) were also cited for collection in 1985. Pick up of clean lumber began in June 1988. Plastic PET soda bottles were first collected in 1984 for 2 months, but this program was discontinued. An expanded program collecting plastic (PET and HDPE) beverage and other containers (including detergent and shampoo bottles, but not oil, window-washing, or anti-freeze bottles) began in February 1988. Residents may also place tires, white goods, and motor oil at the curbside for collection. Leaves, brush, and Christmas trees are also collected.

The Township collects newspaper, corrugated cardboard, scrap metal, glass, plastic, aluminum cans, and tin cans from businesses.

Pick-up Frequency:

Weekly collection of recyclable materials, leaves, and other yard waste materials. Leaves, brush, and clean lumber are collected throughout the year.

Pick-up Same Day as Refuse:

Yes, except for brush and wood waste

Material Set-out Method:

Glass, aluminum, plastic, and ferrous food and beverage containers are stored commingled in a 20-gallon plastic container supplied by the Township. Corrugated cardboard and paperboard must be crushed and bundled. Newspaper and other paper can be mixed, but must be bundled separately from the cardboard. Tires, white goods, and car batteries are placed loose at the curbside. Used motor oil must be contained and clearly identified. Recyclable materials must be placed 5 feet away from refuse. Leaves are collected bagged at curbside except during November and December, when residents must rake them to the curb. Brush and wood waste may be set out either bagged or loose.

Mandatory: Yes (all materials with the exception of white goods, wood waste, and Christmas trees)

Service Provider: Department of Public Works

Collection Vehicles: An Eager Beaver compartmentalized truck (with the compartments removed) is used for collection of commingled recyclable materials. Crushed cardboard is collected in a 1-ton dump truck with paperboard. Newspaper, mixed paper, and metal scraps are collected in a dump truck. A 3/4-ton dump truck is used for collection of tires, batteries, and motor oil. Vacuumed or scooped leaves, chipped brush, and clean lumber are loaded into dump trucks. Finally, a dump truck is sent through the streets after other trucks have gone through to clean up streets and collect any materials that may have been left behind. Each truck is staffed by one person.

Households Served: 1,600 single-family homes and duplexes. Berlin does not service its two apartment complexes.

Participation Rate: 95 percent of the households served (based on a monthly set-out rate)

Businesses Served: Approximately 200 bars, restaurants, schools, offices, gas stations, and stores have recyclable materials collected by the Township.

Economic Incentives: Fines

Enforcement: Residents and businesses that do not separate recyclable materials run the risk of not having their refuse collected. The Township reserves the right to further enforce source separation of mandated materials with a series of fines. First time offenders are fined $25, second time offenders are fined $50, and each subsequent abuse carries a fine of $100. A Public Works staff member makes periodic inspections.

Commercial Materials Recovery Activities

Berlin Township provides collection service of recyclable materials for 200 of its 280 businesses. In 1989, there were two different collection days for businesses. Small businesses located in residential neighborhoods were serviced on the same day as residents, and a special Friday pick-up was provided for bars and restaurants. The collection service is offered to the businesses at no charge, thus creating an incentive for businesses to recycle. This service has been provided since 1981, when the Town adopted its "Garbage, Rubbish, and Refuse" ordinance. In January 1990, the Township began Friday collection from all the businesses it services.

Bars and restaurants are provided with 55-gallon drums for storage of glass. Other businesses may request a 20-gallon container for storage of glass, aluminum and tin cans, and plastic HDPE and PET containers. The Township will also collect newspaper, corrugated cardboard, and scrap metal from businesses. In addition, businesses have the option of bringing their recyclable materials to the drop-off site at the public works yard. The Township provides the commercial establishments with a list of local vendors for materials that are not collected by Berlin. The commercial sector recycled 36 tons of commingled glass, aluminum, and plastic in 1989, most of which was collected by the Township on its Friday route. The Township collected a total of 168 tons of recyclables from businesses in 1989.

The 1981 "Garbage, Refuse, and Recycling" ordinance mandates that businesses must choose three materials for separation from the list of materials collected from residents. Businesses that do not take advantage of the Township's recycling service are required by State law to contract out with private haulers and submit an annual recycled tonnage report to the municipality's recycling coordinator by June 1 of the following fiscal year. In 1989, businesses recycled high-grade paper, mixed paper, and car batteries through private haulers. (The total tonnage of commercial materials recycled is usually not known until shortly before the deadline.)

Berlin Township reviews businesses' recycling plans prior to issuing or renewing the Mercantile Licence necessary for all commercial establishments in the Township. In 1990, the Township will officially make this issuing and renewal process contingent upon submission of a recycling plan. The State and Town ordinances are explained to businesses when they request collection of recyclables by the Township.

The banning of commercial materials from the Winslow Landfill and the mid-summer deadline for reporting materials recycled has made it impossible for the Township to know the tonnage of commercial waste generated in 1989 at this time. The estimated recovery rate for 1989 assumes the tonnage recovered by private haulers in 1989 is the same as that recovered in 1988 (1,466 tons). According to Mike McGee, this assumption is a conservative one.

Materials Processing

The Camden County Recycling Facility (CCRF) has processed Berlin Township's commingled recyclables since the facility became operational in April 1986. The 80 ton-per-day facility processes mixed aluminum, glass, and ferrous beverage and food containers, as well as HDPE and PET containers from some towns, including Berlin Township. No tipping fees are charged. Camden County established this regional processing facility in order to enable its towns to comply with the county-wide mandatory recycling ordinance. Resource Recycling Systems, Inc., designed and built the CCRF for $700,000. Costs were covered by a $200,000 grant from the New Jersey Office of Recycling, $90,000 allocated from the County general funds, and a bond issue of about $400,000. While the County owns the facility, it is managed and operated by Resource Recycling Systems, Inc.

Newspaper and mixed paper are brought to the Newman & Company paper mill in Philadelphia. Newman & Company paid Berlin Township $5 per ton for mixed paper in 1988, and nothing in 1989. Safety Kleen, also located in Pennsylvania, charged the Township 50 cents per gallon of oil in 1988, and 10 cents per gallon in 1989. Corrugated cardboard is delivered to Parisi Brothers in Pennsauken, New Jersey. Scrap metal is collected by either Wade Salvage of Atco, New Jersey, or Camden Iron of Camden, New Jersey, depending on the prices offered. Car batteries are brought to Commercial Recycling, Inc., in Camden.

Public Works personnel remove the doors from white goods and sort heavy metals from aluminum. Their labor cost the Township $9,360 in 1989. Tires are used as storage bins for recyclable materials at the drop-off center.

Composting Activities

Because the New Jersey Statewide Mandatory Source Separation and Recycling Act prohibits landfilling of leaves, Berlin Township has implemented an aggressive yard waste collection program. The Township offers weekly curbside collection of leaves, brush, stumps, tree trunks, and clean lumber throughout the year. In 1989, Berlin's DPW cleared a 2-acre composting site in the public works yard. Before this, materials had been composted in Tansboro, New Jersey.

Leaves are collected loose in April, November, and December. During the remainder of the year, leaves and other yard waste materials must be placed in easily identifiable bags. The Township has two trucks on the road every day during the loose leaf collection months. Workers will pick up the leaves only if they are raked to the curb and separated from other yard waste. Prior to 1989, loose leaves were collected biweekly, but in 1989 collection averaged once a week. The Department of Public Works collects bagged leaves and other yard waste throughout the rest of the year in the course of refuse collection. Residents may bring these materials to the public works yard. The Township asks that leaves brought to the public works yard not be put into plastic bags.

Although the Township purchased two vacuums for leaf collection in 1985, it has since designed its own scoop, which is faster than the vacuums. The scoop, really a 2-cubic-yard container with the end cut out, is attached to the dump truck, and leaves are scooped into it with a front-end loader. Mike McGee claims that this design enables the crew to complete in one day a route that would take a day and a half with the vacuum.

In 1989, Berlin's 2-acre composting site had six and a half windrows, which were 15 feet across, 300 feet long, and 6 feet high. Employees of the Department of Public Works turn the piles monthly. Brush, tree stumps, and clean lumber are chipped on site with a Chipmore chipper, purchased in 1987. By the Spring of 1990 the site will be expanded by 2 acres to become a regional composting facility.

Once the regional composting site is operational, the County will purchase a Scat compost turner for the Township. The new loader will allow the Township to turn its windrows 3 to 5 times a year, and produce a compost in 8 months. The Township will also begin watering the windrows.

Finished compost and mulch are offered to residents free of charge. Whatever residents do not take is given to a farmer in Tabernacle, New Jersey.

Berlin Township is prohibited from collecting grass clippings by the Pinelands Commission.

Amount and Breakdown of Materials Recovered

Material	Total (Tons, 1985)	Total (Tons, 1986)	Total (Tons, 1987)	Total (Tons, 1988)
Newspaper	240	345	489	258
Corrugated	89	106	128	184
Other Paper				1,466
Glass	199	237		
Commingled			200	296
Aluminum		9		
Ferrous Scrap	136	155	185	123
Ferrous Cans		4		
Non-ferrous Scrap		25		
Motor Oil	3	3	13	9
Appliances				22
Batteries				5
Subtotal Recycled	**667**	**884**	**1,015**	**2,363**
Yard Waste*	789	612	711	686
Clean Lumber		273	314	665
Subtotal Composted	**789**	**885**	**1,025**	**1,351**
Total Recovered	**1,456**	**1,769**	**2,040**	**3,714**

*Includes leaves and brush

Material	Commercial (Tons, 1989)	Residential (Tons, 1989)	Total (Tons, 1989)
Newspaper	21.3	†	21.3
Corrugated	30.6	166	196.6
Other Paper	1,466.2 *	300	1,766.2
Commingled	36.3	300	336.3
Aluminum		2	2
Ferrous Scrap	13.9	100	113.9
Motor Oil		5.3	5.3
Tires		3	3
Appliances		52	52
Batteries	1	3.7	4.7
Subtotal Recycled	**1,569.3**	**932**	**2,501.3**
Leaves		683.9	683.9
Brush		493.1	493.1
Clean Lumber	65.1	658.4	723.5
Subtotal Composted	**65.1**	**1,835.4**	**1,900.5**
Total Recovered	**1,634.4**	**2,767.4**	**4,401.8**

*1988 tons reported by private haulers
†Included with other paper

Publicity and Education

The Township publishes a quarterly newsletter for its residents. This newsletter serves as a community calendar, informing readers of important dates and events. It also publishes information about the recycling and composting programs. For instance, the newsletter educates citizens about the preparation of materials for collection, and publishes the Township's recovery rates. The quarterly is circulated by the Department of Public Works at no extra cost to the recycling program.

DPW prints an annual recycling calendar specifying the collection days for the Township's three routes, and distributes it to all residents who receive curbside collection. The 1989 calendar cost the Department $300. The DPW also spends about $200 a year on occasional fliers and mailings for the recycling and composting programs.

Berlin Township schools incorporate the New Jersey State Recycling Curriculum. In addition, the fifth and sixth grade classes produced a short film on recycling in 1989.

Economics

Costs Cover: Capital and operating and maintenance costs given below cover (1) collection of 1,035 tons of recyclables at curbside and at the drop-off center, and (2) collection of 1,901 tons of yard waste at curbside.

Capital Costs: Collection

Item	Cost	Use	Year Incurred
Eager Beaver Trailer	$12,000	Recycling	1981
2 Leaf Loaders @ $4,500	$ 9,000	Composting	1982
Loader @ 5% recycling use and 95% DPW use	$14,000	Recycling/DPW	1985
1-ton Dump Truck @ 20% recycling use and 80% composting use	$ 6,000	Recycling/Composting	1986
Ford 555 Backhoe Loader @ 35% recycling use, 15% composting use and 50% DPW use	$30,000	Recycling/Composting/DPW	1986
Dump Truck @ 35% recycling use, 15% composting use, and 50% DPW use	$10,000	Recycling/Composting/DPW	1987
Ford F800 Dump Truck @ 35% recycling use, 15% composting use, and 50% DPW use	$44,000	Recycling/Composting/DPW	1988
3/4-ton Dump Truck @ 50% recycling use and 50% DPW use	$ 6,000	Recycling/DPW	1988
Stake Body Dump Truck @ 50% recycling use and 50% DPW use	$ 8,400	Recycling/DPW	1989
Eager Beaver Truck	$35,000	Recycling	1989

The only cost the Town has incurred for its drop-off center is the Eager Beaver trailer used for storing sorted glass, aluminum, and tin cans.   Other storage bins are made of tires and 55-gallon drums recovered from the waste stream.   The Town does occasionally use the backhoe loader at the drop-off center for cleanup tasks.

Capital Costs: Processing

Item	Cost	Use	Year Incurred
Chipmore Chipper	$12,000	Composting	1987

Operating and Maintenance Costs (1989)

	Recycling	Composting	Total
Collection	$ 28,982	$ 4,185	$ 33,167
Processing	$ 9,360	$ 864	$ 10,224
Administration	$ 4,000	$ 0	$ 4,000
Education/Publicity	$ 500	$ 0	$ 500
Total	**$ 42,842**	**$ 5,049**	**$ 47,891**

Materials Revenues: $5,159 in 1989
$7,818 in 1988

Source of Funding: Recycling and composting activities are paid for by residents' general taxes. In 1989, Berlin Township received a $7,619.45 State Tonnage Grant from the Office of Recycling, New Jersey Department of Environmental Protection.

Part-time Employees: Seven employees of the Department of Public Works are responsible for the Township's composting and recycling programs. There are no Public Works employees who devote their full time to recycling or composting.

Contact

Mike McGee
Recycling Coordinator
Director of Public Works
Township of Berlin
170 Bate Avenue
West Berlin, NJ 08091
Phone (609) 767-5052
Fax (609) 767-6657

Reference

O'Brien-Kreitzberg & Associates, Inc., *Projected Industrial, Commercial, Residential Trash Tonnage for the Camden Resource Recovery Facility Service Area for the Year 1992*, Pennsauken, New Jersey, August 24, 1988.

LONGMEADOW, MASSACHUSETTS

Demographics

Jurisdiction: Town of Longmeadow

Population: 16,309 (1989 estimate by Selectman's Office)

Total Households: 5,744

Total Businesses: 150

Area: 9 square miles

Other: Largely residential with a small commercial sector

Solid Waste Generation and Collection

(Annual Tonnages for 1989)

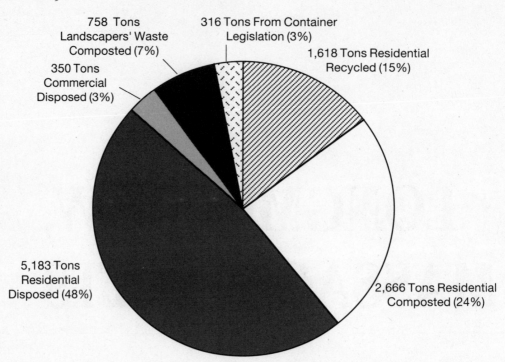

758 Tons Landscapers' Waste Composted (7%)

316 Tons From Container Legislation (3%)

1,618 Tons Residential Recycled (15%)

350 Tons Commercial Disposed (3%)

5,183 Tons Residential Disposed (48%)

2,666 Tons Residential Composted (24%)

Total Waste Generated:	10,891 tons in 1988/1989[1] (including tonnage recovered through deposit legislation, tonnage of landscapers' waste composted, and scrap metal — a small percentage of which is appliances — but excluding most bulky waste such as tires and construction debris)[2]
	10,172 tons in 1987/1988
Residential Waste Generated:	9,467 tons in 1988/1989 (excluding tonnage recovered through container deposit legislation and bulky waste)
	9,922 tons in 1987/1988
Commercial Waste Generated:	350 tons in 1988/1989 (based on estimates from private haulers that service Longmeadow's businesses)
	250 tons in 1987/1988 (estimated by private hauler contracted to collect Longmeadow's waste)
Bulky Waste Generated:	Total tons not available because one of the two bulky waste haulers servicing Longmeadow has not reported tonnages col-

---

[1]Longmeadow's fiscal year is from June 30, 1988 to July 1, 1989.

[2]Yard waste generated by landscapers, like bottle bill tonnage, cannot be broken down into residential and commercial.

lected; however, the Town's contracted refuse collector hauled less than 1 ton of bulky materials in fiscal year 1989.

**% By Weight of Total
Waste Recovered:**

49 percent in 1988/1989 (18 percent recycling including deposit containers, and 31 percent composting)

49 percent in 1987/1988

**% By Weight of
Residential Waste Recovered:**

45 percent in 1988/1989 (17 percent recycling and 28 percent composting, not including deposit containers)

44 percent in 1987/1988

**% By Weight of
Commercial Waste Recovered:**

Not available

**Tipping Fee at
Disposal Facilities:**

$22.79 per ton at Springfield incinerator 1988/1989
$20 per ton at Springfield incinerator 1987/1988
$36.50 per ton at privately owned landfill 1986/1987

Collection of Refuse:

The Town contracts with Waste Control Systems to collect residential refuse and recyclable materials. Longmeadow's small business community contracts with private haulers for waste removal. Residents and businesses contract with Waste Control Systems or Partyka and Sons for collection of bulky materials.

In December 1987, the Town was shut out of a privately owned landfill. Presently, Longmeadow disposes of its refuse at a privately owned incinerator in Springfield, Massachusetts. In 1989, Longmeadow paid $188,455 in contract fees to Waste Control Systems to collect and transport 5,182 tons to the incinerator. (This cost excludes tipping fees.)

The Town also operates a tree stump and lawn clipping drop-off site at the public works yard; these materials are landfilled.

**Future Solid Waste
Management Plans:**

The Town will explore taking its recovered glass to a materials recovery facility in Springfield, Massachusetts.

Materials Recovery

Longmeadow has had a mandatory source-separation ordinance for newspaper, mixed paper, and corrugated cardboard in effect since July 1, 1984. Waste Control Systems, a private hauler under contract with the Town, picks up these items at the curb on a weekly basis. Glass containers, scrap metal, and aluminum are collected at a drop-off center staffed by volunteers. The center is open from 9 a.m. to 12 noon every Saturday. In 1989, it did not accept appliances due to the problems associated with PCBs in the capacitors.

---

[3]In 1989, the average per capita tonnage of beverage containers recovered in Massachusetts was 0.0194 tons. 0.0194 x 16,309 (the population of Longmeadow) = 316 tons.

The Town reported that through recycling it avoided paying $36,851 in tip fees at the incinerator in 1988/1989.

The Commonwealth of Massachusetts implemented a beverage container deposit law in 1983.   Institute for Local Self-Reliance staff estimate that 316 tons of beverage containers were recovered in Longmeadow in 1989 through the State deposit legislation.[3]

As of April 1990, residents and businesses may recycle white goods and tires for a fee ($2 for each tire and $5 for white goods) at the Town's drop-off facility in the public works yard.

Curbside Collection

Start-up Date: July 1, 1984

Private/Public: Municipal program operated under contract with private hauler, Waste Control Systems

Materials Collected: Newspaper, mixed paper (office paper, mail, magazines, and books), paperboard (egg cartons and cereal boxes), corrugated cardboard, and leaves

Pick-up Frequency: Weekly for recyclables (newspaper and mixed paper one week, corrugated cardboard and paperboard the next week).   Leaves are collected twice during November and December

Pick-up Same Day as Refuse: Yes, except for leaves

Material Set-out Method: Newspaper and mixed paper are placed in bags or in a container marked with a white band around it, but NOT tied or bundled. Corrugated and paperboard are flattened and stacked loosely, or placed in a container marked with a white band.   (Residents are responsible for supplying their own containers.) Leaves are raked loose to the curbside.

Mandatory: Yes. (Residents are required to separate newspaper, mixed paper, corrugated cardboard, paperboard, and leaves from their refuse at curbside as indicated above.)

Service Provider: Waste Control Systems

Collection Vehicles: Center loading refuse packer owned by Waste Control Systems and vacuum trucks, owned by the DPW, for leaf collection.   A one-person crew operates the packer for paper collection.

Households Served: 5,744

Participation Rate: 90 percent (private hauler's estimate based on informal count of weekly set-out rates)

Businesses Served: None

Economic Incentives: None

Enforcement: Private contractor has authority to leave refuse with obvious quantities of recyclable material in it.

Commercial Materials Recovery Activities

Private haulers servicing Longmeadow's commercial sector do not offer recycling services.

Materials Processing

The Town sells the glass collected at its drop-off site two or three times per year. The glass is loaded by Town equipment into a trailer provided by the glass buyer. Citizens can put their aluminum cans in four metal trash cans at the drop-off center. A volunteer with a station wagon takes aluminum from the drop-off center to a market once or twice a year. The Town does not weigh the aluminum due to the small amount that is recovered. The Town receives all revenues for these materials.

Waste Control Systems processes and markets the newspaper, mixed paper, paperboard, and corrugated. Sonoco Paper, in Holyoke, Massachusetts, takes Longmeadow's wastepaper, including newspaper, office paper, junk mail, envelopes, magazines, corrugated cardboard, cereal boxes, and egg cartons. However, in June 1989, the Town ceased earning revenue for the wastepaper due to a weak market.

In May 1988, the Massachusetts Department of Environmental Protection warned steel manufacturers that residues from white goods contained PCBs and had to be handled as hazardous waste. This warning caused most companies to stop recovering post-consumer white goods and light metals. The Town of Longmeadow informed residents that it would not accept these items at the drop-off center until a market could be found; however, according to Leslie Haskins, the Recycling Coordinator, some residents continued to bring appliances and scrap metal to the center. Longmeadow stockpiled these materials until a market was found in May 1989. (Although the Town does not officially collect white goods for recycling, it will try to market any materials that are delivered to the drop-off center.) The Town paid $2,015 in 1989 to have 34 tons of scrap metal (and a small amount of appliances) hauled to its vendor, R & R, Inc., in Springfield, Massachusetts.

Composting Activities

A composting program was started in the fall of 1986. The Town collects fall leaves at curbside from October 30 to December 7 and delivers them to a farmer's 100-acre field. The leaves are spread out on the land and tilled into the soil directly. The farmer plants directly onto the field the following year, aiding in the decomposition process. Residential landscapers also deliver leaves and lawn clippings to the fields. A total of 3,424 tons (including the tonnage from landscapers) were brought to the farmer's field in 1988/1989 at a total cost of

$137,545 for collection and processing, including a $62,232 contract with the farmer for the tilling. In addition to the contract fee, the Town pays for all lime that the farmer uses for composting. Three shredders, which are leased by the Town with the expectation that they will be bought, are used at the farm.

Residents are required to rake their loose leaves to the curbside for collection. Two methods of leaf collection are used. Four vacuum "gangs" collect dry leaves. Each gang is made up of two closed dump trucks and one vacuum. A fifth gang collects wet leaves using a small tractor to push the leaves into piles, and a bucket loader to scoop up the leaves and load them into open dump trucks. The Town owns one open dump truck, and hires four additional trucks for the 7-week fall leaf collection season. Each home is serviced twice during the November and December collection period.

Landscapers recovered 758 tons of leaves, brush, and grass clippings for composting from the Town's parklands and residents in 1988/1989. Landscapers are allowed to deliver their yard waste to the farm at no charge. The Town's contract with the farmer covers the tilling of landscapers' yard waste. This represents 7 percent of Longmeadow's waste stream.

Other Activities

A household hazardous waste collection day, which had been sponsored by the Town with matching funds from the Commonwealth during 1986/1987 and 1987/1988, was canceled in fiscal year 1989 due to a lack of State funds. The first collection day in 1986 cost the Town $12,000. The Town plans to start this program again during fiscal year 1990.

Amount and Breakdown of Materials Recovered

Material	Total (Tons, 1985/1986)	Total (Tons, 1987/1988)
Mixed Paper*	1,092	1,123
Corrugated	212	214
Glass†	55	43
Scrap Metal	NA	NA
Aluminum	NA	NA
Subtotal Recycled	**1,359**	**1,380**
Leaves:		
Residential	NA	3,000
Commercial	NA	NA
Subtotal Composted	**NA**	**3,000**
Subtotal Recovered	**NA**	**4,380**
Deposit Containers	NA	616
Total Recovered	**NA**	**4,996**

*Includes newspaper, magazines, high-grade paper, egg cartons, and books
†Glass collected at the drop-off center excludes containers affected by the State's deposit legislation, but does include such items as 1-gallon beverage jars and food containers.

Materials	Commercial (Tons, 1988/1989)	Residential (Tons, 1988/1989)	Total (Tons, 1988/1989)
Mixed Paper*	0	1,299	1,299
Corrugated	0	237	237
Glass†	0	48	48
Scrap Metal	0	34	34
Subtotal Recycled	**0**	**1,618**	**1,618**
Leaves	0	2,666	2,666
Landscaping Yard Waste	NA	NA	758
Subtotal Composted	**NA**	**2,666**	**3,424**
Subtotal Recovered	**NA**	**4,284**	**5,042**
Deposit Containers	NA	NA	316
Total Recovered	**NA**	**NA**	**5,358**

*Includes newspaper, magazines, high-grade paper, egg cartons, and books
†Glass collected at the drop-off center excludes containers affected by the State's deposit legislation, but does include such items as 1-gallon beverage jars and food containers.

Publicity and Education

A local newspaper, *The Reminder,* distributed to residents free of charge, provides publicity for the program. The Town's biweekly subscription newspaper, *The Longmeadow News,* has a regular section set aside for the announcement of activities and changes within the recycling and composting program. In addition, a calendar/flyer is made available at supermarkets and the Town Hall each year with the various collection days marked.

Economics

Costs Cover:

The capital costs given below are those incurred by the Town for its leaf collection program. In 1988/1989, 2,666 tons of leaves were composted. The program has no capital costs for recycling because the Town contracts out for collection and processing of recyclable materials. The Town of Longmeadow has not purchased any processing equipment for either composting or recycling.

The operation and maintenance costs given below are those incurred by the Town for (1) collection and marketing of 1,536 tons of mixed paper and corrugated recovered under contract with Waste Control Systems; and (2) collection of 2,666 tons of leaves and processing of 3,424 tons of leaves, including tons from landscapers.

Capital Costs: Collection

Item	Cost	Use	Year Incurred
Bucket Loader	$ 60,000	Composting	1974
Small Tractor	$ 22,000	Composting	1977
8 6-cu.-yd. Closed Dump Trucks and 4 Vacuum Trucks	$328,000	Composting	1985
6-cu.-yd. Open Dump Truck @ 12% use	$ 35,000	Composting/DPW	1985

Operating and Maintenance Costs (1988/1989)

	Recycling	Composting	Total
Collection	$ 73,340	$ 47,812	$ 121,152
Processing	$ 0	$ 89,733 *	$ 89,733 *
Administration	$ 0	$ 0	$ 0
Education/Publicity	$ 45	$ 0	$ 45
Total	**$ 73,385**	**$ 137,545**	**$ 210,930**

*Includes cost of leasing three shredders, contract fee of $62,232 for tilling, and the cost of the lime applied by the farmer.

Operating and maintenance costs for 1987/1988 were $221,275 ($71,275 for recycling plus $150,000 for composting).

Materials Revenues: $31,872 in 1988/1989
$33,793 in 1987/1988
$35,295 in 1985/1986

Source of Funding: Residents' taxes

Part-time Employees: 25-32 (10-12 DPW and 15-20 temporary workers)

Contacts

Leslie Haskins
Chairperson
Longmeadow Recycling Commission
844 Longmeadow Street
Longmeadow, MA 01106
(413) 567-7454

Ron Perkins
President
Waste Control Systems
81 Randall Place
Springfield, MA 01108
(413) 785-1774

Arlene Miller
Selectperson
Town of Longmeadow
20 Williams Street
Longmeadow, MA 01106
(413) 567-5433

Doug Barron
Superintendent of Public Works
Town of Longmeadow
20 Williams Street
Longmeadow, MA 01106
(413) 567-1281

Alfred Riviere, Jr.
Browning-Ferris Industries
845 Burnett Road
Chicopee, MA 01020
(413) 367-7778

Karl Ekstedt
Commercial Disposal
P.O. Box 389
West Springfield, MA 01090
(413) 737-1129

Reference

Bender, Julie, Administrator of the Massachusetts Beverage Law, Division of Solid Waste Management, Department of Environmental Protection, telephone conversation regarding redeemed beverage containers, Boston, Massachusetts, April 23, 1990.

HADDONFIELD, NEW JERSEY

Demographics

Jurisdiction: Borough of Haddonfield

Population: 12,151 in 1988

Total Households: 4,750 households (4,400 single-residence and 350 multi-unit)

Total Businesses: 270

Area: 2.78 square miles

Other: The Borough of Haddonfield is a fully developed residential suburb of Camden, New Jersey and Philadelphia, Pennsylvania.

Solid Waste Generation and Collection

(Annual Tonnages for 1989)

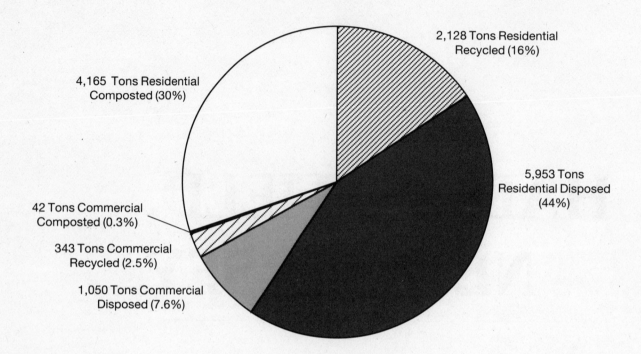

Total Waste Generated:	13,681 tons in 1989 (including bulky waste such as construction debris, tires, and tree trunks) 14,244 tons in 1987
Residential Waste Generated:	Approximately 12,246 tons in 1989 Approximately 12,677 tons in 1987
Commercial Waste Generated:	Approximately 1,435 tons in 1989 Approximately 1,567 tons in 1987
Bulky Waste Generated:	Not available (tree stumps, tires, and construction debris included with residential tonnages)
% By Weight of Total Waste Recovered:	49 percent in 1989 (18 percent recycling, 31 percent composting) 45 percent in 1987
% By Weight of Residential Waste Recovered:	51 percent in 1989 (17 percent recycling, 34 percent from composting)
% By Weight of Commercial Waste Recovered:	27 percent in 1989 (24 percent recycling, 3 percent composting)
Landfill Tipping Fee:	$63 per ton in 1989. The Borough paid $441,189 in 1989 to landfill 7,003 tons of commercial and residential waste. $62 per ton in 1988, up from $42 per ton previously.

Collection of Refuse: Collection is provided by the Borough's Department of Public Works. Some commercial establishments contract with private haulers.

Future Solid Waste Management Plans: Haddonfield plans to add HDPE and PET plastic containers to the materials collected at curbside in the fall of 1990, and to purchase a new, larger capacity (24- cubic-yard) Eager Beaver truck so that more materials can be collected in a shorter period of time.

Materials Recovery

Recycling activity began in 1981 with a Saturday morning drop-off center for newspapers. By mid-1982, 300 to 400 cars dropped off newspapers and glass each Saturday. Local non-profit groups operated the center and loaded Borough trucks. A Borough driver, already scheduled for business district clean-up on Saturday, took the paper to a dealer in nearby Camden. Money from sales went to the groups, after a small deduction for Borough costs.

However, the groups' enthusiasm for operating the drop-off center waned, and the Borough wanted to increase resident participation in recycling. In late 1982 the Borough instituted twice-monthly curbside collection of newspapers and glass on a voluntary basis. The town was divided into two sections, with one receiving pick-up on the first and third Wednesdays of each month, and the other receiving pick-up on the second and fourth Wednesdays. Borough crews of two or three (depending on labor availability and quantity of material) collected the material. Newspaper was collected in a spare 20-cubic-yard refuse packer truck and was taken to a dealer in Camden when the truck was full. Glass was picked up in 55-gallon drums on a small trailer pulled by a pick-up truck. The full barrels were dumped into a 30-cubic-yard container provided by an area glass dealer. Initially, the glass had to be separated into clear and colored. Later, it could be mixed.

Participation grew to 600 stops per week for newspaper and about 300 stops per week for glass. Giving each household a 5- or 6-gallon white plastic bucket with a "Haddonfield Recycles" sticker on it helped boost participation. These were recycled buckets from a dealer, costing $1.00 each. Set out along the curb on collection day, they advertised the program.

By the end of 1983, the quantity of materials left out for recycling was overwhelming the equipment, and the loss of up to six workers each Wednesday was impairing the ability of the Public Works Department to meet normal maintenance obligations. Further, the twice-per-month schedule was confusing to the public, especially when a month had five Wednesdays.

In November 1983, the Borough began to collect recyclables weekly on regular trash collection days. This was made possible, in part, by the purchase of a special trailer manufactured by General Engines, Inc.

The trailer has an all-aluminum body with a 12-cubic-yard capacity (6,500 pounds of glass and newspaper), and is divided into four compartments that can be dumped individually. It is pulled by a 1-ton pick-up truck with an automatic transmission. A "fifth wheel" attachment and a "gooseneck" design make it very maneuverable. Further, the trailer enables one worker to collect all recyclable materials at one time (although a second person is sometimes needed to speed collection).

A State grant helped buy the first trailer and truck. The Public Works Department was now able to schedule one person for 5 days a week recycling (40 labor hours) as opposed to the previous six workers, 1 day per week (48 labor hours). Participation jumped to involve almost 1,500 stops per week for newspaper (and half that for glass) on a voluntary basis.

In late 1983, there was no market for mixed glass, as the Borough's original glass dealer had gone out of business. The program began recycling clear glass only and paid for a 30-cubic-yard container to transport the glass to market. This extra cost equalled the income from sales. The container was located under a ramp where the recycling trailer could dump directly into it to avoid double handling. All glass was collected in the rear compartment of the trailer and emptied into the container three times a day. The rest of the trailer held newspapers, which it took directly to the dealer once per day. The Borough's goal was to avoid double handling at all costs.

In March 1985, participation in the municipal curbside recycling program became mandatory, and was expanded to include aluminum cans and colored glass. A second recycling trailer and truck were purchased. Bins were constructed at the Public Works Department yard to store color-separated glass. There are two refuse collection crews, and each recycling truck/trailer covers a refuse collection route, putting newspaper, clear glass, green glass, and brown glass into the trailer, and aluminum cans into the large cardboard boxes on the bed of the truck. When the collection containers were full, the recycling crew dumped materials at the public works yard.

A North Jersey glass dealer provided two 30-cubic-yard containers, one for clear glass and one for colored glass. A loader scooped the glass from the bins in the public works yard and filled these containers, which the glass dealer picked up as needed. A Philadelphia paper mill provided a 30-cubic-yard container for newspapers. Borough crews could dump newspapers directly into it from the trailer. Paper mill employees picked up the container when it was full, enabling the Borough to avoid the trip to the paper dealer in Camden. The Borough crews transferred aluminum from the cardboard boxes to 55-gallon barrels on the old trailer and took them to an area dealer once per week.

Following the mandatory ordinance, participation increased to an average of 2,300 weekly stops for newspaper (31,000 lbs), 1,900 stops for glass (15,000 lbs), plus 20 barrels (200 lbs) of aluminum cans. Income from sales was $10 per ton for newspaper, $14 per ton for glass, and 23 cents per pound for aluminum.

In May 1986, the program changed again. The Camden County Recycling Facility (CCRF) opened to accept all glass and metal food and beverage containers. This meant that tin cans, steel cans, and mixed metal cans could also be recycled. All these items could be received mixed. The Borough now had a stable market, and the County handled the separation, processing, storage, and marketing of these items.

Residents were told they could put all glass and metal together in one or more buckets. Newspaper collection remained the same. The front three-fifths of the trailers are used for glass and cans. The rear two-fifths hold newspapers. Newspapers are emptied from the truck/trailer into the dumpster at the Borough yard two or three times per day. After 6 to 7 hours to complete the route, bottles and cans are hauled to the Camden facility — a 1-hour round trip. The trailers are then cleaned and made ready for the next day.

Following the announcement of this convenient way to store and put out recyclable materials for collection, the number of stops increased to over 3,000 per week (70 percent of a total of 4,400 households). The Borough also undertook an enforcement program. Recycling buckets were distributed with a strong letter to those still not participating. Further, the drivers had become familiar with their routes and their "customers"; their records showed that only a handful, perhaps 5 percent, of the households never put out any recyclable materials. Many did not have the quantities to justify putting materials out weekly (senior citizens in particular) and did so biweekly or even monthly. Some shared buckets. Therefore, the Borough estimates that, while 70 percent of its households put material out on any given week, 95 percent of its households put material out at least monthly.

In May 1988, the Borough began collection of mixed paper: telephone books, magazines, advertising supplements, hardbound and paperback books, junk mail (including envelopes), kraft paper (e.g., brown grocery bags), office, school, notebook, computer, and similar types of paper. Residents were instructed to put these added paper products into paper grocery bags with their newspapers for weekly curbside collection. Newspaper and other paper products could also be put into small cardboard boxes, if the boxes were clearly marked "Recycling" and were closed securely so the paper could not blow around.

Haddonfield's outstanding recycling program has earned several awards. In 1988, the Borough received the New Jersey Recycling Association's 1988 *Glass Recycling Award* for recycling 65.2 pounds per capita that year, more than any other New Jersey municipality. Haddonfield was also given the *Best Data Collection Award* in the *Record Setting Recycling Contest 1989* conducted by the Institute for Local Self-Reliance.

In September 1989, a publicly run drop-off center for PET and HDPE plastic containers was opened. It is open for 2 hours each Saturday morning, and accepts any plastic container that held a liquid. The rationale behind this rule is that containers holding liquids are easier to clean than containers holding other substances. Participation in the drop-off program has been tremendous, resulting in collection of as much as 900 pounds of plastic in one 2-hour period.

Haddonfield's recycling collection program is integrated with its trash collection system. Recycling is treated as simply another type of trash collection. For years prior to the current program, the Borough made separate collections of appliances, leaves, and brush. The appliances are sold to scrap dealers, while the leaves and brush are composted and used by residents and the Borough.

The Borough has found that, for a recycling program to succeed, elected officials must initiate it, or strongly identify with it and back it. Separating trash may not be popular with residents initially, but with support from public officials, it comes to be seen as a positive thing.

Curbside Collection

Start-up Date: Voluntary from 1980 until March 1985

Private/Public: Public

Materials Collected: Glass, metals (tin, aluminum, ferrous), newspapers, mixed paper (telephone books, magazines, advertising supplements, books, junk mail, kraft paper, corrugated boxes, office, school, notebook, computer and similar paper), used motor oil, appliances and other white goods, leaves, brush, and Christmas trees

Pick-up Frequency: Weekly for residential recyclables and brush. Leaves are collected two to three times per household in the fall and spring. Appliances are collected on designated days throughout the year.

Pick-up Same Day as Refuse: Yes

Material Set-out Method: Newspaper and mixed paper must be placed in brown paper bags or secured in bundles not to exceed 50 pounds, and must not be contained in plastic bags. Used glass and cans must be contained in one or more reusable metal or plastic container that is owner-, occupant-, or Borough-supplied, each not to exceed 6 gallons in capacity. Glass must not be broken. Corrugated boxes must be flattened and tied securely in bundles not to exceed 50 pounds. Motor oil must be stored in an easily identifiable, closed container. Leaves are piled between the sidewalk and the curb. Brush and wood waste must be set out neatly at the curb.

Mandatory: Yes. Residential households must recycle all materials listed above except motor oil, corrugated cardboard, and white goods, which may be recycled voluntarily.

Service Provider: Department of Public Works

Collection Vehicles: Two General Engines, Inc. (Eager Beaver) 12-cubic-yard trailers with five compartments, each pulled by a 1-ton pick-up truck, collect glass, metal containers, residential corrugated cardboard, motor oil, newspapers, and mixed paper. One person per truck/trailer does collection. A separate packer truck picks up both bundled corrugated cardboard and bagged office paper from commercial establishments.

A dump truck equipped with a trailer-mounted vacuum picks up leaves. A dump truck equipped with a chipper and a box to receive chips is used for brush.

During regular trash collection, the trash crew notes households where appliances have been set out. The crew comes back later in a pick-up truck to collect the appliances.

Households Served: 4,750 households (4,400 single family residences and 350 multi-family units). The tallest buildings are 4-story.

Participation Rate: 95 percent (70 percent of the households put out recyclable materials weekly, but 95 percent of households put materials out at least monthly. The stops per week are counted and divided by the total households served). There has been no significant change in this rate for the last several years.

Businesses Served: All except two of Haddonfield's 270 businesses. (The business district is served by the curbside collection program if no private contractor is involved.)

Economic Incentives: Fines

Enforcement: Any person who violates or neglects to comply with any provision of the mandatory recycling ordinance can be fined up to $100. Regular trash will not be picked up if there are any recyclable materials in it.

Commercial Materials Recovery Activities

In 1988, Haddonfield's mandatory recycling ordinance was amended to comply with State law. The amendment, which went into effect in January 1989, requires commercial establishments to recycle corrugated cardboard and high-grade paper. It applies both to establishments for which the Borough provides refuse collection and to those that contract with a private hauler. Commercial and institutional solid waste generators may be exempted from the source separation requirements of the ordinance if satisfactory proof of an acceptable alternate plan for recycling materials is submitted to and approved by the Commissioner of Public Works. In such cases, the generator has to submit written documentation to the Borough of the total number of tons recycled. To date, this mandate has not been enforced. Richard Schwab, the Recycling Coordinator, states that businesses are fairly good about recycling. However, he estimates that retail stores and offices could easily double their output of recyclables. Volunteers are going door to door to retail establishments and encouraging them to recycle.

Before recycling of corrugated cardboard and office paper from business and commercial establishments became mandatory on January 1, 1989, the Borough had been collecting trash daily from these generators. It is now collecting recyclable materials daily as well. The materials collected and the set-out method are similar to those of the residential curbside program. The voluntary materials (newspaper, mixed paper, glass, and metals) are collected in the same trailers that serve the residential districts. However, corrugated cardboard, flattened and bundled, and high-grade computer and ledger paper in clear plastic bags, are collected separately due to the higher volumes of these materials generated by the commercial sector.

Some commercial establishments recycle privately, and then report tons recovered to the Recycling Coordinator. In 1989, the ACME grocery stores reported 17.77 tons of food waste and 123.6 tons of corrugated cardboard recycled, and New Jersey Bell reported 1.2 tons of office paper recycled.

Materials Processing

Glass, metal, and plastic food and beverage containers are hauled to the Camden County Recycling Facility — a 1-hour round trip — for processing. Commercial cardboard and office paper are taken to Ponte Brothers, a scrap dealer in Camden. Newspapers, mixed paper, and residential cardboard are dumped directly into a container provided by a Philadelphia paper mill. The yard wastes collected are composted. Brush is chopped into wood chips and used by the Borough and its residents. In the past, tree trunks were stored at the public works yard, where residents could chop them for use as firewood, and the excess were buried. In 1989, the Borough had a particularly large number of tree trunks, which it could not process by the usual method, so it paid Winzinger Recycling Systems, which recovers construction debris and wood waste, to grind them into wood chips. The Borough will continue to utilize Winzinger rather than reverting to the old, more haphazard system.

Composting Activities

The Borough of Haddonfield has been collecting leaves separately for 20 years. Throughout the year, leaves and other yard waste (excluding grass clippings) are collected for composting during specific periods announced by the Borough (two to three collection days per household in the fall, and two more in spring). Between October 1 and December 31, and during the month of April, leaves are collected regularly by dump trucks with trailer-mounted vacuums to handle the additional volume. Residents must pile the leaves between the sidewalk and the curb, or just behind the sidewalk if there is not space between the sidewalk and curb. Leaves must not be placed in the street or gutter.   Leaves put out for collection may be placed at the curb only during collection periods announced by the Borough.   The Borough reports that participation is 100 percent.

At other times of the year, leaves must be placed in plastic or biodegradable bags and be clearly identifiable as leaves.   Only large quantities are actually composted.   Smaller quantities end up being landfilled.

Leaves are composted at the former landfill site, which has been reclaimed as a park.   The compost produced is used by the residents and the Borough — most of it on-site, as part of the landfill reclamation project.   Approximately 2,500 tons of leaves are composted per year.

Brush, tree limbs, and Christmas trees have also been collected separately for many years.   The Borough collects brush weekly throughout the year.   These items must be laid out neatly at the curb. Brush is chipped and used to maintain the dirt road at the composting site.   No chipping is done during the October 15-December 31 leaf collection period.

The Borough of Haddonfield owns the approximately 10,000 trees lining its streets, and has a "shade tree department" with two 2-person crews to maintain them.   High-quality wood chips are produced from the tree maintenance debris.   These chips are in high demand among schools, public facilities, and residents.

Amount and Breakdown of Materials Recovered

The following chart includes the total tonnage of materials recovered in the Borough of Haddonfield from 1985 to 1988.   Breakdowns of materials collected into commercial and residential categories were not available until 1988.   Mixed paper was added to the materials collected for recycling in 1988.   Recycling of corrugated cardboard and office paper from business and commercial establishments became mandatory in January 1989.   Also, the Borough began collecting PET and HDPE plastic containers via a publicly run drop-off center in September of 1989.   All three of these initiatives increased the tonnage collected for recycling.

Material	Total (Tons, 1985)	Total (Tons, 1986)	Total (Tons, 1987)	Total (Tons, 1988)
Newspaper	771.53	1,094.43	1,051.31	1,281
Glass, Aluminum, & Ferrous Cans	308.40	520.38	520.61	538
White Goods	34.20	33.19	32.70	51
Borough Motor Oil	3.00	1.10	2.98	6
Commercial Motor Oil	4.40	3.82	7.32	4
Corrugated Cardboard	86.30	88.28	101.17	110
ACME Food Waste	18.70	15.85	18.72	18
Subtotal Recycled	**1,226.53**	**1,757.05**	**1,734.81**	**2,008**
Leaves	2,458.80	2,184.60	2,057.72	2,308
Wood Chips	1,731.63	1,055.93	2,559.13	1,348
Subtotal Composted	**4,190.43**	**3,240.53**	**4,616.85**	**3,656**
Total Recovered	**5,416.96**	**4,997.58**	**6,351.66**	**5,664**

Material	Commercial (Tons, 1989)	Residential (Tons, 1989)	Total (Tons, 1989)
Newspaper*	76.2	1,515.41	1,591.61
Glass, Aluminum, & Ferrous Cans	20	527.31	547.31
White Goods		40.29	40.29
Motor Oil		3.05	3.05
Corrugated Cardboard	228.6		228.60§
ACME Food Waste	17.77		17.77
Plastic Containers		2.5	2.5
Concrete		40	40
Subtotal Recycled	**342.57**	**2,128.56**	**2,471.13**
Leaves†	20.69	2,048.06	2,068.75
Wood Chips†	21.38	2,116.72	2,138.1
Subtotal Composted	**42.07**	**4,164.78**	**4,206.85**
Total Recovered	**384.64**	**6,293.34**	**6,677.98**

*Includes mixed paper
†Based on estimated breakdown of 99 percent residential, 1 percent commercial
§Includes high-grade office paper

Publicity and Education

The Borough's publicity and education program for recycling in-cludes mailers, pamphlets, and an annual calendar, as well as ads in the local newspaper. Two new brochures were recently produced: one on commercial recycling, and one on the plastics drop-off program. A mini-curriculum on recycling is taught in schools throughout the state of New Jersey. The schools use a video on recycling that was produced by the New Jersey Office of Recycling. In Haddonfield, the 4th grade class goes on a trip to the Borough Hall to learn about recycling and the Borough government.

Economics

Costs Cover: Publicly sponsored recycling and composting (6,495 tons in 1989) not including 123.6 tons of corrugated cardboard, 17.77 tons of ACME supermarket food waste, 40 tons of concrete recycled by Winzinger, and 1.2 tons office paper recycled by NJ Bell.

Capital Costs: Collection

Item	Cost	Use	Year Incurred
Truck (for wood chipping)	$ 6,000	Chipping	1973
4 Long Body Dump Trucks @ 50% of use	$ 120,000	Composting	1981
Long Body Dump Truck @ 30% of use	$ 30,000	Composting	1981
6 Trailer Mounted Vacuums @ $15,000 each	$ 90,000	Composting	1981-1983
1-Ton Pick-up Truck (used for backup only)	$ 9,000	Recycling	1983
General Engines 24' Trailer	$ 10,000	Recycling	1983
"Pan" Attachment for trash trucks	$ 2,500	Composting	1983
Truck Modification for Pan Attachment	$ 2,500	Composting	1983
1-Ton Pick-up Truck and Eager Beaver Trailer	$ 23,000	Recycling	1985
"Pan" Attachment for trash trucks	$ 2,500	Composting	1986
Truck Modification for Pan Attachment	$ 2,500	Composting	1986
Construction of 2 Glass Storage Bins	$ 5,000	Recycling	1987
Chip Receiving Box on Specialized Tree Maintenance Truck	$ 15,000	Chipping	1987
Bucket Loader for Leaf Collection on Tractor	$ 4,500	Composting	1987
Front-end Loader @ 25% of use	$ 55,000	Composting	1988
Long Body Dump Truck @ 50% of use	$ 40,000	Composting	1988
Replacement 1-Ton Pick-up Truck	$ 15,000	Recycling	1988
Recycling Buckets	$ 18,000	Recycling	1985-1989

Capital Costs: Processing

Item	Cost	Use	Year Incurred
2 Trailer Mounted Chippers @ $12,000 each	$24,000	Chipping	1987
Trailer Mounted Brush Chipper	$17,000	Chipping	1988

Capital costs are paid directly out of the annual budget, and are depreciated over 5 years for accounting purposes. There are no new capital costs for the plastics drop-off center. The same trash truck that picks up office paper and corrugated is parked in the Borough Hall parking lot for 2 hours every Saturday morning, and plastic containers are loaded directly into the truck. One person supervises and runs the compactor when there is enough plastic to warrant its use. Monday mornings, the truck is driven to the processing facility in Camden. O&M costs for plastics recycling are included with other recycling O&M costs.

Operating and Maintenance Costs (1989)

Item	Recycling	Composting	Total
Collection	$109,855	$150,000	$259,855
Processing	0	$ 19,425	$ 19,425
Administration	$ 500	0	$ 500
Education/Publicity	$ 500	0	$ 500
Total	**$110,855**	**$169,425**	**$280,280**

Operating and maintenance costs for 1987 were $221,425 ($77,500 for recycling and $143,925 for composting).

The large increase in recycling costs is attributed to the addition of more personnel for business district collection and the fact that the Borough now has to pay to recycle newspaper and mixed paper. Tree chipping costs have increased since 1987 because the Borough now pays to have tree trunks chipped.

Materials Revenues:

$ 4,000 in 1989
$12,231 in 1987
$20,250 in 1986

Revenues listed above do not include basic State tonnage grants, which average about $7,000 per year. Revenues dropped in 1989 because the Borough now must pay to recycle newspaper and mixed paper. In 1989 and 1990, Haddonfield received a $20,000 bonus grant from the State of New Jersey for its high per capita recycling rate.

Source of Funding: State tonnage grants, averaging about $7,000 per year, special State grants, and the local budget

Employees: 2 full-time and 1 part-time employee year-round, plus one person hired for 2 hours per week to staff the drop-off center for plastics. In addition, 15 temporary workers are hired during the 8 weeks of leaf season, and occasional part-time or temporary employees are hired as needed for the holiday season.

Contact

Richard Schwab
Borough Administrator
Borough of Haddonfield
242 Kings Highway East
Haddonfield, NJ 08033
Phone (609) 429-4700
Fax (609) 427-0920

Reference

Borough of Haddonfield, "Recycling Collection System, Haddonfield, New Jersey," unpublished document, May 1987.

PERKASIE, PENNSYLVANIA

Demographics

Jurisdiction: Borough of Perkasie

Population: 7,005 in 1989

Total Households: 3,600 in 1989 (3,200 single-family homes and 400 multi-unit residences, including approximately 150 condominium units)

Total Businesses: 75 (estimate from the Mayor of Perkasie)

Area: 2.6 square miles

Other: Perkasie is a rapidly developing suburb of Philadelphia. The population and number of households are growing.

Solid Waste Generation and Collection

(Annual Tonnages for 1989)

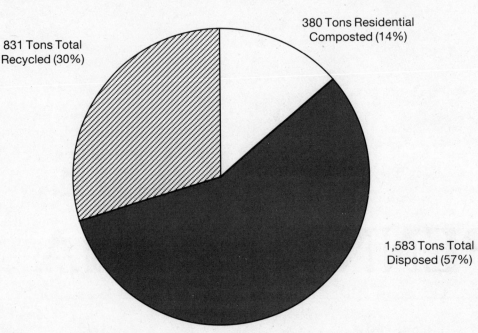

380 Tons Residential Composted (14%)

831 Tons Total Recycled (30%)

1,583 Tons Total Disposed (57%)

Total Waste Generated: 2,794 tons in 1989 (includes 218 tons of bulky waste disposed by Borough, but not bulky waste disposed by private hauler; excludes commercial waste collected by private haulers and waste generated by condominiums and apartments, which is collected by private haulers)

1,868 tons in 1988

Residential Waste Generated: 2,235 tons in 1989 (estimated to be 80 percent of total waste generated)

1,494 tons in 1988

Commercial Waste Generated: 559 tons in 1989 (estimated to be 20 percent of total waste generated; this tonnage includes the 218 tons of bulky waste disposed by the Borough and excludes tonnage collected by private haulers)

374 tons in 1988

Bulky Waste Generated: 218 tons in 1989 (includes mattresses and furniture, which are hauled by Borough, but not construction debris, tires, or appliances, which are disposed by a private hauler with a municipal contract)

122 tons in 1988

% By Weight of Total Waste Recovered: 43 percent in 1989 (29.7 percent recycling and 13.6 percent composting)

44 percent in 1988 (38 percent recycling and 6 percent composting)

% By Weight of Residential Waste Recovered:	Not available
% By Weight of Commercial Waste Recovered:	Not available
Landfill Tipping Fee:	$64.50 per ton in 1989 $59 per ton in 1988 $ 8 per ton in 1980
Collection of Refuse:	The Department of Public Works collects refuse from residents and 35 businesses. Businesses not served by the Borough, condominiums, and apartments over four units must contract with private haulers. The Borough pays a private hauler $200 each month for collection of white goods and scrap metal. The Borough DPW collects mattresses and furniture.
Future Solid Waste Management Plans:	The Borough of Perkasie does not have any plans at this time to change or expand its solid waste management program.

Materials Recovery

Effective January 4, 1988, all wastes collected and disposed by the Borough of Perkasie must be contained in green 20- or 40-pound plastic bags sold by the Borough. Bags are sold at the Borough Hall during normal business hours, as well as at a number of local stores and markets for the convenience of residents. The 20-pound bags sell for 80 cents; 40-pound bags sell for $1.50. The sale of these bags is exempt from Pennsylvania State sales tax. Bulky trash is collected once a month by a private hauler who disposes of the white goods, scrap metal, and motorized appliances. White goods and motorized appliances must have a tag attached for pick-up.

The per-bag fee program replaced a flat annual fee of $120 per residence for refuse collection and disposal.

Participation in the Borough's recycling program became mandatory in October 1987. Residents are required to recycle aluminum beverage cans, glass, corrugated cardboard, magazines, and newspapers. The Borough has distributed 5-gallon buckets to residents living in single-family homes, to hold recyclable materials. The 1987 law does not mandate that private haulers offer per-bag fees or collection of recyclables to residents of condominiums and apartments. Neil Fosbenner, the Recycling Coordinator and Public Works Director, reports that no private haulers offer the per-bag rate at this time.

Before 1988, solid waste was collected twice a week. In January 1988, the Borough cut down solid waste collection to one day a week, and started collecting recyclables once a week, on a different day. Glass and aluminum are collected weekly. Newspaper, junk mail, and corrugated cardboard are collected once a month.

Glass and aluminum cans are collected in a compartmentalized trailer pulled by a pick-up truck. Wastepaper is collected in a packer truck. The Department of Public Works crew sorts glass from aluminum at the curbside.

The Borough of Perkasie also runs a drop-off recycling center that is open 24 hours a day, 7 days a week. In October 1989, the Borough began a plastics recycling pilot program at its drop-off center. This program, which has been extended into 1990, recovered 3.7 tons of HDPE and PET plastic beverage containers in 1989. Perkasie estimates that 75 percent of residents participated in the plastics pilot study. This estimate is based on a comparison of the tons recovered in the Borough with the tons recovered by a community of similar size and demographics that has mandatory curbside collection of HDPE and PET beverage containers. The drop-off center also accepts aluminium, glass, newspaper, and corrugated cardboard.

The Borough collects leaves and brush from residents in October and November for composting.

The Borough is already in compliance with the 1997 goals of the Pennsylvania recycling bill passed on April 12, 1988. The law, entitled the Municipal Waste Planning, Recycling, and Waste Reduction Act, calls for planning procedures for the processing and disposal of municipal waste, and mandates recycling. It states that at least 25 percent of all municipal waste and source-separated materials in the Commonwealth must be recycled by January 1, 1997. Municipalities must schedule at least 1 day a month for the collection of at least 3 recyclable materials, and must provide containers to be used for sorting the refuse.

In February 1990, the Borough of Perkasie won the *Highest Residential Recovery Rate* award from the *Record Setting Recycling Contest 1989*, sponsored by the Institute for Local Self-Reliance.

Curbside Collection

Start-up Date: January 1, 1988

Private/Public: Public

Materials Collected: Newspaper, magazines, junk mail, corrugated cardboard, glass, aluminum cans, leaves, and brush

Pick-up Frequency: Glass and aluminum are collected weekly. Newspaper, magazines, junk mail, and corrugated cardboard are collected once a month. Leaves and brush are collected from residents weekly during October and November.

Pick-up Same Day as Refuse: No

Material Set-out Method: Newspapers are stacked and tied or put into paper grocery bags. Aluminum cans are put in bags or boxes. Large corrugated cardboard is stacked and tied into bundles. Residents can voluntarily separate glass bottles and jars by color (clear, green, and amber) with metal caps and rings removed or put them together in an open bucket (available through the Borough). Leaves and brush are collected loose at the curbside.

Mandatory: Yes (except for junk mail, leaves, and brush; condominiums, apartments, and businesses do not have to comply)

Service Provider: Public Works Department

Collection Vehicles: Glass and aluminum are collected in a compartmentalized trailer pulled by a pick-up truck. Wastepaper is collected in packer trucks. Leaves and brush are collected in a 14-cubic-yard dump truck.

Households Served: 3,200

Participation Rate: 100 percent of households served (based on data collected in Public Works survey)

Businesses Served: Approximately 12

Economic Incentives: The per-bag disposal fee program encourages residents and businesses served by the Borough to generate less waste, thus providing a direct economic incentive to recycle.

Enforcement: None

Commercial Materials Recovery Activities

The Borough of Perkasie does not mandate that businesses recycle or subscribe to the per-bag rate structure. The Borough will, however, collect recyclable materials and refuse from any business desiring service. The Borough will collect newspaper, junk mail, corrugated cardboard, glass, and aluminum cans from the commercial sector. Commercial establishments are serviced on the same day and with the same trucks as the residential sector. The Borough picks up refuse from 35 businesses. Of these, about 12 recycle. Some private haulers of commercial waste are recovering corrugated cardboard from the waste stream for recycling; these tonnages are not available.

Materials Processing

Collection workers separate all glass and aluminum collected at the curbside, put them into a compartmentalized trailer, and deliver them directly to their respective markets. Aluminum cans are delivered to Aluminum Cans of America. Wellman Incorporated buys the plastic beverage containers. The Borough had difficulty selling its paper in 1989 due to poor markets. It changed paper vendors three times that year in an effort to get the best possible price. The Borough paid vendors a total of $5,125 in 1989 for its wastepaper.

Glass bottles, color-sorted at the curbside by collection personnel, are donated to the Brothers of the Brush, a local civic organization, for cleaning, crushing, and shipment to glass manufacturers. The Borough has provided the Brothers of the Brush with a storage area for crushed glass in the public works yard, adjacent to the Borough Hall. The civic group had previously conducted a once-a-month volunteer glass collection program. Since quality control and markets had already been established, the Borough allowed the organization to continue processing and selling glass after municipal collection and sorting were instituted. The Brothers of the Brush incurred $10,188 in 1989 in operation and maintenance costs for glass processing, and sold the glass for $8,643. The Borough realizes no direct income from the sale of glass.

Residents from surrounding communities have been using the drop-off center, creating extra maintenance work for DPW employees. Perkasie is staffing the drop-off center in order to limit drop-off privileges to local residents only. Staff check labels on junk mail collected at the center to see who is using facilities. According to Neil Fosbenner, it is difficult to assess the success of this effort because some out-of-town residents may be tearing the address labels off their mail.

Composting Activities

The Borough tried to initiate a yard waste materials collection program in May 1988, but cancelled the program in June of that year due to difficulty locating a site to compost the materials. Collection was started again in October 1989, when the Borough began windrowing leaves and brush at an organic farm outside of Perkasie. In exchange for the use of the land, the farmer can use the compost materials on the farm. The piles are turned monthly with a Borough-owned back-hoe.

The Borough collects leaves and brush from residents weekly during October and November. Department of Public Works employees vacuum leaves that residents have raked to the curbside. Brush is raked and loaded into a 14-cubic-yard Borough dump truck with the leaves.

The Borough does not weigh the yard waste materials collected, but it does keep a record of the number of loads taken to the farm. In 1989, the Borough tipped 155 loads at the organic farm. Multiplying the 155 14-cubic-yard loads by the conversion factor of 350 pounds per uncompacted cubic yard yields a tonnage of 380 in 1989. This represents a 68 percent increase from the 120 tons estimated collected in May and June of 1988. Neil Fosbenner attributes this drastic increase to enforcement of the ban on burning, and collection of yard waste in the fall instead of the spring.

Amount and Breakdown of Materials Recovered

Material	Total (Tons, 1988)
Mixed Paper*	474
Glass	225
Aluminum	10
Subtotal Recycled	**709**
Yard Waste Materials	120
Subtotal Composted	**120**
Total Recovered	**829**

*Newspaper, junk mail, and corrugated cardboard

Material	Commercial (Tons, 1989)	Residential (Tons, 1989)	Total (Tons, 1989)
Mixed Paper*	NA	NA	600.7
Glass	NA	NA	216.1
Aluminum	NA	NA	10.7
Plastic Containers	NA	NA	3.7
Subtotal Recycled	**NA**	**NA**	**831.2**
Yard Materials	NA	380	380
Subtotal Composted	**NA**	**380**	**380**
Total Recovered	**NA**	**NA**	**1,211.2**

*Newspaper, junk mail, and corrugated cardboard

Publicity and Education

Rules and regulations for the storage, collection, and disposal of refuse have been distributed to all residences. A brochure describing the program was mailed to all residents in December 1987.

In 1988, key Borough personnel made door-to-door visits to provide information and answer questions about the overall program. In 1989, the Borough conducted public education through direct mailings, public meetings, newspaper articles and advertising, and radio broadcasts and advertising.

Source Reduction

Refuse collection and disposal data in tons (excluding bulky waste collection and waste generated from apartments and condominiums) recorded from 1985 to 1989 are summarized below:

Year	Waste Landfilled	Waste Generated
1985	2,407	2,407
1986	2,585	2,585
1987	2,573	2,573
Average	**2,522**	**2,522**
1988	1,038	1,868
1989	1,583	2,576

These data show that the amount of waste landfilled in 1989 was 59 percent less than the average amount of waste landfilled in the 3 years prior to implementation of the per-bag ordinance.   Adding recovered materials to the amount of waste disposed in 1988 gives a total waste generation figure of 1,868 tons (excluding bulky waste and waste generated in apartments and condominiums).   A comparison of 1988 municipal solid waste generation with the average generated from 1985 to 1987 indicates a 26 percent reduction by weight in municipal solid waste generated.

This 26 percent source reduction is believed to be due to the following:

(1) Public awareness of waste generation and disposal problems, resulting in improved purchasing habits.

(2) Attrition of commercial customers not wanting to participate in the bag program.   Commercial establishments are free to contract with private haulers.   On this basis, attrition is responsible for at least 3.1 percent of the reduction in the waste collected.

(3) Home burning — backyard, fireplace, and wood stoves.   In 1988, the Borough did not enforce an ordinance banning backyard burning.   Quantities of waste disposed in 1988 by household burning through stoves, fireplaces, or backyard facilities are unknown.   No complaints of smoke or odor were received.

(4) Exporting waste from the Borough to nearby municipalities or depositing in commercial containers.   However, there were only four reports of such instances in 1988.   The names of the offenders were reported in the local newspaper.   Illegal dumping was not reported in 1988.

Adding materials recovered in 1989 to the total waste disposed in 1989 gives a total of 2,576 tons of municipal solid waste generated (excluding all bulky waste and waste generated in condominiums and apartments) in 1989. Comparing this figure with the 1988 municipal solid waste generation tonnage (excluding bulky waste and materials generated in condominiums and apartments) indicates a 38 percent increase over 1988.

This 38 percent increase in municipal solid waste is believed to be due to the following:

(1) The Borough collected refuse from 600 more households in 1989 than in 1988 — a 23 percent increase.

(2) In 1989, the Borough began enforcing an old ordinance banning backyard burning. Although residents may still be burning wastepaper in stoves and fireplaces, the ban on backyard burning of yard waste materials and refuse is actively enforced.

(3) The Borough reports that there has not been a single incidence of illegal exportation of waste in 1989 since it publicized the names of the four residents caught exporting refuse to other municipalities in 1988.

While the number of households served by the Borough has increased 23 percent, total waste generated in 1989 has only increased 2 percent over the average amount generated from 1985 to 1987. This is remarkable.

Economics

Costs Cover: Capital and operating and maintenance costs cover the collection of 831 tons of recyclable materials (1) through the curbside collection program, and (2) at the drop-off center. The Borough has not kept records on the costs of the composting program.

Capital Costs: Collection

Item	Cost	Use	Year Incurred
Recycling Trailer	$ 15,807	Recycling	1988
Modifications to Truck	$ 600	Recycling	1988
Security Fence	$ 500	Recycling	1988
Steel Barrels	$ 400	Recycling	1988
Recycling Buckets	$ 2,500	Recycling	1988

The following costs are representative of both refuse collection and recycling. Perkasie does not separate costs incurred for the recycling program from costs incurred for regular trash pick-up. The programs use the same trucks and employees.

Refuse and Recycling Operating and Maintenance Costs

Item	Expense (1988)	Expense (1989)
Collection Labor	$ 54,586	$ 61,830
Truck Expenses	$ 6,349	$ 4,220
Fuel	$ 2,009	$ 2,788
Subtotal Collection Costs	**$ 62,944**	**$ 68,838**
Miscellaneous Supplies	$ 15,581	$ 1,741
Consulting Fees	$ 0	$ 534
Subtotal Administration Costs	**$ 15,581**	**$ 2,275**
Total Shared Expenses	**$ 78,525**	**$ 71,113**
Bags*	$ 19,764	$ 16,231
Total	**$ 98,289**	**$ 87,344**

*The cost of the bags is not included as shared expenses because they are used solely for refuse collection purposes.

Although the costs to recycle are combined with the cost of regular trash collection, the Borough has divided worker-hours into the following percentages: 34 percent of worker-hours are spent collecting solid waste, 12 percent are spent collecting bulky waste, and 54 percent are spent collecting recyclable materials.

Operating and Maintenance Costs (1989)

	Recycling	Composting	Total
Collection	$ 37,173	NA	NA
Processing	$ 5,129 *	NA	NA
Administration	$ 1,229	NA	NA
Education/Publicity	$ 2,000	NA	NA
Total	**$ 45,531**	**NA**	**NA**

*Price paid to vendor for wastepaper

Materials Revenues:	$10,586 in 1989
	$15,546 in 1988
Source of Funding:	Bag-fee structure
Full-time Employees:	4
Part-time Employees:	1

Contact

Neil H.   Fosbenner
Recycling Coordinator/Director
Public Works Department
311 9th Street
Perkasie, Pennsylvania 18944
Phone (215) 257-5065
Fax (215) 257-5010

References

Good, Linda C., *Annual Report on the Borough of Perkasie: Per Bag Disposal Fee, Waste Reduction and Recycling Program*, Perkasie, PA, 1989.

Woodruff, Kenneth L., *Preliminary Report on the Borough of Perkasie, Per Bag Disposal Fee, Waste Reduction and Recycling Program*, Morrisville, PA, July 1988.

RODMAN, NEW YORK

Demographics

Jurisdiction: Township of Rodman

Population: 850 in 1989 (estimate based on 1980 census, which indicated population was 850; no new homes have been built since)

Total Households: 270

Total Businesses: 2

Area: 42.25 square miles

Other: Largely a rural farm community. The only commercial establishments are a restaurant and the Township government building.

Solid Waste Generation and Collection

(Annual tonnages for 1989)

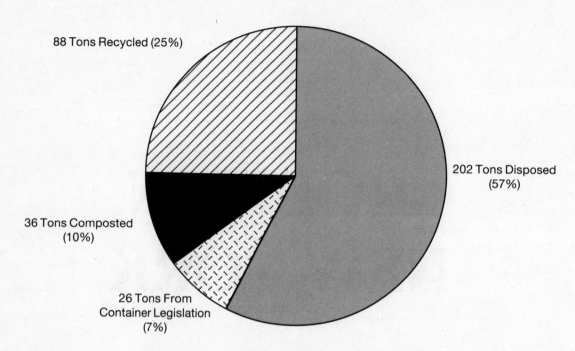

88 Tons Recycled (25%)

202 Tons Disposed
(57%)

36 Tons Composted
(10%)

26 Tons From
Container Legislation
(7%)

Total Waste Generated:	352 tons in 1989 (includes bulky materials, 142 tons landfilled, 60 tons burned, 26 tons estimated collected through deposit container legislation, 88 tons recycled, and 36 tons estimated composted in backyards)
Residential Waste Generated:	Exact breakdown is not known, although more than 99 percent of the 352 tons generated is believed to be residential materials. (This assumption is used to calculate per capita residential waste generation.)
Commercial Waste Generated:	Exact breakdown is not known, although less than 1 percent of the 352 tons generated is believed to be commercial materials.
Bulky Waste Generated:	60 tons in 1989 (including tires, appliances, and construction debris)
% By Weight of Total Waste Recovered:	43 percent in 1989 (32.4 percent recycling including deposit containers, and an estimated 10.2 percent composting)
% By Weight of Residential Waste Recovered:	Not available
% By Weight of Commercial Waste Recovered:	Not available
Landfill Tipping Fee:	$48 per ton

Collection of Refuse:

The Township of Rodman has never provided curbside collection service for refuse or recyclable materials. Rodman residents haul their own refuse to the Township transfer station.

The State of New York allows communities of 20,000 or fewer residents to burn their yard waste. The Township of Rodman does burn tree stumps and clean lumber from construction waste twice a year. The tonnage estimated burned in 1989 was 60 tons. Residents burn some wastepaper in wood burning stoves.

The Township has a contract with a disposal company, Tri-Cil, to collect refuse at the transfer station and haul it to the company's landfill. Rodman pays $154 per load to have the refuse hauled and a $48-per-cubic-yard tip fee at the landfill. In 1989, Tri-Cil hauled 22 loads (141.5 tons).

In 1986, the Township spent $25,000 on refuse disposal. With the implementation of the recycling law, this cost dropped to $12,500 in 1987. The budget in 1989 for refuse disposal was $12,000. Disposal costs that year totalled $10,701 (transportation and tipping fees). Tri-Cil has added $10 per week to Rodman's hauling bills as a surcharge to offset the company's loss of revenue due to the reduction in refuse.

Future Solid Waste Management Plans:

The Township of Rodman does not have any plans at this time to change or expand its solid waste management program.

Materials Recovery

The Township of Rodman is located in the Tug Hill region, a 1.25 million acre plateau next to Lake Ontario. This largely undeveloped region, which includes 200,000 acres without roads, has been the target of many recent attempts by the Development Authority of the North County (DANC) to site a 1,100-acre landfill in the Town. Motivated by a desire to stop the landfill, the Township of Rodman began a campaign with neighboring communities to gain control over the development that occurs in the Tug Hill region, especially in regard to landfill siting.

DANC's 1987 attempt to site a landfill prompted the Township to implement one of the first mandatory recycling ordinances in New York State on August 15, 1987. The ordinance, which is based on a recycling mandate for the Village of Hamburg, New York, designates glass, tin and aluminum cans, all types of plastics (including HDPE and PET plastic beverage containers, LDPE, PVC, and plastic toys), scrap metal, newspaper, corrugated cardboard, car batteries, paperboard, and non-ferrous scrap metals for separation from refuse by residents and by workers at the one restaurant and the government building. Magazines are not specified in the ordinance as mandatory, but they may be recycled at the transfer station.

In 1987, the Township purchased a prefabricated building and a baler for a recycling center. Once the Township Board approved the recycling law, a non-profit environmental group, Pure Water For Life, designed and mailed an educational flier to all residents. The flier notified residents of a public hearing to discuss the law, and also contained specifics about the types of materials affected by the law and how they should be prepared. Despite a poor turn-out at the public meeting, the Board decided to implement the recycling law in August 1987. The Township and members of Pure Water For Life erected a recycling center at the transfer station, and it became operational that September. Although no opposition to the recycling law was voiced at the Township meeting, some residents later said they had not known about the public hearing process. The Township held another public meeting, which included a demonstration of how and what to separate for recycling. The meeting was well attended, and afterwards the Township reported a 90 to 95 percent participation rate at the recycling center.

A loft divides the recycling center into two levels to facilitate long-term storage of materials before they are marketed. Glass is stored below the loft in 40 55-gallon steel drums, which were discarded by the Kraft Corporation. Hand-crushed metal scraps, tin cans, and aluminum cans are stored next to the glass in 40 55-gallon fiber drums, which were donated by a company in a nearby city. Residents place crushed plastics in 50-gallon plastic bags, which are stored in the loft when full. Paper products are piled on the floor across from the glass and cans. Batteries, tires, and oil are stored behind the building. A shelf in the recycling center holds products that may be of use to other residents, such as books, egg cartons, and glass gallon jugs. Newspapers are piled in a separate corner to be taken by farmers for use as animal bedding and as a bulking agent for composting. Residents separate their own materials, although a small bag of commingled glass, plastic, and metal containers can be left to be separated by the one part-time employee at the facility.

The Township of Rodman belongs to a recycling cooperative with seven other local rural towns. The towns in the cooperative share equipment loaned to them by vendors. For instance, the towns share a roll-off container that is used as a mobile drop-off center for tin can collection. The roll-off stays in each town until the container is ready to be collected by the dealer. The towns do not receive revenue from the sale of the tin cans.

The State of New York implemented a beverage container deposit law in 1983. Specified beverage containers are returned to the point of purchase or to a redemption center for refund of the 5-cent deposit. Rodman's recycling center is not a redemption center. Institute for Local Self-Reliance staff estimate that 26 tons of beverage containers were recovered in Rodman in 1989 through the State's deposit legislation.[1]

---

[1] In 1989, the average per capita tonnage of beverage containers recovered in New York State was 0.03 tons. 0.03 x 850 (the population of Rodman) = 26 tons.

Drop-Off Collection Program

Start-up Date: August 1987

Private/Public: Public

Materials Collected: Glass, aluminum and tin cans, plastics (including HDPE and PET beverage containers, plastic bags, hoses, and toys), scrap metal and aluminum, newspaper, high-grade paper, magazines, corrugated cardboard, paperboard (such as cereal boxes, but _not_ milk containers), appliances, motor oil, car batteries, tires, and books

Separation Method: Small quantities of paper products (including newspaper, high-grade paper, magazines, paperboard, and corrugated cardboard) can be placed in a box or paper bag. Large quantities must be separated. Glass bottles (with caps removed), cans (crushed and with both ends removed from tin cans, if possible), and plastic containers should be carried in boxes or kraft paper bags. Motor oil must be brought in sealed containers. Tires, appliances, and batteries may be left behind the center.

Mandatory: Yes. (High-grade paper, motor oil, tires, scrap metal, white goods, and reusable items are voluntary.)

Service Provider: Township of Rodman

Collection Vehicles: One Highway Department dump truck is used approximately twice a year to take glass to Owens-Illinois in Fulton, New York.

Households Served: 270

Participation Rate: 90 percent (estimate by Charles Valentine, Chairman of the Township, based on his familiarity with all the Township's residents)

Businesses Served: 2 (including Township government building)

Economic Incentives: None

Enforcement: None

Commercial Materials Recovery Activities

The restaurant and the municipal office haul their own recyclable materials to the facility. There are no private haulers that service the Township. (These tonnages cannot be broken out from total tonnages recovered.)

Materials Processing

The Township of Rodman has joined a cooperative with seven other towns to ensure that the supply of newspapers matches farmers' animal bedding and composting needs. The cooperative, the Original Recycling Cooperative Association (ORCA), works with Cornell University Extension Services to supply 10,000 pounds of newspapers per week. In the Spring of 1990, Cornell's Extension Service will conduct educational tours for local farmers of farms in Rodman that use old newspaper as bedding or as a bulking agent in compost.

The Township asks residents to crush all cans and plastic beverage containers at home, but glass is taken to the center whole and broken in a 55-gallon drum. Corrugated cardboard, paperboard, plastics, and high-grade paper are baled. The Township separates the plastics into six groups for baling: milk jugs, mixed color HDPE bottles, mixed color PET bottles, LDPE, PVC, and all other plastics (including toys and hoses). The Township found that it is necessary to place the miscellaneous loads in a plastic bag prior to baling in order to keep the finished bale together.

Local firms pick up recyclables and pay Rodman for materials hauled; the Township does not pay for the hauling. Dealers pick up large appliances and tires in bulk quantity; the Township receives no revenues for these items. The Township delivers glass to Owens-Illinois in Fulton, New York, which is approximately 40 miles from Rodman. All plastics collected for recycling are picked up by Empire Recycling in Syracuse, New York.

Jefferson County is building a materials processing center, to which Rodman will have access. However, the Township does not plan to use the facility, which will be operational in the Fall of 1990, because the Township will not receive revenue for materials brought there, and it will incur higher transportation and labor costs for delivery of the materials.

Composting Activities

The Township of Rodman does not provide a public composting site for residents, but it does encourage residents to set up their own backyard composting bins. Pure Water For Life provides volunteer technical assistance to anyone interested in setting up their own bin. A survey of the Township conducted in 1989 revealed that 55 percent of residents were composting at home. Throughout 1989, the Township, with the help of Pure Water For Life, monitored 10 homes with backyard composting bins, studying the amount and types of materials that were being composted. The findings were then extrapolated to the total number of homes that were composting in order to estimate the amount of materials being composted in Rodman. The Township estimates that 36 tons of leaves, brush, field and lawn clippings, and food waste were composted in 1989.

Amount and Breakdown of Materials Recovered

Material	Total (Tons, 1988)	Total (Tons, 1989)
Newspaper	17	16.8
Corrugated	6	11.2
Mixed Paper*	7	11.3
Glass	10	16.8
Plastics	3	2.9
Ferrous and Aluminum Cans	4	4.9
Ferrous Scrap	16	10.5
Non-ferrous Scrap	1	0.9
Appliances	†	5.7
Batteries	1	3.6
Tires	2	1.3
Reusable Items§		2.1
Subtotal Recycled	**67**	**88**
Yard Materials	NA	36
Subtotal Composted	**NA**	**36**
Subtotal Recovered	**67**	**124**
Deposit Containers	NA	26
Total Recovered	**NA**	**150**

*Includes magazines, high-grade paper, and paperboard
†Included under ferrous scrap
§Includes egg cartons, books, and 1-gallon glass jugs

Publicity and Education

Prior to the enactment of the Township recycling law, Pure Water For Life designed and mailed educational fliers to all residents. The fliers contained information on what materials would be collected at the recycling center, and how they should be prepared. Money for the fliers was raised through fundraisers. Pure Water For Life also provided a demonstration of the separation and preparation process at the second Township Meeting where the proposed law was discussed.

A part-time employee at the recycling center answers questions and advises residents where the materials for recycling should be stored in the center.

Economics

Costs Cover: The capital and operating and maintenance costs given below cover the collection and processing of 88 tons of recyclable materials. An additional 36 tons of yard waste were composted at no cost to the Town.

Capital Costs: Collection

Item	Cost	Use	Year Incurred
24' x 48' Building	$11,000	Recycling	1987
40 55-gallon Steel Drums	Donated	Recycling	1987
40 55-gallon Fiber Drums	Donated	Recycling	1987
Dump Truck	Borrowed	Recycling	1987

The Township of Rodman borrows a truck from the Highway Department to take glass to Owens-Illinois in Fulton, New York.

Capital Costs: Processing

Item	Cost	Use	Year Incurred
Baler	$6,800	Recycling	1989

Operating and Maintenance Costs (1989)

	Recycling	Composting	Total
Collection	$ 200	$0	$ 200
Processing	$ 3,791	$0	$ 3,791
Administration	$ 0	$0	$ 0
Education/Publicity	$ 500	$0	$ 500
Total	**$ 4,491**	**$0**	**$ 4,491**

The Township spent $3,791 processing recyclables as follows: (1) $360 in wages, including time spent delivering materials to markets; (2) $1,667 in salaries for program supervision, including part-time employee at drop-off and supervision of delivery trips; and (3) $1,764 for gas and oil. The Town's only collection expense for 1989 was $200 for plastic bags, purchased for storage of plastic containers.

Materials Revenues:	$1,970
Source of Funding:	Residents' taxes
Part-time Employees:	1

Contacts

Charles Valentine
Chairman of Township of Rodman
Solid Waste Committee
RD 1 Box 3
Rodman, New York 13682
(315) 232-2242

Robert Hutchinson
President
Pure Water For Life
Box D
Rodman, New York 13682
(315) 232-2390

Reference

Philips, Joe, New York State Department of Conservation, telephone conversation regarding redeemed beverage containers, Albany, New York, April 26, 1990.

WELLESLEY, MASSACHUSETTS

Demographics

Jurisdiction:	Town of Wellesley
Population:	26,590 in 1988 (from the Census Bureau)
Total Households:	8,500
Total Businesses:	1,000
Area:	10.39 square miles

Solid Waste Generation and Collection

(Annual Tonnages for 1989)

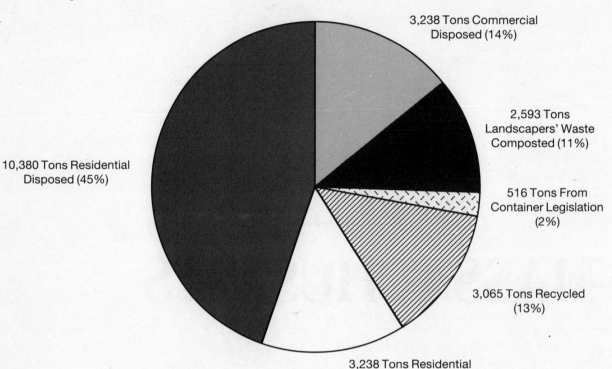

3,238 Tons Commercial Disposed (14%)

2,593 Tons Landscapers' Waste Composted (11%)

516 Tons From Container Legislation (2%)

3,065 Tons Recycled (13%)

10,380 Tons Residential Disposed (45%)

3,238 Tons Residential Composted (14%)

Total Waste Generated:
23,030 tons in 1988/1989[1] (includes bulky materials — such as tires, white goods, scrap metal, and other waste, but not construction debris — generated by the residential and commercial population that uses the Recycling and Disposal Facility, but excluding the commercial tonnage taken to other disposal facilities by private haulers)

21,972 tons in 1987/1988

Residential Waste Generated:
Tonnage in 1988/1989 not available due to the impossibility of determining the breakdown between residential and commercial materials recycled, although 10,380 tons of residential materials were disposed (excluding residential materials collected by private haulers).

Commercial Waste Generated:
Tonnage in 1988/1989 not available due to the impossibility of determining the breakdown between residential and commercial materials recycled, and the unavailability of commercial tonnages hauled by private haulers that do not use the Town facility. There were 3,238 tons commercial waste disposed at the facility (including waste generated by apartments and local government agencies, but excluding the materials collected by the large haulers of commercial waste, such as BFI).

---

[1]Wellesley's fiscal year is from July 1, 1988 to June 30, 1989.

Bulky Waste Generated:	Tonnage breakdown not available
% By Weight of Total Waste Recovered:	41 percent in 1988/1989 (16 percent recycling, including deposit containers, and 25 percent composting) 42 percent in 1987/88
% By Weight of Residential Waste Recovered:	Not available
% By Weight of Commercial Waste Recovered:	Not available
Landfill/Transfer Station Tipping Fees:	$80 per ton in 1989 at Wellesley Recycling and Disposal Facility (transfer station) $29.90 per ton in 1989 at landfill 25 miles away $28.23 per ton in 1988 at landfill 25 miles away
Collection of Refuse:	The Town of Wellesley offers no curbside collection service for either refuse or recyclables. Ninety percent of Town residents haul their own waste to the Wellesley Recycling and Disposal Facility (RDF), which is both a drop-off center for recyclable and compostable materials, and a transfer station for refuse. The rest of the residents contract with private haulers. The Town issues stickers to residents and private haulers (including the businesses that self-haul) who use the transfer station. The stickers, green for residents and white for private haulers, are required for entry into the RDF, preventing outside waste from being disposed on site.
	The Town weighs all incoming loads from private haulers twice — first for a total weight, including recyclable materials, and a second time after these materials have been sorted out. The tonnage bill is based on the weight to be disposed, thus providing an incentive for private haulers using the facility to recycle.
	Three major haulers of commercial waste service the Town's residents and businesses: Browning-Ferris Industries (BFI), H.A. SanComb Trucking, and Wellesley Trucking. These haulers do not use the Town's transfer station. BFI is the main hauler of commercial waste.
Future Solid Waste Management Plans:	The Town intends to increase its 40 percent recovery rate (excluding materials diverted through container legislation) to 50 percent by 1993.
	Wellesley is currently seeking a consulting firm to conduct a waste composition study and to help the Town develop a solid waste management plan for the next 20 years. The plan will help the Town reach a 50 percent rate of recovery by maximizing source reduction and materials recovery.
	Wellesley is also considering mixing yard waste with sludge dredged from small ponds and sand from road sweeps. The product will be used as a replacement for topsoil.

The Town has a 5-year contract with a privately owned landfill 25 miles away, which will end November 1990. At the end of the contract, tipping fees may be raised to $150 per ton. Wellesley's Department of Public Works proposes a hierarchy of strategies for waste management: reduction of the waste stream through consumer awareness, reuse, and composting and recycling.

Materials Recovery

A local volunteer non-profit group, Action for Ecology, started a source-separation recycling program behind the Town's original municipal incinerator building in February 1971, with the help and cooperation of the Department of Public Works. Since that time the program has grown from using 55-gallon drums, to 10-cubic-yard dumpsters, to the present system that employs 40-cubic-yard open-top transfer haul containers and a pit baler.

The Recycling and Disposal Facility at Wellesley is known as one of the most successful drop-off centers in the country. It is beautifully landscaped, with the different collection bins and areas situated among manicured lawns. Each bin is clearly marked with neatly lettered signs. The facility is open Monday through Friday, 7:00 a.m. to 3:00 p.m., and Saturday 7:00 a.m. to 4:00 p.m.

The facility is used by 90 percent of the Town's residents, who haul their own waste and recyclable materials to the site. Of the residents who use the facility, 90 percent report that they separate recyclables from their other waste. Participation is totally voluntary. The balance of the households in the Town contract to private haulers for collection.

The DPW conducted a one-house solid waste composition study in order to determine the amount of recyclable materials in the residential waste stream. This study analyzed the waste materials generated from one average home in the Town (20,000-square-foot lot with 5,000 square feet of grass and shrubbery, 60 evergreen and deciduous trees, and a 2-story colonial home) from August 13, 1987 to October 13, 1987. The household studied did recycle. The participants weighed all outgoing wastes for 2 months and recorded the types (i.e., recyclable, reusable, and refuse) and the respective weights, although no records were kept of the amount of food waste discarded through the kitchen sink disposal. The Town of Wellesley concluded from this study that 80 percent of household waste can be diverted from the landfill through reduction, reuse, composting, and recycling. This study was instrumental in the Town's decision to establish 50 percent recovery as its goal.

The Commonwealth of Massachusetts implemented a beverage container deposit law in 1983. Institute for Local Self-Reliance staff estimate that 516 tons of beverage containers were recovered in Wellesley through the Commonwealth's deposit legislation.[2] The Wellesley Recycling and Disposal Facility accepts all types of returnable containers as tax-deductible charitable contributions.   Revenue received from returnable containers goes to the Town fund.   Approximately 13 tons of returnable containers were collected at the RDF in 1989.

In 1990, Wellesley won the *Best Overall Program for a Small City* award in *The Record Setting Recycling Contest 1989,* conducted by the Institute for Local Self-Reliance.

Drop-off Collection Program

Start-up Date:	February 1971
Private/Public:	Public
Materials Collected:	Corrugated cardboard, paperboard (such as shoe boxes), newspaper, high-grade paper, mixed paper (magazines, junk mail, and miscellaneous paper), books, kraft paper bags, metal cans, aluminum foil and trays, glass separated by color (clear, green, and brown), returnable bottles and cans, HDPE and PET plastic food and beverage containers, plastic flower pots, used oil, batteries (wet cell and car batteries), clothing, reusable items, appliances, metals (aluminum, copper, brass, lead, cast iron, #1 and #2 unprepared iron and light iron), firewood, leaves, brush, other wood waste, and grass clippings
Separation Method:	Each material is source separated by the user and dropped off at the facility. Materials are deposited in roll-off containers, in containers moved by fork lift, or at specific locations at the facility. Deposit containers are collected in a separate bin from other containers.
Mandatory:	No
Households Served:	8,500
Participation Rate:	82 percent overall (92 percent of residents self-haul discards to the Recycling and Disposal Facility, while another 3 percent have a private refuse hauler but bring their recyclable materials to the RDF. Of those residents who use the facility, 86 percent report that they separate recyclables from other waste. This information is based on a comprehensive marketing survey conducted in June 1989 by the DPW in conjunction with Boston College students.)
Businesses Served:	200 white disposal stickers have been issued to private haulers and businesses hauling their own waste. The exact number of businesses using the facility, as distinct from private haulers (some of whom are serving residents) cannot be determined.

---

[2]In 1989, the average per capita tonnage of beverage containers recovered in Massachusetts was 0.0194 tons.   0.0194 tons x 26,590 (the population of Wellesley) = 516 tons.

Economic Incentives:

There are no direct economic incentives for residents to recycle at the RDF. Private haulers do not have to pay tipping fees for properly separated recyclable materials. The remainder of the waste is charged at a rate of $80 per ton. Compostable leaves and grass clippings may be tipped for $35 per ton.

Commercial Materials Recovery Activities

Businesses in the Town of Wellesley are not required to recycle or to haul materials to the RDF. While most businesses that bring recyclable materials to the facility do so as they dispose of refuse, some small businesses collect recyclable materials to bring to the facility with their household waste. This latter practice makes it difficult for the Town to ascertain the number of businesses that recycle at the facility.

The RDF is able to attract approximately 200 private haulers (including self-hauling businesses) by offering disposal of recyclable materials at no extra charge. Its $80 per ton tip fee acts as an incentive for businesses that haul materials there to recycle, and as a disincentive for large haulers to use the facility. Currently, some of the largest haulers of commercial waste in Wellesley, such as BFI, do not tip at the site.

Materials Processing

Residents separate materials into the appropriate roll-off. From there materials are transported to markets or backhauled. The RDF has one pit baler, which was used to bale 648 tons of the 1,774 tons of newspaper and 11 tons of the 227 tons of corrugated cardboard collected in 1988/1989. The Town has found that it is more cost-effective to sell the corrugated cardboard loose than baled. Newspaper would be more valuable baled, according to the Director of Public Works, but the labor required to process all of the newspaper with the old baler is not available on a regular basis.

Many items, such as firewood, reusable items, books, and compost, are redistributed to the residents at the site at no charge. In addition, the Salvation Army has bins, and Goodwill Industries has a staffed trailer, at the site.

During the Spring of 1989 the Town could not find a market for its clean, baled newspaper, and stockpiled it until there was no more space available. Wellesley then landfilled 25 tons of newspaper in July 1989. The Town now markets its newspaper, but receives no revenues for it.

In May 1988, the Massachusetts Department of Environmental Protection warned steel manufacturers that residues from white goods contained PCBs and had to be handled as hazardous waste.   This warning caused most companies to stop recovering post-consumer white goods and light metals.   Wellesley continued to collect these materials, however, and stockpiled them in the public works yard until June 1989, when the Town found a vendor to take these materials.   These materials are still collected for recovery, but no longer earn revenue.

Composting Activities

Leaves, brush, grass clippings, and other wood waste are composted in one large windrow, approximately 10 feet high by 30 feet wide, at the Recycling and Disposal Facility site.   Ashes from wood-burning stoves are mixed with the compost and leaves.   An estimated 3,831 tons of material (3,238 tons of which are considered residential) are being composted on the 1.5-acre site.   Residents are allowed to take the unscreened compost for free.   The Town sometimes barters or sells the compost to nurseries, or gives it away to community gardening projects.

Materials are added to the windrow with a front-end loader which is also used to turn the windrow about once a year.   The windrow is not watered.   Wellesley is considering purchasing a tub grinder for shredding brush.

In addition, the Town operates a separate composting program on a 1-acre plot in the public works yard.   The Town sells dumping permits to commercial landscapers at $225 per vehicle for the leaf season, or until the yard is filled.   The permits can be revoked if incoming loads are contaminated.   The leaves are formed into windrows and allowed to compost for one year.   They are then consolidated into a curing pile, screened, and used on municipal landscaping projects. The Town, which had been renting its composting screen, purchased a Screen-All in 1989 for $75,000.   It was not delivered until 1990.   A calculation taken at the end of August 1987, indicated a total of 2,552 cubic yards, or 1,387 tons.   At the end of 1988, there were four large windrows, 10 to 12 feet high and over 100 feet long.   In 1989, 2,000 tons of leaves were composted in the four windrows.

A 1988 survey conducted by the Department of Public Works and Boston College students indicates that 39 percent of Wellesley residents are composting leaves in their backyards.   The Town provides residents with information on composting through articles in the local newspaper.

In an effort to encourage backyard composting the Town enclosed fliers in 1985 utility bills recommending that garden scraps and fruit that have fallen from trees be added to backyard compost piles. However, that same year the Massachusetts Department of Health informed the Town that composting food waste is against State regulations.   Wellesley no longer encourages composting of food waste.

Other Recycling Activities

The Town also collects and recycles materials from various municipal operations. Metals and engine oils are collected from the automotive garage. High-grade metals such as copper, wire, lead-covered copper cable, aluminum poles, and miscellaneous iron and steel are collected from the DPW Electric Division. Pipe and used water meters are collected from the DPW Water and Sewer Divisions.

In February 1990, schools in Wellesley began separating their polystyrene cafeteria trays and cups for recycling at Plastics Again, a plastics processing plant in Leominster, Massachusetts. Plastics Again provides bins for the collection of polystyrene, and New England CRINC picks up the material. No costs are incurred by the schools or the Town.

Amount and Breakdown of Materials Recovered

Material	Total (Tons, 1984/85)	Total (Tons, 1985/86)	Total (Tons, 1986/87)	Total (Tons, 1987/88)
Newspaper	1,266	1,421	1,654	1,795
Corrugated	119	119	101	210
Glass	209	212	213	209
Ferrous Metal	469	580	606	584
Aluminum	*	*	*	*
Misc. Metal	3	4	6	49
Tires	11	3	*	0
Batteries	3	7	8	10
Waste Oil	9	10	11	12
Deposit Containers	5	8	11	12
Misc†	165	196	239	166
Subtotal Recycled	**2,259**	**2,560**	**2,850**	**3,047**
Yard debris, leaves, and wood chips:				
Residential	NA	NA	NA	2,400
Commercial	564	439	622	2,513
Subtotal Composted	**NA**	**NA**	**NA**	**4,913**
Subtotal Recovered#	**NA**	**NA**	**NA**	**7,960**

*Less than 1 ton recovered
†Includes books, firewood, eyeglasses, clothing, and other reusable items
#Excludes tonnage recovered from deposit legislation

Material	Commercial (Tons, 1988/1989)	Residential (Tons, 1988/1989)	Total (Tons, 1988/89)
Newspaper	NA	NA	1,774
Corrugated	NA	NA	227
Glass	NA	NA	272
Ferrous Metal	NA	NA	472
Aluminum	NA	NA	*
Misc. Metal	NA	NA	106
Batteries	NA	NA	5
Waste Oil	NA	NA	16
Misc†	NA	NA	193
Subtotal Recycled	**NA**	**NA**	**3,065**
Yard debris, leaves, and wood chips	2,593 #	3,238	5,831
Subtotal Composted	**2,593**	**3,238**	**5,831**
Subtotal Recovered	**NA**	**NA**	**8,896**
Deposit Containers	NA	NA	516 §
Total Recovered	**NA**	**NA**	**9,412**

*Tonnages included with miscellaneous metals
†Includes books, firewood, eyeglasses, clothing, and other reusable items
§Includes 13 tons redeemed at RDF
#Tonnage of yard waste delivered by landscapers

Publicity and Education

An extensive 3-year public education program targeting all types of waste generators began in fiscal year 1986. Because of its success the program was extended through the year 1990. Its objective is to increase awareness and establish principles that will lead to "conservation of natural resources and environmentally sound disposal of solid waste through: reduction of wastes; reuse of materials; and recycling of materials from the waste stream as a source of raw materials for the same or other products." The campaign theme is "Recycle. Join the Team!" Promotional activities have included a kickoff campaign, a poster that was displayed all over town, news articles, letters to the editor, advertisements, utility bill inserts, redesigned facility signs, and the country's first art show — with music — held at a recycling facility.

The Town hired a consultant in 1989 to help design a recycling education program that was presented to third grade classes in all of the schools. The budget for the public education program was $14,000 for the first year, and $3,220 the following year.

Economics

Costs Cover: Capital and operating and maintenance costs cover the 3,078 tons of materials recycled at the drop-off center, and 5,831 tons of yard waste composted.

Capital Costs: Processing

Item	Cost	Use	Year Incurred
1 used Pit Baler	$ 14,000	Recycling	1978
9 2.5-Cubic-Yard Containers	$ 6,750 *	Recycling	1988
1 Front-end Loader w/ Forklift	$ 45,000 *	Compost/Recycling	1988
5 40-Cubic-Yard Containers	$ 24,000 *	Recycling	1989
2 2.5-Cubic-Yard Containers @ $500 each	$ 1,000	Recycling	1989
Screen-All	$ 75,000	Composting	1989

*Replacement costs

Operating and Maintenance Costs (1988/1989)

	Recycling	Composting	Total
Collection	$ 0	$ 0	$ 0
Processing	$ 38,385	$ 39,439	$ 77,824
Administration	$ 8,668	$ 10,668	$ 19,336
Publicity/Education	$ 2,000	$ 0	$ 2,000
Total	**$ 49,053**	**$ 50,107**	**$ 99,160**

Materials Revenues: $75,453 in 1988/89
$76,468 in 1987/88
$72,246 in 1986/87
$55,098 in 1985/86
$72,133 in 1984/85

Source of Funding: Town funds and tipping fees at the Recycling and Disposal Facility

Full-time Employees: 8 (for all waste disposal functions including recycling, composting, transfer haul station operations, and trucking)

Contact

M.R. "Pat" Berdan
Director of Public Works
Town of Wellesley DPW
455 Worcester Street
Wellesley Hills, MA 02181
Phone (617) 235-7600
Fax (617) 237-1936

References

Bender, Julie, Administrator of the Massachusetts Beverage Law, Division of Solid Waste Management, Department of Environmental Protection, telephone conversation regarding redeemed beverage containers, Boston, Massachusetts, April 23, 1990.

Berdan, M.R., "Efficiency in the Windrow," *Biocycle*, November/December 1987.

Boston College Consulting Group, *Report to Wellesley Department of Public Works: Development of a Marketing Plan to Increase Participation in Wellesley From 25 Percent to 50 Percent*, May 13, 1988.

Kashmanian, Richard M., and Alison Taylor, *Study of Eight Yard Waste Composting Programs Across the United States*, U.S. Environmental Protection Agency, December 30, 1988.

Town of Wellesley Source Separation Recycling, reported at the NSWMA - Municipal Wastes Alternatives '87: Waste to Energy Conference Proceedings, September 9 - 11, 1989.

LINCOLN PARK, NEW JERSEY

Demographics

Jurisdiction: Borough of Lincoln Park

Population: 11,337 (1989)

Total Households: 5,500 (1,050 condominium units, 3,400 single-family and duplex residences, and 1,050 small apartment units)

Total Businesses: 200

Area: 6.94 square miles

Other: Lincoln Park is a suburban residential community. Much of its land is wetlands protected from further development.

Solid Waste Generation and Collection

(Annual Tonnages for 1988)[1]

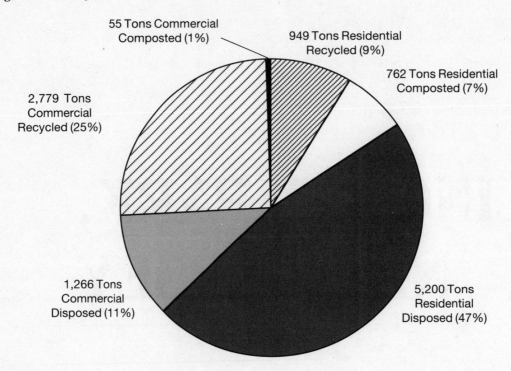

55 Tons Commercial Composted (1%)

949 Tons Residential Recycled (9%)

762 Tons Residential Composted (7%)

2,779 Tons Commercial Recycled (25%)

5,200 Tons Residential Disposed (47%)

1,266 Tons Commercial Disposed (11%)

Total Waste Generated:	11,011 tons in 1988 (includes bulky waste such as construction debris and tires)
Residential Waste Generated:	6,911 tons in 1988
Commercial Waste Generated:	4,100 tons in 1988 (includes tonnages generated and recovered from condominiums)
Bulky Waste Generated:	2,335 tons of tires, appliances, other white goods, and construction debris (2,142 tons are bulky residential waste and are included in residential waste generation tonnage. The other 193 tons are bulky commercial waste, included in commercial waste generation tonnage.)
% By Weight of Total Waste Recovered:	41 percent in 1988 (34 percent recycling and 7 percent composting)
% By Weight of Residential Waste Recovered:	25 percent in 1988 (14 percent recycling and 11 percent composting)

---

[1] 1989 tonnages only became available at press time.

% By Weight of Commercial Waste Recovered:	69 percent in 1988 (68 percent recycling and 1 percent composting)

Transfer Station Tipping Fee: $122.70 per ton in 1988

Collection of Refuse: Lincoln Park contracts out for collection of its residential solid waste. The Borough is responsible for paying the tip fee at the transfer station. In 1989, Lincoln Park paid Suburban Disposal Company $191,346 for the collection and transportation of 4,207 tons of refuse. Businesses contract with private refuse haulers. All refuse generated in Lincoln Park must go to the Morris County Transfer Station, according to Borough and State law.

Future Solid Waste Management Plans: In April 1990, the Borough will expand its drop-off center to 3 acres, and organize the storage bins so as to cut down on the amount of traveling residents must do within the center.

In 1990, the Borough will require residents to recycle 12 designated materials.

Materials Recovery

The Borough of Lincoln Park recovers recyclable materials through a curbside program and a drop-off center. While the Department of Public Works' curbside program provides monthly collection of newspaper only, 14 materials can be recycled at the drop-off center: HDPE and PET plastic beverage and detergent containers, newspaper, high-grade paper, corrugated cardboard, magazines, glass, aluminum cans, appliances, scrap metal and aluminum, tires, oil, car batteries, Christmas trees, and leaves.

The Borough's recycling program began in 1983 with a drop-off center for newspaper, glass, and aluminum cans in the public works yard. Curbside collection of newspaper began in January 1987. Lincoln Park is in the process of revising its recycling law to require citizens to bring a total of 12 materials (newspaper, high-grade paper, corrugated cardboard, magazines, glass, aluminum cans, appliances, scrap metal, tires, oil, car batteries, and leaves) to the drop-off center. As of 1988, the law mandated that residents recycle newspaper, glass, and aluminum cans, but did not specify that newspaper be placed at the curbside for collection.

In 1989, the Borough purchased a roll-off truck and eight roll-off containers, which were delivered in 1990. This equipment enables the materials to be collected in the same containers that will be shipped to vendors.

Curbside Collection

Start-up Date:	January 1987
Private/Public:	Public
Materials Collected:	Newspaper, brush, and leaves
Pick-up Frequency:	Monthly collection of newspaper. Leaves and brush are collected on average once a month during April, May, October, and November.
Pick-up Same Day as Refuse:	No
Material Set-out Method:	Newspaper must be bundled with twine or put in a kraft paper bag. Leaves and brush are raked loose to the curbside.
Mandatory:	Residents are required to separate newspaper, leaves, and brush for recycling/composting; however, set out at the curbside is not mandatory. Residents have the option of using the drop-off center.
Service Provider:	The Department of Public Works provides curbside collection. A three-person crew operates the DPW truck during the monthly collection of newspaper. The collection of leaves is handled by one paid employee. Inmates from the Sheriff's Labor Assistance Program aid in the collection of brush.
Collection Vehicles:	A DPW dump truck is used to collect newspaper. Brush and leaves are also collected with DPW dump trucks.
Households Served:	4,450 single-family residences, duplexes, and apartment units
Participation Rate:[2]	85 percent of the population recycles at the drop-off center (based on sign-in sheets)
	95 percent recycles newspaper (based on monthly set-out rates and sign-in sheets)
	85 percent composts yard waste (based on set-out rates and sign-in sheets)
Businesses Served:	25 to 30 businesses use the drop-off center, but no businesses receive curbside collection of recyclables.
Economic Incentives:	Fines
Enforcement:	A series of fines is assessed by the Borough Administrator and/or designee for improper separation of materials.

---

[2] Participation rate for just curbside program is not available.

Commercial Materials Recovery Activities

The Borough of Lincoln Park has mandated that businesses recycle glass, aluminum, high-grade paper, newspaper, and corrugated cardboard. Approximately 25 to 30 businesses self-haul recyclable materials to the drop-off center. The remainder contract out with private haulers for collection. In 1988, commercial enterprises recovered 76 tons of food waste through private haulers. Materials recycled privately are reported to the Town with commercial tonnages.

Condominiums have curbside collection of recyclable materials through private haulers, although many residents bring their recyclable materials to the drop-off center. According to Recycling Coordinator Richard Lavallo, condominiums recycle HDPE and PET plastic beverage containers, glass, aluminum and other metal cans, newspaper, high-grade paper, and magazines at the curbside through private haulers.

In 1988, 50 tons of automobile scrap were recycled. This tonnage is excluded from the waste generation figures and the tonnage recovered data.

Materials Processing

Elf Recycling, a volunteer organization, and the Borough collect aluminum cans, scrap metal (including appliances), car batteries, and scrap aluminum from the drop-off center. The Borough delivers corrugated cardboard unbaled to Lobosco and Sons, and clear and colored glass to REI Distributors. Vendors supply all equipment at the drop-off center. Revenues from the sale of scrap metal ($2.50 per ton) are used to offset Elf's cost for tolls and gas incurred in the delivery of the scrap metal. No revenues are earned from the sale of batteries or plastic. Lincoln Park does receive revenue from its aluminum, but donates 80 percent of this money to a local food pantry and puts the remainder into a scholarship fund. In 1988, the Borough received $7,000 for the sale of newspaper, glass, and aluminum, of which the Borough donated $5,500. Revenues from the sale of glass and newspaper are used to cover the costs charged to the Borough for recycling corrugated cardboard.

Composting Activities

Lincoln Park Borough recovers leaves and brush for composting through a seasonal curbside collection program and a year-round drop-off program at the recycling center. According to Richard Lavallo, the Recycling Coordinator, 50 percent of the residents bring their leaves and brush to the drop-off center. The DPW provides curbside collection according to a schedule, which is published in the local newspapers.

This collection takes place about once a month during April, May, October, and November. Loose leaves are raked to the curbside and are collected by means of a vacuum pulled by a dump truck. Once the dump truck is full, the materials are brought to a public composting facility in Montville, New Jersey. The Borough is not charged a tipping fee at this site.

DPW collects brush and tree stumps on an on-call basis, with the help of the Sheriff's Labor Assistance Program. Brush and tree stumps are taken to Ox Stump Factory in Ledgewood, New Jersey, where they are chipped for composting.

The Borough also collects and chips Christmas trees at the drop-off center. The chipped trees are brought to Ox Stump Factory. In 1990, the Borough began collecting grass clippings at the drop-off center.

Amount and Breakdown of Materials Recovered

Material	Commercial* (Tons, 1988)	Residential (Tons, 1988)	Total (Tons, 1988)
Newspaper	90.6	603.6	694.2
High-grade Paper	46.3	1.3	47.6
Corrugated	1,407.7	93.8	1,501.5
Other Paper	1,041.4	6.4	1,047.8
Commingled†	8.9	0	8.9
Glass	19.6	169.9	189.5
Aluminum	0.2	5.8	6
Plastic Containers	19.3	3.1	22.4
Non-ferrous Scrap	13.1	2.8	15.9
Ferrous Scrap	15.6	38.1	53.7
Batteries	0	3.1	3.1
Tires	0	21	21
Food Waste	75.8	0	75.8
Motor Oil	40.5	0	40.5
Subtotal Recycled	**2,779.0**	**948.9**	**3,727.9**
Leaves	55	675	730
Brush	0	86.7	86.7
Subtotal Composted	**55**	**761.7**	**816.7**
Total Recovered	**2,834.0**	**1,710.6**	**4,544.6**

*Includes materials recovered from condominiums
†Includes glass and aluminum

Publicity and Education

Every year the Borough sends a flier to all residents detailing what materials are mandated for separation, what materials may be recycled voluntarily at the drop-off center, and how to prepare all materials. In 1988, the Borough spent $400 on its mailing. The local newspaper advertises Lincoln Park's recycling successes. Articles include information about the percentage of materials recovered and photographs of residents at the recycling center. The photographs help to create a feeling of pride in the recycling program. The newspaper also prints the collection schedule for leaves and brush.

In May 1988, fourth-grade children in Lincoln Park were treated to a 50-minute lesson on recycling, reuse, and reduction by "Glinda Garbajh," a character conceived and developed in 1987 by Penny Jones, the County Recycling Education Specialist. The education specialist supplies teachers with news articles, a brochure of books and educational videos, the New Jersey Teachers Guide on Recycling, and an evaluation form.

Economics

Costs Cover:	Costs for capital equipment and operating and maintenance given below cover 931 tons of recyclables and 675 tons of leaves collected at curbside and accepted at the drop-off center.

Capital Costs: Collection

Item	Cost	Use	Year Incurred
2 Vacuums @ $2,500 each	$ 5,000	Composting	1974
Dump Truck @ 30% composting use	$ 19,000	Composting/DPW	1982
Dump Truck @ 30% recycling use	$ 19,000	Recycling/DPW	1982
Roll-off Truck*	$ 78,000	Recycling	1989
8 Roll-off Containers @ $2,500 each*	$ 18,000	Recycling	1989
Repairs to Vacuums*	$ 3,200	Composting	1989

*This equipment was bought in 1989, but was not delivered until 1990.

Capital Costs: Processing

Item	Cost	Use	Year Incurred
2 Chippers @ $8,000 each	$16,000	Composting	1982

Operating and Maintenance Costs (1988)*

	Recycling	Composting	Total
Collection	$ 57,000	$31,000	$ 88,000
Processing	$ 8,000	$ 0	$ 8,000
Administration	$ 12,400	$ 0	$ 12,400
Education/Publicity	$ 400	$ 0	$ 400
Total	**$ 77,800**	**$31,000**	**$ 108,800**

*1988 costs are estimated to be the same as the costs for 1989, according to Richard Lavallo.

Materials Revenues: $7,000 from the sale of glass, newspaper, and aluminum. The Borough donated $5,500 of this to a food pantry and a scholarship fund.

Source of Funding: The recycling program is paid for out of residents' taxes and a State Tonnage Grant.

Part-time Employees: 1 (DPW workers are also used on an as-needed basis.)

Contacts

Richard Lavallo
Recycling Coordinator
Municipal Building
34 Chapel Hill Road
Lincoln Park, New Jersey 07035
Phone (201) 694-6100
Fax (201) 628-9512
(Drop-off center contact only)

Paul A. Sarames
Management Specialist
Municipal Building
34 Chapel Hill Road
Lincoln Park, New Jersey 07035
Phone (201) 694-6100
Fax (201) 628-9512
(Overall program contact)

Penny Jones
Recycling Education Specialist
Morris County MUA
P.O. Box 900
Morristown, New Jersey 07963-0900
Phone (201) 285-8390
Fax (201) 285-8397

WEST LINN, OREGON

Demographics

Jurisdiction: City of West Linn

Population: 14,030 in 1989 (in 1987, population was reported at 13,000)

Total Households: 5,900 (5,000 single residences and 900 multi-unit dwellings)

Total Businesses: 379 (including home businesses such as Avon distributors)

Area: 7 square miles

Other: West Linn is a suburban commuter community in the Portland metropolitan area with a small commercial sector. The only industrial establishment is a paper mill.

Solid Waste Generation and Collection

(Annual Tonnages for 1989)

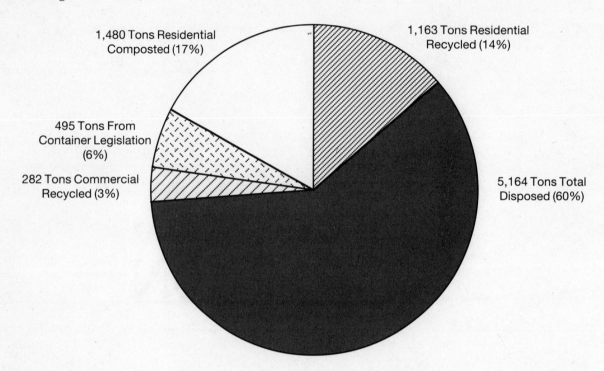

1,480 Tons Residential Composted (17%)

1,163 Tons Residential Recycled (14%)

495 Tons From Container Legislation (6%)

282 Tons Commercial Recycled (3%)

5,164 Tons Total Disposed (60%)

Total Waste Generated:	8,584 tons in 1989 (includes materials recovered through the container deposit system and bulky waste such as tires, white goods, and construction debris) 7,042 tons in 1987 (includes materials recovered through the beverage container deposit system, but does not include bulky waste)
Residential Waste Generated:	Not available, but most of the total waste generated is residential
Commercial Waste Generated:	Not available, but only a small portion of the total waste generated (approximately 5 or 6 percent) is commercial
Bulky Waste Generated:	Not available because the City does not keep track of bulky waste separate from other waste
% By Weight of Total Waste Recovered:	40 percent in 1989 (23 percent recycling, including deposit containers, and 17 percent composting) 34 percent in 1987 (18 percent recycling, including deposit containers, and 16 percent composting)
% By Weight of Residential Waste Recovered:	Not available
% By Weight of Commercial Waste Recovered:	Not available

Transfer Station Tipping Fee:

$45.75 per ton since November 1, 1988 at the transfer station. The tipping fee will rise to $55.50 per ton on July 1, 1990, and is expected to continue increasing.

$19.90 per ton in 1987

Collection of Refuse:

The City has a franchise agreement with West Linn Disposal, a private hauler, for collection of residential and commercial solid waste. The franchise agreement entitles West Linn Disposal to be the only solid waste hauler in the City, and requires the hauler to pay the City a flat yearly fee for this privilege.

The Portland metropolitan government (Metro) operates the area's only general purpose landfill, and has authority over solid waste planning and disposal. West Linn retains control over local refuse collection. Waste generated in West Linn is transported to a transfer station, owned by Metro, located within 2 miles of the City. Metro then transports the waste from the transfer station to a privately owned landfill in Arlington, Oregon, 140 miles away.

West Linn Disposal incurs approximately $130 per ton for refuse collection and tipping fees. The costs of transporting the refuse to the landfill and the landfill's operation costs are covered by the transfer station tip fee.

In recent years, landfill tipping fees have increased significantly and are expected to continue to rise. Metro is exploring "alternative technologies" to deal with portions of the waste stream. Both increasing tipping fees and this research effort will seriously impact the cost of waste disposal in West Linn.

West Linn Disposal charges residents by volume for collection of their refuse. Weekly collection of one 32-gallon container of refuse costs $11.30 per month. Two containers cost $22.60 per month. Recyclers can choose a reduced rate of $9.65 per month for weekly pick-up of a 20-gallon mini-can. Currently, only about 25 households, mostly senior citizens, have chosen this option.

In addition to the flat fee that it pays the City, West Linn Disposal must pay the City $0.95 per month for a household that sets out one 32-gallon can, $3.60 for 2 cans, $6.25 for 3 cans, $8.70 for 4 cans, and $11.35 for 5 cans. The hauler pays a slightly lower amount for every 20-gallon mini-can. The City uses this money to fund its recycling activities (drop-off center, publicity/education).

Future Solid Waste Management Plans:

The state has mandated a solid waste management hierarchy of reduce, reuse, recycle, recover, and, as a last resort, landfill. Oregon has several laws that encourage recycling, including bottle bill legislation, a requirement that local jurisdictions provide the "opportunity to recycle" to all residents, and a law requiring that metropolitan Portland develop a regional plan to achieve the maximum extent of solid waste reduction that is economically feasible.

West Linn recently received a grant for a demonstration program to distribute reusable plastic bags to 10 percent of residences for collection of junk mail, low-grade paper of all sorts, and high-grade paper. These materials will be separated by color and grade, and then marketed. The goal is to find out how much of the paper in the waste stream can be recovered, and how much can be earned in revenues from this endeavor.

West Linn Disposal plans to begin on-call collection of yard debris at curbside by July 1, 1990.

Materials Recovery

In the early 1980s, the Portland Metropolitan government (Metro) proposed building a garbage incinerator in a town adjacent to West Linn. In response to citizen concerns, the West Linn City Council withdrew its support for the incinerator and instead established a Solid Waste Reduction Task Force to make recommendations on ways to reduce the City's solid waste output by 50 percent. In June 1983, the Task Force presented 15 recommendations, including the implementation of a curbside collection program.

Each recommendation fell into one of four general categories: (1) implementing programs, (2) education and promotion, (3) funding, and (4) supervision. The primary goal of these recommendations was to provide a quality service that was constant in the types of materials collected and the days of collection. Another goal was to provide support for the service with sufficient promotion, education, and staff time to guarantee its success.

In July 1983, West Linn Sanitary, the franchised solid waste hauler, began offering free curbside collection of residential recyclable materials including newspaper, corrugated cardboard, kraft paper, three colors of glass, tin, and motor oil.

In December 1984, West Linn Sanitary began placing multi-material recycling collection boxes at multi-family complexes in the City. By the end of 1986, just under 90 percent of all residents living in complexes of ten or more units were served by the collection program. Since 1987, the hauler has been serving the multi-family complexes in the course of collection from single residences on the same routes.

In March 1985, the hauler began collecting corrugated cardboard and bulk quantities of other materials from commercial sources. The only institutions that recycle are schools, which recycle paper. Curbside recycling service is provided to all residents and all commercial establishments in West Linn, whether or not they are customers of the hauler.

The City of West Linn operates a drop-off center for recyclables once a week at its composting site. The truck that collects recyclables at curbside picks up the same types of materials from the drop-off center. In addition to these types of materials, the center accepts magazines, white and colored ledger paper, computer paper, HDPE plastic milk jugs, and polystyrene. Leaves and yard debris are accepted for composting.

The State of Oregon has had a beverage container deposit system since 1972. West Linn's recycling coordinator reports that 495 tons of aluminum and glass beverage containers were returned to grocery stores for deposit refund in the City in 1989. These containers were then recycled.

The Lions Club of West Linn has placed large trailers for newspapers at three shopping centers. The Boy Scouts and other groups have four smaller drop boxes for newspapers across the City. These groups report the tonnage they recover to the City.

The City sponsors two clean-up days a year, one in the fall and one in the spring. Any recyclable material collected from the clean-up days is taken to the drop-off and composting site; from there, it is sent to local brokers.

Residents have three options for recycling appliances: (1) to haul them for no fee to the drop-off center open during the twice-yearly City clean-up days, (2) to haul them any day of the year for no fee to the regional transfer station, and (3) to call the private hauler, who collects appliances in his flat-bed truck for a $10.00 fee.

Similarly, residents may dispose of tires by taking them to a drop-off center open during the semiannual clean-up days, or by hauling them to the regional transfer station. The tires are recycled at Waste Recovery Systems, a company that grinds them and markets the product.

In April 1989, West Linn Sanitary was bought out. The new owner changed the name of the company to West Linn Disposal. West Linn's Recycling Coordinator, Ed Druback, attributes the 6 percent increase in tonnages recovered in 1989 over that recovered in 1987 to the new owner's aggressive recycling activities.

In April 1990 West Linn Disposal began providing 14-gallon containers to residents for source separation of recyclable materials.

The West Linn recovery program has been commended by the League of Oregon Cities for reducing waste disposal costs and improving the overall quality of life of the community.

Curbside Collection

Start-up Date: 1983

Private/Public: Private hauler has agreed to provide curbside collection of recyclable materials as part of its franchise agreement with the City.

Materials Collected: Newspaper, corrugated cardboard, kraft paper, three colors of glass, aluminum, ferrous cans, motor oil, and appliances

Pick-up Frequency: Weekly for all materials, except for appliances, which are collected on an on-call basis

Pick-up Same Day as Refuse: Yes

Material Set-out Method: Materials are bagged or bundled separately and placed at least 5 feet from non-recyclables. Newspaper is placed in one bag, all colors of glass in another, and tin and aluminum in a third.

Mandatory: No. The State of Oregon has implemented the Recycling Opportunity Act, which mandates that municipalities with populations of 4,000 or more provide curbside collection of recyclable materials at least once a month.

Service Provider: West Linn Disposal, a private hauler

Collection Vehicles: 2 modified 16-cubic-yard garbage trucks equipped with 10 bins for recyclables. The bins have a capacity of 1/2 to 2 cubic yards and can be removed with a forklift. Appliances are collected in a flat-bed truck.

Households Served: 5,900 in 1989

Participation Rate: 84 percent[1] of all single-family households (estimated)

Businesses Served: 379

Economic Incentives: The variable can rate is a direct economic incentive for residents to generate as little waste as possible and to recycle as much as possible.

---

[1]Participation rate is calculated as follows: two counters are kept in the collection truck. One records the number of set-outs that are just newspaper, and the other records set-outs that include newspaper and at least one other material. It is assumed that every home sets out materials once every 2.5 weeks, which would be 20.8 set-outs per year (52/2.5). There were 87,440 set-outs in 1989, which were divided by 20.8 set-outs per household to yield 4,204 participating households. Dividing this by 5,000 single-family households yields a participation rate of 84%.

Commercial Materials Recovery Activities

The franchised solid waste hauler began collecting corrugated cardboard and bulk quantities of other materials from commercial establishments in March 1985. The program has regular weekly routing to collect corrugated cardboard from more than 40 small businesses and an on-call program for commercially generated high-grade computer and ledger paper. The three larger retail groceries each recycle corrugated cardboard in cooperation with their suppliers. Volumes from the groceries are reported to the City and are included in waste generated and recovered figures.

Materials Processing

Materials collected through the curbside program are unloaded from the 10-bin truck with a forklift. Since materials are already separated, the hauler delivers them directly to K&B Recycling, a buy-back center that processes the materials. Revenues are retained by the private hauler.

The City markets the materials collected at its drop-off center, and receives the revenues. The Environmental Learning Center at Clackamas Community College grinds the City's HDPE plastic milk jugs and polystyrene and delivers them to Denton Plastics, where they are manufactured into items such as flower pots. The tonnage of plastics recovered is not tracked.

Composting Activities

In 1983, it was estimated that yard debris constituted 25 percent of the total waste generated in West Linn. Based on recommendations made by the Solid Waste Reduction Task Force, the City encouraged home composting, arranged for the franchised solid waste hauler to provide on-call collection of yard debris, and set up a drop-off/composting site for yard debris. In cooperation with the private hauler, the City has attempted to make disposal of yard debris as garbage more expensive than source separation.

The City's drop-off center for yard waste is open on Saturdays, from February through November. Materials accepted include leaves, grass clippings, brush, wood waste (non-dimensional lumber), and all the materials collected at curbside. All wood material is ground in a tub grinder and composted in windrows. The composted material is sold back to residents or used by the City in parks. The City also sponsors a yearly Christmas tree drop-off program. The Christmas trees are chipped.

The most cost-effective and desirable solution to yard waste is home composting. Since 1984, West Linn has offered 2-hour seminars on how to compost at home, taught four times a year by the staff of the local community college. Attendance has dropped off in recent years. It is estimated that 15 to 20 percent of all yard debris is composted in backyards.

In September of 1987, Oregon's Environmental Quality Commission adopted rules requiring all jurisdictions in the area to develop a recycling plan that provides either curbside collection or drop-off centers for yard debris. West Linn Disposal is planning to provide year-round on-call collection of source-separated yard debris for a nominal charge: $3.50 for each bag of leaves (not to exceed 60 pounds) and $7.50 for each bundle of brush (not to exceed 3 feet by 4 feet). This is less than the charge for refuse collection. The residents of West Linn tend to haul their yard waste to the drop-off center, because doing so costs less ($0.50 per bag of leaves and $3.00 per cubic yard of brush) than having the private hauler pick up these materials.

Amount and Breakdown of Materials Recovered

Material	Total (Tons, 1987)
High-Grade Paper	2
Newspaper	616
Corrugated Cardboard	103
Glass	80
Tin Cans	18
Motor Oil	7
Scrap Metal	19
Subtotal Recycled	**845**
Yard Debris	1,123
Subtotal Composted	**1,123**
Deposit Containers	400
Total Recovered	**2,368**

Note: Of the materials listed above, 1,172 tons were recovered through the City's recycling and composting drop-off center (1,100 tons of yard debris, 23 tons from Christmas tree collection, 19 tons of scrap metal from the clean-up programs, and 30 tons of other materials). 796 tons were collected through the curbside program, Lions Club, and commercial paper recycling.

Material	Commercial (Tons, 1989)	Residential (Tons, 1989)	Total (Tons, 1989)
Newspaper	0	839.8	839.8
Corrugated Cardboard	278.9	133.7	412.6
High Grade Paper	2.7	0	2.7
Magazines	0	5.1	5.1
Glass	0	128.8	128.8
Motor Oil	0	15.3	15.3
Tires	0	4.4	4.4
Appliances	0	10.3	10.3
Ferrous Cans	0	25.7	25.7
Subtotal Recycled	**281.6**	**1,163.1**	**1,444.7**
Yard waste	0	1,454	1,454
Christmas trees	0	26	26
Subtotal Composted	**0**	**1,480**	**1,480**
Subtotal Recovered	**281.6**	**2,643.1**	**2,924.7**
Deposit Containers	NA	NA	495
Total Recovered	**NA**	**NA**	**3,419.7**

Note: Of the materials listed above, 1,454 tons of yard debris were collected at the drop-off center.   26 tons of Christmas trees, and 923 tons of recyclables were collected at the drop-off and at curbside, and 240 tons of newspapers were collected by the Lions Club and the Boy Scouts.   281.6 tons were collected through commercial curbside recycling.

Publicity and Education

The State's Recycling Opportunity Act requires that municipalities send out notices of the recycling program every 6 months.   Recycling Coordinator Ed Druback believes that West Linn's program is more aggressive than the State rules require.   He attributes the program's success to promotion and education.

Promotional activities have included direct mail flyers, utility bill inserts, City newsletter features, stickers placed on garbage lids, yard signs, buttons, handbooks distributed through Welcome Wagon (an organization sponsored by local businesses to orient newcomers to various businesses and their services), and an exhibit booth at the City fair.   The program has also given presentations to all kindergarten through fifth grade classes, and has a commercial on the local cable television channel.

Citizen input has also been an important part of the success of West Linn's materials recovery program.   The original Solid Waste Task Force polled the residents on the type of program they wanted to see instituted and shaped the materials recovery programs accordingly. The City recognizes individuals and organizations that support recycling through a Certificate of Appreciation awards program.

Economics

Costs Cover:

The capital and operating and maintenance costs given below cover (1) the curbside and drop-off collection of 923 tons of recyclables from households, and (2) the composting of 1,480 tons of yard waste at the City drop-off site. Curbside collection costs are incurred by West Linn Disposal, and drop-off costs are incurred by the City.

Capital Costs: Collection

Item	Cost	Use	Year Incurred
16-Cubic-Yard, 10-Bin Recycling Truck*	$ 14,000	Recycling	1985
16-Cubic-Yard, 10-Bin Recycling Truck*	$ 14,000	Recycling	1989
20-Cubic-Yard Packer Truck for Yard Waste*	$ 20,000	Composting	1990

*Note: West Linn Disposal purchased and owns these trucks.

Capital Costs: Processing

Item	Cost	Use	Year Incurred
Front-End Loader @ 20% of use	$40,000	Recycling	1985
Composting Equipment	$10,000	Composting	1985
Land Improvements	$22,000	Composting	1985
Tub Grinder/Power Unit	$33,000	Composting	1989

Since the front-end loader is only used for recycling on Saturdays, the recycling program only paid 20 percent ($8,000) of its total cost. The Public Works Department paid the remaining 80 percent. The recycling program also receives in-kind labor from other departments, and occasionally has inmates from correctional facilities work several hours at the drop-off center.

Operating and Maintenance Costs (1989)

	Recycling	Composting	Total
Collection	$ 112,807 *	$ 0	$ 112,807
Processing	$ 0	$ 30,398	$ 30,398
Administration	$ 23,131	$ 7,322	$ 30,453
Education/Publicity	$ 8,200 †	$ 0	$ 8,200
Total	**$ 144,138**	**$ 37,720**	**$ 181,858**

*West Linn Disposal reported $112,807 for this cost.
†Includes education/publicity expenses for composting.

Materials Revenues: $37,700 in 1989 ($16,000 from sales of composted materials by the City, and $21,700 from sales of recyclable materials by West Linn Disposal)

$10,000 in 1987 (sale of composted materials only)

Source of Funding: Funding for the City comes from several sources: income from operation of the yard debris and composting site; franchise fee paid by the solid waste hauler ($6,000); surcharge on multiple can customers of the solid waste hauler;[2] 5 percent rate increase from July 1987; and general funds.   General funds supplied 8 percent of the total recycling budget in fiscal year 1986-87 and 18 percent in 1987-88.

Funding for West Linn Disposal's recycling program comes from revenue received for refuse collection in West Linn and in four other jurisdictions that also have variable can rates.

Full-time Employees: 3 employees of West Linn Disposal and 1 City employee (the City recycling coordinator)

Part-time Employees: 4 City employees (1 operator at drop-off/composting site, 2 people to grind yard waste and Christmas trees, 1 person contracted to do educational presentations)

---

[2]The difference between the monthly rates charged for one waste can and two or more waste cans is dedicated to funding the recycling program.   Between April 1989 and March 1990 this difference totalled $63,410.

Contacts

Ed Druback
Recycling Program Coordinator
Engineering Department
City of West Linn
2042 Eighth Avenue
West Linn, Oregon 97068
Phone (503) 656-4211
Fax (503) 656-8756

Pamela Bloom
West Linn Disposal
820 7th Street
Oregon City, Oregon 97045
Phone (503) 654-4048
Fax (503) 656-0320

Reference

Solid Waste & Recycling in West Linn, Oregon, City of West Linn, March 1989, West Linn, Oregon.

HAMBURG, NEW YORK

Demographics

Jurisdiction: Village of Hamburg

Population: 11,000 in 1989 (based on estimated growth since 1980 census, which reported 10,500 people)

Total Households: 3,350 (single-family households and multi-unit dwellings up to two stories tall. Households in the one high-rise apartment are not included in the total.)

Total Businesses: 100 to 120 (estimated)

Area: 2.5 square miles

Other: The Village of Hamburg is a small municipality contained within the larger Town of Hamburg. The two have separate refuse collection and recycling systems.

Solid Waste Generation and Collection

(Annual Tonnages for 1989)

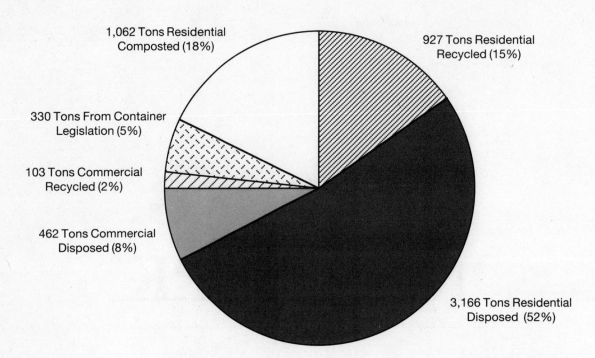

1,062 Tons Residential Composted (18%)

927 Tons Residential Recycled (15%)

330 Tons From Container Legislation (5%)

103 Tons Commercial Recycled (2%)

462 Tons Commercial Disposed (8%)

3,166 Tons Residential Disposed (52%)

Total Waste Generated: 6,050 tons in 1989 (3,518 tons disposed by Village, 1,030 tons recycled, 60 tons commercial waste and 50 tons construction debris disposed as reported by private hauler, 330 tons estimated recovered through the beverage container deposit system, and an estimated 1,062 tons of yard waste. Tonnages for tires and scrap metal are not included.)

3,851 tons in 1987 (3,658 tons reported by the Village, plus 193 tons estimated recovered through the beverage container deposit system)

Residential Waste Generated: Estimated at 5,155 tons in 1989 (based on an estimated breakdown of the waste recycled and disposed by the Village of Hamburg into 90 percent residential and 10 percent commercial.[1] Yard waste recovered is all considered residential. Excludes materials recycled under the beverage container deposit system.)

Commercial Waste Generated: Estimated at 565 tons (based on 10 percent of waste disposed and recycled by the Village,[2] plus 60 tons commercial waste disposed and 50 tons of construction debris disposed, as reported by BFI)

---

[1] 90 percent of 3,518 tons waste disposed (3,166 tons), plus 90 percent of 1,030 tons of materials recycled (927 tons), plus 1,062 tons estimated composted (see footnote on page 163).

[2] 10 percent of 3,518 tons waste disposed (352 tons), plus 10 percent of 1,030 tons of materials recycled (103 tons), plus 60 tons reported disposed by BFI and 50 tons of construction debris disposed.

Bulky Waste Generated:

50 tons of construction debris were estimated disposed by the private hauler. Construction and demolition waste is taken to the Construction and Demolition Debris (C&D) Landfill for $42 per ton. Tires are taken to a tire recycling facility, and items such as non-metal furniture are taken to a transfer station for $50 per ton. Tonnages of tires and furniture are not available.

% By Weight of Total Waste Recovered:

40 percent in 1989 (22 percent recycling and 18 percent composting)

30 percent in 1987 (30 percent recycling; composting percentage not available and composting tonnage not included in the 1987 figure for total waste generated)

% By Weight of Residential Waste Recovered:

39 percent in 1989 (18 percent recycling, excluding tonnage recycled under the beverage container deposit system, and 21 percent composting)

% By Weight of Commercial Waste Recovered:

18 percent in 1989 (excluding tonnage recycled under the beverage container deposit system)

Landfill/Incinerator Tipping Fee:

$4.80 per cubic yard (approximately $10 per ton) in 1989 at the Chaffee landfill, $45 per ton at the Niagara Falls incinerator, $42 per ton at the C&D Landfill, and $50 per ton at the transfer station (where some bulky waste is taken)

Approximately $8 per ton ($4.20 per cubic yard) at the landfill in 1987

Collection of Refuse:

The Village of Hamburg Department of Public Works collects recyclable materials and waste at the same time with the same crews by using packer trucks with specially designed trailers. The Village collects refuse and recyclables from small businesses, and BFI hauls the refuse for the other commercial establishments.

Future Solid Waste Management Plans:

The Village of Hamburg is planning to start a joint compost site with the larger Town of Hamburg in the next few years, so that more yard waste can be recovered. Once this is started, the Village's goal is a 60 percent reduction of waste disposed.

In the middle of 1989, the Village ceased to dispose of any refuse at the Chaffee Landfill, where it had previously taken much of its refuse, and entered into a contract with the Niagara Falls waste incinerator. Both of these facilities are approximately an hour's drive from the Village. The goal of the Village was to negotiate a 25-year contract. The Chaffee Landfill preferred not to commit to this length of time, but the Niagara Falls incinerator agreed to do so. Also, the Chaffee Landfill's bid for the contract was $59 per ton for refuse minus recyclables and $79 per ton for refuse including recyclables. The Niagara Falls incinerator agreed to charge $45 per ton for refuse the first year of the contract, and $46.50 the second year, followed by small increases for the next few years, with the charge for the 11th through the 25th years to be negotiated after 10 years.

Materials Recovery

The Village Board of Hamburg, with the help of volunteer committees, developed a voluntary recycling program in the early 1970s. This program encouraged residents of Hamburg and a neighboring town to separate newspapers, bottles, and cans from their household refuse. These materials could then be dropped off at the Village of Hamburg Recycling Center, which was located at the public works garage site. Local firms picked up and disposed of the recyclables, paying the Village for the materials they received.

In 1978, rising landfill costs, decreased availability of raw materials, and increasing demands to conserve energy by any means possible, moved the Village to consider changing the voluntary recycling program into a compulsory program for all residents. After approximately 2 years of in-depth study by the local recycling committee, the Village Board in 1981 passed a law requiring Hamburg residents to separate refuse at their homes and to place it at the curb. The Village Sanitation Division of the Department of Public Works picks up the separated garbage and delivers the recyclable materials to the Village Recycling Center.

The recycling program was started in order to (1) reduce the amount of material being delivered to the landfill, thus reducing landfill costs incurred by the Village of Hamburg, (2) contribute positively to the environmental movement by recycling various materials, (3) slow down the use of landfill space, and (4) reduce the overall cost of the sanitation operation. The reduction in landfill costs combined with the savings on labor, fuel, repairs, and wear and tear on equipment attributable to recycling was approximately $29,332 in 1989.

Many of the costs associated with recycling are included in the total cost of sanitation services for the Village. The same crews collect recyclable materials and garbage with the same trucks on the same days, so there are no additional collection costs for recycling. In fact, the revenues received and landfill costs avoided by adding recycling to sanitation services have actually reduced the overall cost per stop of sanitation services. According to Gerald Knoll, Superintendent of Public Works for the Village of Hamburg, the total cost of sanitation services for 1984, not including recycling, amounted to $221,165 — or $67 per stop. Adding the costs for recycling increases the figure to $251,146. Factoring in revenues from the sale of recycled materials and the landfill savings reduces the total figure to $196,659 — or $59 per stop. Thus, in 1984, the investment of $29,981 resulted in revenues and avoided costs (totalling $54,487) that produced a net savings of $24,506 in sanitation services costs.

The State of New York implemented a beverage container deposit law in 1983. Specified beverage containers are returned to the point of purchase for redemption of the 5 cent deposit. These materials are not included in the waste generation and recycling figures reported by the Village because they bypass the local waste management system. ILSR staff estimate that 330 tons of beverage containers were recovered in 1989 through the state's deposit legislation.[3]

Bulky waste is handled separately from other waste. It is usually hauled for disposal by BFI. Records of this are kept separately from records of materials handled by the Village. Construction and demolition debris is taken to the C&D landfill, tires are taken to a tire recycling facility, and other bulky waste is taken to a transfer station. An estimate of the tonnage of construction debris is included with the figure for waste generated.

Curbside Collection

Start-up Date: Early 1970s; mandatory in 1981

Private/Public: Municipally run program

Materials Collected: Newspaper, corrugated cardboard, glass, bi-metal containers, aluminum, PET and HDPE plastic beverage and detergent containers, waste oil, appliances, metal furniture, brush, and leaves

Pick-up Frequency: Weekly for newspaper, corrugated cardboard, glass, bi-metal containers, aluminum, PET and HDPE plastic containers, and waste oil. Appliances and metal furniture are collected four times per year. Brush is collected once a month all year round. Leaves are collected separately in the fall; during the 2-month collection period, each household can expect to have its leaves collected two or three times.

Pick-up Same Day as Refuse: Yes, for all materials except leaves and brush

Material Set-out Method: Newspapers in one container or bundle; glass, plastic, and metal in another container; cardboard flattened and placed next to glass and cans; and the balance of the refuse in a third container. The Village provides residents with special plastic containers that hold one oil change for curbside collection of waste oil. Leaves must be put loose next to the curb so that they may be easily collected by the leaf vacuums, and brush is stacked.

Mandatory: Yes, for all materials except waste oil, metal furniture, and appliances

Service Provider: Municipal crews

Collection Vehicles: Specially designed trailers and bins attached to the packer truck are used for newspaper, corrugated cardboard, glass, metals, waste oil, and plastics. Materials are not sorted until they reach the recycling center. Vacuums attached to dump trucks

---

[3]The tonnage of containers redeemed in New York in 1989 divided by the total population of the state of New York yields 0.03 tons per capita. For Hamburg, 0.03 times 11,000 = 330 tons in 1989.

are used for leaves, and chippers attached to dump trucks are used for brush. The Village collects appliances and scrap metal in dump trucks.

Households Served: 3,350 single-family households and multi-unit dwellings up to two stories tall. The one high-rise apartment in the Village has a dumpster that is not serviced by the Village.

Participation Rate: 98 percent of households put out recyclable materials every week.

Businesses Served: The Village picks up recyclable and compostable materials from small businesses, but the number served is not available

Economic Incentives: None

Enforcement: If recyclables are not separated from the rest of a household's refuse, its trash is not picked up at all. Enforcement has not been a major problem and is handled on a case-by-case basis.

Commercial Materials Recovery Activities

The Village collects recyclables from small businesses. Commercial establishments are required to recycle the same materials as households, and the set-out method is the same. However, the Village of Hamburg will not collect brush or tree parts discarded by commercial contractors.

Materials Processing

The Recycling Center is operated and staffed by the Association of Retarded Children (ARC) under supervision of the Department of Public Works, which owns the Center. It is located in a building that was donated in the 1970s when the recycling program first began. The source-separated materials are delivered to this recycling center, where they are separated further. Glass is divided into clear and colored, cans into aluminum and tin, plastic into PET and HDPE containers, and paper into newsprint and corrugated cardboard. The materials are then stored in either exterior bins or 40-foot trailers to be hauled away by contractors who have agreements with the Village for these services.

Most beverage containers that can be returned for a deposit are not included with materials set out at curbside. Occasionally, however, they end up at the Recycling Center, where the staff separates them from other materials and returns them for the deposit, which they are allowed to keep. The staff does not keep track of the amount of bottle bill containers handled in this way.

Appliances (white goods) and metal lawn furniture are taken to a scrap yard. Waste oil is re-refined at a local waste oil company.

Composting Activities

The Village has mandated the separation of leaves and brush from other refuse.   Village crews collect leaves separately in the fall and deliver them to local farmers, who handle the composting.   Crews deliver brush to a pile near the landfill, where it is informally composted. The Village does not keep records of the amount of leaves or brush collected.   By converting volume amounts, based on truckloads, to tonnage,[4] ILSR staff have estimated that 1,008 tons of leaves and 54 tons of brush were collected in 1989.

Brush is collected on the last Friday of the month, all year.   Grass clippings are currently not collected, although they will be when the new compost site opens.   The farmers who accept leaves from the Village do not accept grass clippings for fear that they will be contaminated with pesticides.

Commercial landscapers, such as the Water Valley Nursery and Wanakah Landscaping, compost their yard waste on their own sites or use it in their own growing plots.   These tonnages are not tracked and therefore are excluded from waste recovery and waste generation figures.

Amount and Breakdown of Materials Recovered

Material	Total (Tons, 1987)*
Newspaper	569.52
Corrugated Cardboard	50.63
Glass	144.14
White Goods	58.67
Ferrous Metal	50.20
Waste Oil	3.82
Total	**876.98**

*Recovery in 1987 was estimated to be approximately the same as recovery in 1985.

[4]During the fall season, four Village trucks collect leaves each day for about 40 days (2 months containing eight 5-day weeks).   Each 8-cubic-yard truck picks up 4 to 5 full loads each day.   Using a density of 5,714 cubic yards per ton for compacted leaves yields an average of 1,008 tons of leaves collected per year.

In addition, the Village collects 18 to 36 full truck loads of brush per year. Using a conversion factor of 4 cubic yards per ton for brush yields an average of 54 tons of brush collected per year.

Material	Commercial (Tons, 1989)	Residential (Tons, 1989)	Total (Tons, 1989)
Newspaper & Corrugated Cardboard	NA	NA	600
Glass	NA	NA	250
White Goods	NA	NA	NA
Ferrous Metal	NA	NA	159
Waste Oil	NA	NA	8.75
Aluminum	NA	NA	6
Plastics	NA	NA	6
Subtotal Recycled	**102.97**	**926.78 ***	**1,029.75**
Leaves	0	1,008 †	1,008
Brush	0	54 †	54
Subtotal Composted	**0**	**1,062**	**1,062**
Subtotal Recovered	**102.97**	**1,988.77**	**2,091.75**
Deposit Containers	NA	NA	330
Total Recovered	**NA**	**NA**	**2,421.75**

*Based on an estimate that 90 percent of recyclables are collected from the residential sector and 10 percent from the commercial sector
†Based on ILSR estimates.   See footnote on previous page.

Publicity and Education

The recycling program no longer has a publicity and education program.   According to Gerald Knoll, residents are already educated.   Only $100 per year is spent on publicity.

Economics

Costs Cover:

Capital costs given below cover the equipment used to recycle the 1,030 tons in 1989. Incomplete capital costs for composting the 1,062 tons are provided. Estimated operating and maintenance costs are provided only for the recycling of the 1,030 tons collected by the Village.

Capital Costs: Collection

Item	Cost	Use	Year Incurred
Recycling Center Building	Donated	Recycling	1981
3 Trailers	$ 7,500	Recycling	1981/82
Skidsteer Loader	$ 12,738	Recycling	1981/82
1.25-Cubic-Yard Bins	$ 7,068	Recycling	1981/82
Misc.	$ 10,208	Recycling	1981/82
Waste Oil Containers	$ 3,500	Recycling	1983
18 1.25-Cu.-Yd. Replacement Bins	$ 8,766	Recycling	1988
18 1.25-Cu.-Yd. Replacement Bins	$ 11,565	Recycling	1989
Leaf Collection Vacuum	$ 16,000	Composting	1989
Leaf Collection Vacuum*	NA	Composting	NA
4 Dump Trucks (not full time)*	NA	Composting	NA

*The second vacuum for leaf collection and the four dump trucks were purchased many years ago and the cost is not known. For purposes of the chart in the beginning of this report, the cost of the second front-end loader is assumed to be the same as the first.

Capital Costs: Processing

Item	Cost	Use	Year Incurred
Sorting Table	$ 200	Recycling	1981
12 Bins	$ 3,696	Recycling	1981/82
Brush Chipper	$ 8,000	Chipping	1982
Brush Chipper	$ 12,000	Chipping	1986

Operating and Maintenance Costs (1989)

	Recycling	Composting	Total
Collection	$49,183 *	NA	NA
Processing	$33,267	NA	NA
Administration		NA	NA
Education/Publicity	$ 100	NA	NA
Total	**$82,550**	**NA**	**NA**

*O&M costs for collection of recyclables in 1989 are estimated at $49,183 as follows:

Total cost of collection services for refuse and recyclables	$337,348
Less landfill dumping costs	$115,813
Less gasoline to landfill costs	$ 4,368
	$217,167

Divided by total waste handled by the Village: $217,167/4,548 tons = $47.75 per ton
Multiplied by the tons recycled: $47.75 per ton x 1,030 = $49,183

Materials Revenues: $12,413 in 1989
                                 $16,297 in 1987
                                 $13,407 in 1985

Source of Funding: Local budget

Full-time Employees: 5 for collection. This is the same number employed before the curbside recycling program was implemented.

Contacts

Gerald E. Knoll
Superintendent, Department of Public Works
Village of Hamburg
100 Main Street
Hamburg, NY 14075
(716) 649-4953

Ann Kankolenski
Secretary
Village of Hamburg
100 Main Street
Hamburg, NY 14075
(716) 649-4953

Reference

Philips, Joe, New York State Department of Conservation, telephone conversation regarding redeemed beverage containers, Albany, New York, April 26, 1990.

WILTON, WISCONSIN

Demographics

Jurisdiction:	Village of Wilton
Population:	473 (1989 estimate)
Total Households:	200
Total Businesses:	9
Area:	Approximately 8 square miles
Other:	The Village of Wilton is a small rural community located in Monroe County, a dairy farming area of west-central Wisconsin.

Solid Waste Generation and Collection

(Annual Tonnages for 1989)

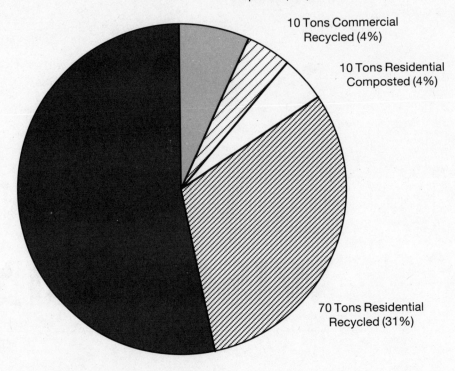

16 Tons Commercial Disposed (7%)

10 Tons Commercial Recycled (4%)

10 Tons Residential Composted (4%)

120 Tons Residential Disposed (53%)

70 Tons Residential Recycled (31%)

Total Waste Generated:	226 tons in 1989 (excluding bulky waste such as tires, construction debris, and appliances)
Residential Waste Generated:	200 tons in 1989
Commercial Waste Generated:	26 tons in 1989
Bulky Waste Generated:	Not available — very little is generated and the private hauler, Martin's Disposal, Inc., does not keep records of the amount.
% By Weight of Total Waste Recovered:	40 percent in 1989 (35.4 percent recycled and 4.4 percent composted)
% By Weight of Residential Waste Recovered:	40 percent in 1989 (35 percent recycled and 5 percent composted)
% By Weight of Commercial Waste Recovered:	38 percent in 1989 (38 percent recycled, none composted)
Landfill Tipping Fee:	$31 per ton in 1989 at the Monroe County Landfill
Collection of Refuse:	A private hauler, Martin's Disposal Service, Inc., collects refuse from all residential and commercial establishments in the Village. Martin's also used to haul recyclables (collected by volunteers from the Village) from the storage site to market at

no charge above that of regular refuse service. However, beginning on May 15, 1990, Martin's is charging $40 per ton to haul recyclables.

Future Solid Waste Management Plans:

The State of Wisconsin recently passed recycling legislation. In response, the Village of Wilton is currently developing a recycling ordinance. Nalani Bever, the Village President, anticipates that recycling will become mandatory in Wilton beginning on January 1, 1991.

The Monroe County Landfill, at which the Village of Wilton now disposes of its refuse, will close in 1992 if current filling rates continue unabated. Nalani Bever hopes that all communities in Monroe County that use the landfill will implement recycling programs, thus decreasing the amount of refuse being sent to the landfill and extending its lifespan by about 10 years. The Lacrosse incinerator is the only other local waste disposal option. The County is unlikely to build a new landfill after the current one closes, because the Lacrosse incinerator is operating under capacity due to insufficient waste. As a result, Wilton may be pressured into sending its refuse there.

The Village is setting up a compost site, which will begin operation in the summer of 1990. When the new compost site is open, the Village will occasionally pick up yard waste on a scheduled day in addition to the regular once-a-week collection. The Village is also building a drop-off center, with the help of a $1,500 County grant. It will open by July 1, 1990. The new compost site will be located behind the drop-off center.

Materials Recovery

The Village of Wilton implemented voluntary curbside collection of recyclables on July 1, 1988, after the Monroe County Landfill abandoned its flat fee and began charging a tipping fee of $31 per ton for refuse. The Village decided that a recycling program, staffed by volunteers, would save a great deal of money.

Through July and August of 1988, an entrepreneur doing curbside recycling pick-up in four or five nearby towns picked up recyclables from the curbside in Wilton for no charge, in exchange for being able to keep the revenues from the materials collected. He soon found that four or five towns were too many, and was forced to drop Wilton. The Village President was notified of this the night before recyclables were scheduled to be picked up. She decided to round up some volunteers who would handle the collection themselves.

Currently, recyclables are collected the second and fourth Saturdays of each month in Wilton. Lori Brueggen, a Village Board member, handles the scheduling of volunteer recycling crews. Volunteers are drawn from a list of 40 to 50 regular participants; each crew consists of four or five volunteers. Lori Brueggen acts as the crew leader, coordinating the pick-up and sorting of recyclables. One person drives, and two others fan out to pick up recyclables from the curbside. Two people remain on the back of the truck, sorting materials into bins on the trailer. Materials are set out in separate grocery bags and are then emptied directly into the appropriate bin on the back of the trailer. Materials are not always completely separate, so some sorting is required.

In the future, the Village President hopes to organize the list of regular volunteers into crews of 5 or 6 people, each with its own leader. Each crew would be assigned to staff the curbside program once every 3 months. This would save Lori Brueggen the effort of finding volunteers every other week. Finding volunteers is generally no problem, however, because the biweekly recycling endeavor is known to be lighthearted and enjoyable, and the President need only go to the Village restaurant to recruit extra labor. The recycling program has greatly raised awareness in the community about solid waste issues and the need for source reduction and recycling.

Curbside Collection

Start-up Date: July 1, 1988

Private/Public: Public

Materials Collected: Glass, plastic containers of all kinds (including milk jugs, beverage containers, shampoo and detergent bottles), film plastic (bread wrappers, saran wrap, shopping bags, and milk bags), tin, aluminum, corrugated cardboard, newspaper, magazines, leaves, grass clippings, brush, and other wood waste

Pick-up Frequency: Weekly for yard waste, biweekly for all other materials

Pick-up Same Day as Refuse: No

Material Set-out Method: Items must be separated at the curb and placed in cardboard boxes, sacks, or some other reusable container. Each color of glass is put in its own grocery bag; aluminum in another, ferrous cans in yet another. Plastic bottles with handles are strung together with string; other plastic containers and film plastic are put in their own bag. Newspapers and magazines are bundled. Grass clippings and leaves are bagged, and brush and wood waste are bundled.

Mandatory: Separation of recyclables is voluntary; separation of yard waste is mandatory.

Service Provider: Volunteer haulers and sorters collect recyclables. The Village pays for fuel for the truck. A paid Village employee picks up yard waste and spreads it on the Village farm.

Collection Vehicles: A dump truck owned by the Village pulls a trailer with bins on it for recyclables. The dump truck alone is used to haul yard waste.

Households Served: Approximately 200

Participation Rate:	50 to 60 percent (roughly estimated by the Village President, who is generally on the truck helping to collect recyclables)
Businesses Served:	The Village collects corrugated cardboard from five businesses.
Economic Incentives:	None
Enforcement:	None

Commercial Materials Recovery Activities

The local co-op recycles corrugated cardboard, as do all business facilities. The three taverns sell their aluminum and glass to outside recyclers independently of the Village. Tonnage figures for this aluminum and glass recycling are not available.

Materials Processing

The volunteers separate materials into large barrels on the trailer during recyclable collection. The barrels are then stored in a small donated building until the private hauler can take them to be marketed.

Composting Activities

It is illegal for residents to set out yard waste for disposal. The Village refuse hauler does not pick up yard waste, even when it is set out with regular refuse. A paid Village worker, driving the Village dump truck, picks up leaves, grass clippings, brush, and other wood waste at the curbside once per week, year-round. (During this weekly route, the Village worker will also pick up miscellaneous other items such as appliances or old furniture.) If set out, leaves and grass clippings must be bagged; brush and wood waste must be bundled. Although leaves and grass clippings are targeted for collection, brush and garden waste (such as corn stalks or flower trimmings) comprise most of the yard waste collected. Residents tend to leave grass clippings on their lawns rather than raking and bagging them. In addition, residents tend to rake the leaves from trees in their yards and along the streets, and burn them in burn barrels that they keep in their backyards. The Village's current system of collection would be unable to handle the quantity generated if this were not the case.

The Village worker takes all yard waste collected to a farm owned by the Village and spreads it out there. This farm became the property of the Village when its owner defaulted on his taxes in the 1920s or '30s. Some of the land is rented out for grazing to local farmers; the rest contains cornfields and ponds. The Village is planning to begin formal composting of its yard waste in the summer of 1990 when the new compost site behind the new drop-off center opens. Very few people do their own backyard composting.

Amount and Breakdown of Materials Recovered

Material	Commercial (Tons, 1989)	Residential (Tons, 1989)	Total (Tons, 1989)
Newspaper & Magazines	0	10	10
Corrugated Cardboard	10	10	20
Glass	0	20	20
PET Plastic	0	10	10
HDPE Plastic*	0	5	5
Aluminum	0	NA	NA
Ferrous Metals	0	15	15
Subtotal Recycled	**10**	**70**	**80**
Yard Waste	0	10	10
Subtotal Composted	**0**	**10**	**10**
Total Recovered	**10**	**80**	**90**

*Film plastics are included with HDPE plastic.

Publicity and Education

The Village has sent several letters to residents encouraging recycling and including a recycling guide. Reminders are occasionally published in the local shopping guide.

Also, the Village requires the local schools to teach kindergarten through 8th grade students about recycling. Students will take a field trip to the landfill, located 8 to 10 miles from the Village and surrounded by farmland. The Village President hopes that children will thus learn to value recycling and source reduction, and will influence their parents to do the same.

Economics

Costs Cover: 90 tons recovered through Village-sponsored recycling and composting activities.

Capital Costs: Collection

Item	Cost	Use	Year Incurred
Village Dump Truck	NA*	Recycling/Composting	1970
Trailer and Frame Rack	$300	Recycling	1989

*There are no records surviving of the cost of the truck. This cost was completely depreciated long before the recycling program began.

Capital Costs: Processing

Item	Cost	Use	Year Incurred
Storage Building	Donated	Recycling	1988
Storage Barrels	Donated	Recycling	1988

Operating and Maintenance Costs (1989)

	Recycling	Composting	Total
Collection	$ 200	$ 380	$ 380
Processing	$ 0	$ 0	$ 0
Administration	$ 0	$ 0	$ 0
Education/Publicity	$ 0	$ 0	$ 0
Total	**$ 200**	**$ 380**	**$ 580**

The $200 in recycling collection covers the cost of gasoline and oil for the Village dump truck.

The $380 in composting costs is incurred as follows: $120 per year for truck fuel ($10 per month; 12 months in the year) plus $260 for the wages of the Village worker who handles compost collection ($5 per hour multiplied by an average of 1 hour per week).

Materials Revenues: None — materials are not sold. A recycler hauls the materials for no charge.

Source of Funding: County grant for $1,500 and local budget

Full-time Employees: None

Part-time Employees: An estimated 40 to 50 volunteers staff the recycling program at various times throughout the year. One Village employee spends about one hour per week collecting yard waste and spreading it on the Village farm.

Contact

Nalani Bever
Village President
Village of Wilton
P.O. Box 70
Wilton, Wisconsin 54670
Phone (608) 435-6666
Fax (608) 372-5492

SEATTLE, WASHINGTON

Demographics

Jurisdiction:	City of Seattle
Population:	497,000 (1989 estimate)
Total Households:	250,913 (1989 estimate)
Total Businesses:	30,000 (estimated by the Citizens Service Bureau)
Area:	92 square miles

Solid Waste Generation and Collection

(Annual Tonnages for 1989)

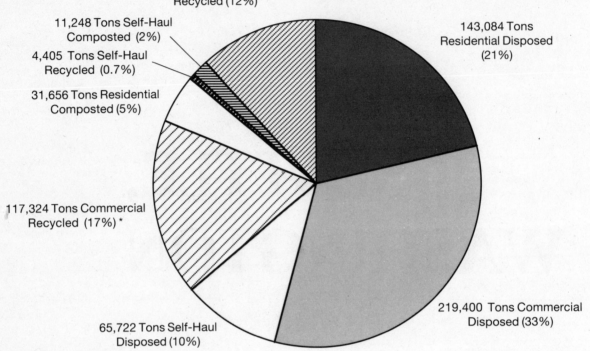

79,185 Tons Residential Recycled (12%)

11,248 Tons Self-Haul Composted (2%)

4,405 Tons Self-Haul Recycled (0.7%)

31,656 Tons Residential Composted (5%)

117,324 Tons Commercial Recycled (17%) *

65,722 Tons Self-Haul Disposed (10%)

143,084 Tons Residential Disposed (21%)

219,400 Tons Commercial Disposed (33%)

*Based on 1988 data, the most recent available.

Total Waste Generated:	672,024 tons estimated in 1989 (excluding most bulky waste such as construction debris and tires, but including appliances and small amounts of demolition debris)
Residential Waste Generated:	253,925 tons in 1989 (excludes residential waste self-hauled)[1]
Commercial Waste Generated:	336,724 tons in 1988 (most recent data available; excludes commercial waste self-hauled)
Bulky Waste Generated:	Not available (private haulers haul to a private landfill and the amount is not tracked)
% By Weight of Total Waste Recovered:	36 percent estimated in 1989 (30 percent recycling, 6 percent composting)
% By Weight of Residential Waste Recovered:	44 percent in 1989 (31.2 percent recycling, 12.4 percent composting)
% By Weight of Commercial Waste Recovered:	35 percent in 1988 (35 percent recycling, no composting)

---

[1]Per capita residential waste generation figure is based on estimate by the City that half of self-hauled waste is residential.

Landfill Tipping Fee:

$31.50 per ton in 1989
$31.50 per ton in 1987
$11.00 per ton in 1986

Transfer Station Tipping Fee:

$62 per ton for commercial waste in 1989

Collection of Refuse:

Seattle's residential waste is collected by private contractors, brought to either of two City-owned transfer stations, and then long-hauled by truck to King County's Cedar Hills Landfill. Commercial waste is collected by two private haulers who have franchises enabling them to collect refuse in Seattle. The haulers transport commercial waste to two privately owned transfer stations in the City.

The City has had a variable can rate, as opposed to a flat monthly garbage rate, since 1980. It offers four different sized containers: a 19-gallon "mini-can" at $10.70 per month; a 32-gallon can at $13.75 a month; a 60-gallon can at $22.75 per month; and the largest container, a 90-gallon can, at $31.75 per month.

An analysis, *Volume-Based Rates in Solid Waste: Seattle's Experience*, showed that more garbage would have been generated and disposed if the City had not imposed a variable rate structure. In 1986 and 1987, the City increased rates. This led to significantly more customers subscribing to fewer cans. The new curbside recycling, which became available early in 1988, further influenced the downward shift in subscriptions. In fact, the weighted average number of cans subscribed by single-family customers decreased from 3.5 to 1.4 per customer between 1981 and 1988.

Future Solid Waste Management Plans:

Seattle has chosen a non-incineration future until at least 1998, and has set the goal of recovering 60 percent of its total waste by that time. In 1998 progress towards the 60 percent goal will be evaluated. The City Council decided in October 1988 to terminate its disposal contract with the King County Cedar Hills Landfill and contract for disposal at a landfill east of the Cascade Mountains by 1993. It took this step because it believes landfills in that arid, sparsely populated region present fewer environmental hazards than landfills in the Puget Sound region.

The City may study collection of commercial food waste for composting at an in-vessel compost facility in 1991. If an economically feasible collection system can be devised, the City will also collect residential food waste.

The City may consider additional mandatory legislation on recycling if the 60 percent goal is not met by 1998. In the future, the City may also combine collection of residential refuse, commercial refuse, and recyclables. This will enable the City to set all rates in a way that most encourages waste reduction and recycling. It will also increase the recycling program's base of funding, which is derived from garbage rate revenues (the revenue that the City receives for providing refuse collection service).

In addition, Seattle plans to lobby for Federal and State legislation aimed at reducing the amount or toxicity of waste being generated.

If neither Federal nor State waste reduction legislation is passed by July 1993, the City will consider adopting waste reduction legislation itself. The City will also work with local retailers to promote the use of products that are durable, reusable, recyclable, or made of recycled materials.

Further, the City will work aggressively to achieve stable markets for recycled materials.

The City's plans are best summarized in its August 1989 report, On *The Road to Recovery: Seattle's Integrated Solid Waste Management Plan:*

> With this Plan, the City of Seattle sets itself firmly on the road towards a future quite different than the present. The Plan envisions the future as it could be 20 years from now if the solid waste management policies described here are successfully implemented.

> The scene is Seattle in the year 2010. People are throwing away much less than they did in 1989. They are buying more durable products rather than disposable products. They are buying products with little or no packaging. Most people now choose the half-can garbage collection option and many weeks don't set out a can at all.

> Recycling has become a way of life in Seattle. Most homes have only one waste can, but every room has a recycle can. Many homes have a compost bin in the back yard. Every home has a special container for food waste. At work, in school, in shopping malls and on street corners, people casually toss their pop cans, bottles, newspapers and paper into recycling containers and their scraps of food into compost buckets.

> To make waste reduction and recycling easier, dozens of products, invented by enterprising small businesses, are now manufactured and distributed widely. Recycling is a flourishing business, with many firms competing to collect a wide variety of recyclable materials. Recyclables are collected at least once a week from nearly every home, office and industry in the City.

> Processing of recyclables has become a major industry in Seattle, employing hundreds of people. The brightest, most creative young men and women often choose careers in developing new recycling technology and designing new products from recycled materials, using minimal, easily recyclable packaging. Recycled products and secondary materials are among the Port's fastest growing exports.

These days, so much material is recycled, or never thrown away in the first place, that relatively little is left over that can be called "waste." That remaining nonrecycled waste is shipped by train to a landfill in Eastern Washington or Oregon where it is buried safely. For 20 years, Seattle's old landfill sites have been carefully monitored. The engineered closures were so successful that there is no evidence of air or water pollution from the landfills.

After 20 years of steadily learning how to reduce and recover more and more of their waste, citizens of Seattle are proud of what they have accomplished. Their City has led the way with programs and policies that many other cities in the U.S. and overseas have since copied.

Materials Recovery

The City began developing recycling plans in 1985, after plans to build a mass burn incinerator were derailed by citizen protest. In September of 1986, after the closure of two City-operated landfills, Seattle had to renegotiate its disposal options. The City decided to transport its waste to a county-operated landfill, where the disposal fees were $31.50 per ton (as compared to $11 per ton at the City-operated landfills). In 1987, the City renewed the incinerator option. Continued citizen objections to the new incinerator plan prompted additional recycling and waste reduction research by the City Solid Waste Utility. This research yielded an analysis of existing recovery activities and potential additional recovery strategies that the City could implement.

The report *Waste Reduction, Recycling and Disposal Alternatives* reviewed several recovery scenarios. The sixth scenario, on which the Mayor's recommendations were based, indicated that the City could recover 64 percent of its waste stream by the year 2000. This scenario was adapted to form scenario "8b," which has been adopted as the official plan to recover 60 percent by 1998. This goal is based on the following recovery strategies: with existing private recycling activities the City recovers 24 percent of its waste stream. Waste reduction would bring the recovery rate to 26 percent. The new city-wide residential curbside collection program will increase the recovery rate to 34 percent. By adding yard waste collection, the City could recover a total of 43 percent. Processing the remaining waste would lead to a 48 percent recovery rate. Finally, by pursuing commercial recycling activities the City could recover 60 percent of its total waste stream. This scenario helped convince the City Council to abandon plans for incineration and adopt a recycling/landfilling waste management strategy.

In February of 1988, Seattle began a city-wide residential recycling program. The collection services are offered to approximately 146,950 single- through four-unit residences, and involve two different approaches provided by two different collection contractors. In the north section of the City, residents (65,000 eligible households) receive three stackable

containers for recyclable materials, which are collected weekly.   In the
south section of the City, participants (82,000 eligible households) are
provided with 90-gallon containers, and the collection service is maintained monthly.   In 1989, the amount of recyclables collected per participating household was 18 percent greater in the north section than in the
south section.

Recycle America, a subsidiary of Waste Management, Inc., provides
collection services in the north section of the City.   Recycle Seattle, a
subsidiary of Rabanco, Inc.   (a locally owned waste management company), collects materials in the south section of the City.

, The City of Seattle is very interested in how the two different
methods of service perform, but believes that it is too early to draw any
conclusions.   The south end of the City is different demographically from
the north end.   The City has done a study, which is not yet published,
to determine the different demographics.   In general, the north section of
the City is a higher-income area than the south section.   The north
section is considered the university area.

The City Solid Waste Utility also provides recycling drop-off containers
at its two transfer stations.   Large appliances, scrap metal, mattresses,
and motor oil are accepted, as well as tin, glass, aluminum, newspapers,
mixed paper, plastic bottles, car batteries, and corrugated cardboard.
Approximately 4,405 tons of materials (excluding yard waste) were collected through these drop-off centers in 1989.

A pilot collection program for mixed plastic servicing 4,500 households
began in November 1988.   As a result of this pilot program, the City in
1989 implemented curbside collection of PET plastic containers only,
although PET, LDPE, and HDPE plastic containers are accepted at eight
City drop-off centers.   A ban on the use of polystyrene and plastic
beverage containers at all City facilities went into effect in 1988.

Before the establishment of the recycling goals, the City relied on a
network of independently owned, for-profit and non-profit recycling centers
that purchased, accepted, or collected household and commercial recyclable materials.[2] In 1985, this network alone recovered a remarkable 22
percent of the City's waste.   This level of recycling is attributed to the
City's variable can rate, which has been in effect since 1981.

It has been estimated that 25 percent of Seattle's waste stream is
currently recycled through these efforts.   There are hundreds of private
drop boxes throughout the City for newspaper collection, as well as multi-
material drop-off sites for glass, aluminum, and newspaper and buy-back
centers for some materials, including high-grade paper.   They are located
throughout the City and vary in complexity of operation and in the
materials they process.   Buy-back facilities pay customers for some of the
materials; drop-offs do not.   Numerous drop boxes sponsored by schools,

---

[2]One of two private recyclers that formerly operated small curbside collection
routes was bought out by the two main contractors that now operate the residential
curbside program.

churches, scout troops, clubs, and other charities are located throughout the City to collect newspapers and/or aluminum only.   Many are in grocery store parking lots for easy access to residents.

The City Solid Waste Utility has set up a mitigation committee to analyze the effect of the new program on the independently owned, for-profit and non-profit recycling centers.   Thus far, they have found that the recyclers operating drop-off centers and buy-back centers in the City may have seen their recovery rates go down, but the recyclers operating outside the City limits have experienced an increase in material.   A study quantifying these results has not been completed, but one possible reason for the increase in materials collected outside of town is the increased education and advertising for recycling and waste reduction.

In 1988, a full-time coordinator was hired to develop and implement an apartment recycling program.   The coordinator has been responsible for informing apartment owners, managers, and dwellers how to recycle; promoting the availability of the program throughout the City; and coordinating with the City, recyclers, and apartment building owners, managers, and tenants.

The City initiated an apartment recycling program in the fall of 1989 in order to offer recycling services to the remaining households that were formerly ineligible.   The Seattle Solid Waste Utility initially planned to supply haulers with an economic incentive for providing recycling to multi-family housing with five or more units.   The haulers that provided refuse collection services to multi-dwelling housing units were to receive a diversion credit of $30 to $40 per ton for recyclable materials collected.   Only one small hauler signed up for this program, however.   The City then approached the current curbside recycling contractors about adding apartments to their routes; it also opened negotiations with two other private contractors.   A satisfactory price could not be negotiated, so the City is currently preparing an RFP asking only for proposals that do not exceed $75 per ton, the approximate avoided cost.   The City expects to receive proposals in late 1990 and to begin implementation in late 1991. The small hauler that signed up for the diversion credit program has been allowed to utilize it.   In 1989, this hauler reported 305 tons recycled; it has increased this amount to 75 tons per month in 1990.

Seattle has had a recycling program in City offices for 10 years.   The City has contracted with Seadrunar Recycling, a non-profit organization committed to drug rehabilitation of juveniles and adults, for weekly pick-up of paper and cardboard at City offices.   Employees typically keep a recycling box at their work stations.   Periodically, they empty the boxes into centralized collection stations, usually blue 55-gallon drums.   On pick-up day, the recycling operator empties the barrels and takes the paper for baling and marketing.

As part of the office-paper recycling program, the City procures envelopes, letterhead, and copier paper made from recycled paper fiber. On August 11, 1987, the Mayor directed all Departments of the City to print letterhead on 100 percent recycled paper.

In 1989, the City signed new contracts for a multi-material recycling collection program of office paper, newspaper, aluminum, glass, and cardboard. Collection services were expanded to include smaller City facilities not previously served. The new program includes employee education, promotion, and additional sign-ups.

The City also encourages departments to reduce and recycle through interdepartmental recycling grants. In 1989 the Solid Waste Utility provided grants totalling $77,500 for the following projects: outdoor recycling containers, cardboard baler, and yard waste chipper for Seattle Center; a compost site for the Parks Department; and an intern to coordinate City office recycling for Administrative Services.

Through its Environmental Allowance Program, the Utility has funded many projects to test innovative recycling techniques, including:

- mixed waste paper collection from small businesses and apartment buildings ($99,000, Paper Fibres);

- a pilot plastics recycling program with drop-off sites and collection offered to 4,500 households in conjunction with the existing curbside collection program ($86,000, O'Neil & Company and First Line Plastics);

- a program to test methods for the recycling, reuse, and safe disposal of latex paint ($21,000, Morley and Associates);

- Cash for Trash, a monthly garbage lottery that paid participants for having recyclable-free garbage ($30,000, Metrocenter YMCA);

- waste reduction/recycling brochure for distribution to commercial and industrial sectors ($25,000, Greater Seattle Chamber of Commerce); and

- purchase of a shredder-chipper for loan to neighborhood residents for backyard composting ($2,000, Duwamish Peninsula Community Commission).

The City of Seattle was awarded the *Best Overall Program in a Large City* award in the Institute for Local Self-Reliance's *Record Setting Recycling Contest 1989*. The City received similar awards from the National Recycling Coalition and the Washington State Department of Ecology.

Curbside Collection

Start-up Date: February 1988 for the north section, April 1988 for the south

Private/Public: Private haulers under municipal contract

Materials Collected: Newspaper, mixed wastepaper (magazines, junk mail, coupons, flyers, wrapping paper, used envelopes, cereal boxes, cancelled checks, old bills, old papers, phone books, paper tubes, paper egg cartons, and brochures), glass, aluminum, tin, PET plastic containers, corrugated cardboard, leaves, grass clippings, brush, and other wood waste

Pick-up Frequency: Recyclables are picked up weekly in the north section of the City and monthly in the south section. Leaves, grass clippings, brush, and other wood waste are collected weekly, year-round, on the same day as refuse in the northern two-thirds of the City. These same yard waste materials are collected monthly November through February, and biweekly during the remainder of the year, in the southern third of the City.

Pick-up Same Day as Refuse: Different day for recyclables, same day for yard waste

Material Set-out Method: Recyclable materials in both the north and the south sections are collected in containers provided to households. In the north section of the City residents are furnished with three stacking containers (about 12 gallons each). One holds glass containers, aluminum, PET plastic containers, and tin cans. Another holds mixed scrap paper. The third holds newspaper. Corrugated cardboard is set out next to the containers. In the south section, a 90-gallon or 60-gallon container holds commingled materials (glass containers, aluminum and tin cans, newspapers, and mixed paper). Yard waste can be bagged, bundled, or put in cans.

Mandatory: Separation of recyclables is voluntary. Separation of yard waste is mandatory.

Service Provider: In the north section, Recycle America collects recyclables and Recycle Seattle collects yard waste. In the south section, Recycle Seattle collects recyclables and U.S. Disposal collects yard waste.

Collection Vehicles: A compartmentalized recycling truck is used for collection of recyclables in the north section of the City. Rear-loading trucks are used in the south section. In both, a one-person crew operates the recycling trucks. Yard waste is collected in rear-loading packer trucks in both sections of the City.

Households Served: 147,000 households are eligible for curbside collection service (65,000 in the north section, and 82,000 in the south section); 77.2 percent of these have signed up.

Participation Rate: 77.2 percent (89.8 percent in the north section, and 67.3 percent in the south section). Participation rate is defined as sign-up rate — the ratio of the number of households registered for the program to the number of households eligible.

Businesses Served: No businesses are served under the municipal contract, but all
                            have the opportunity to have their recyclables picked up by
                            private haulers.

Economic Incentives: The variable can rate is a direct incentive for residents to generate
                            as little waste as possible and to recycle as much as possible.

Enforcement: None for the voluntary recycling program. It is illegal to discard
                            yard waste with refuse. The private haulers will not pick up
                            refuse that contains yard waste. (In such cases, they leave a
                            note explaining why the refuse was not collected.) The program
                            seems to be successful. A recent waste stream composition study
                            indicated that only 1 percent of the waste stream disposed con-
                            sists of yard waste.

Commercial Materials Recovery Activities

A number of private recyclers provide collection services to businesses and paper drives for schools and charities. The City does not
regulate or fund these services. The private firms provide pick-up of
corrugated cardboard, office paper, computer paper, aluminum, ferrous
cans, plastic containers, and glass from any business that requests it.

The commercial and industrial sector of Seattle is serviced by four
collection companies that hold certificates from the Washington Utility
Transportation Commission (WUTC), which regulates rates. Commercial
haulers asked for and received a special recycling rate. Seattle Disposal
(a Rabanco company) and Bayside Disposal (a Waste Management company) both collect mixed waste and demolition debris as well as recyclable materials. These two companies compete for customers through
service, but have identical territories and rates. They both provide
regular route service and drop-box service for on-call customers. Both
provide reduced rates for collection of source-separated materials —
typically a 45 percent price reduction. One reason they may do this may
be because the City currently excludes collection of commercial recyclables
from the City Business and Occupation tax that the companies must pay
on garbage collection revenues.

The City plans to encourage commercial waste recovery by ensuring
that recycling service is as readily available to businesses as regular
refuse service. The City plans to work with the WUTC in order to
establish a rate structure that supports the City's waste reduction and
recycling goals. The WUTC currently monitors tonnage recycled in the
commercial sector. The City requires ready access to this information.

Materials Processing

Recyclable materials collected through the City's residential curbside collection program and private commercial garbage collection services are processed in three private facilities: the Rabanco Recycling Center, the Recycle America Processing Center, and the Eastmont Development Transfer Station.

The Rabanco Recycling Center was built and began operating in 1988. It is a 80,000-square-foot processing facility on 5 acres. The plant is designed to process 500 to 700 tons per day of recyclables from a variety of waste streams including clean paper, cardboard, newspaper, and plastic loads, paper-rich loads of commercial waste collected from selected commercial garbage routes, and commingled recyclables from Recycle Seattle's residential curbside collection program in the south end of the City and certain commercial accounts. It uses a combination of conveyors, trommel, disc screens, magnetic separation, air classification, hand picking, and baling to recover and process the recyclable materials. About 0.51 percent by weight of the materials collected at curbside are reported rejected as contaminants. The overall rejection rate may be as high as 3.5 percent.

The Recycle America Processing Center was opened by Waste Management in 1988 to process recyclables collected by Recycle America from the north end of Seattle. The 43,000-square-foot facility processes newspaper, cardboard, mixed paper, tin, glass, and aluminum. Since recyclables are partially separated by the generators and collected in compartmentalized trucks, the facility is primarily used for baling, with a maximum capacity of 400 tons per day. Glass, tin, and aluminum are sorted on a pick line through a combination of magnets and hand sorting. The facility is also designed to process commercial loads rich in cardboard and paper. About 0.3 percent by weight of the materials collected at curbside are reported rejected as contaminants.

The Eastmont Development Transfer Station is owned and operated by Waste Management. Commercial waste collected by Bayside Disposal is dumped at Eastmont Development Transfer Station. The facility uses a conveyor belt to spread out dry commercial loads and allow hand picking of cardboard and aluminum.

Composting Activities

The City of Seattle has undertaken numerous demonstration projects and experiments with composting since 1980. Pilot projects have provided data and experience that helped the City in planning its comprehensive composting program, which began in 1989. Initial composting projects included composting demonstration sites at 12 Pea Patch gardens, the community composting education program, the Zoo Doo program, Christmas tree chipping, and a 3-month pilot "Clean Green" program in 1987 at the City's two transfer stations.

The two transfer stations accept clean yard waste (grass clippings, leaves and brush, trees and branches up to 12 inches in diameter) through the "Clean Green" program at a discounted fee to customers. The City began this program on a 3-month pilot basis in 1987. In 1988 it expanded service to City residents and businesses during designated daily hours. In 1989, 11,248 tons were collected at the drop-off sites and transferred to a private composting facility, Cedar Grove, for processing. Transportation averages $15 per ton, while processing costs average $22.50.

The City sponsors four composting demonstration sites throughout Seattle. Three of the sites are in flourishing urban gardens, and one is next to an urban market. The City also funds a backyard composting education program run by Seattle Tilth, a local organization of urban gardeners. This program trains volunteers to be proficient at composting. Then the volunteers, called master composters, perform 40 hours of outreach to neighborhood and business groups, schools, and street fairs. They also give presentations and tours at the City's compost demonstration sites. In 1988, with a program budget of $27,500, master composters responded to over 2,000 calls on the compost hotline and made over 20,000 contacts with citizens.

In 1986, the City began a program of collecting compost pen waste and pen straw from the Woodland Park Zoo, in cooperation with the Parks Department. This material is composted and sold to the public under the name of "Zoo Doo." The Parks Department budgets and manages the program, which generates enough revenue to cover its own costs, as well as avoiding disposal costs for pen wastes.

In October 1988, Seattle passed an ordinance mandating separation of yard waste. To handle this yard waste, the City has a three-pronged strategy of backyard composting, curbside yard waste collection, and expansion of the transfer station "Clean Green" collection program.

The Utility has budgeted $530,000 for the first year of the backyard composting program, with 75 percent of the cost expected to be covered by a Department of Ecology grant. The City will hire a consultant to coordinate the program, which will employ the equivalent of six full-time trainers to reach 6,000 residents. Each participant will receive in-home instruction on composting techniques and a free composting bin or $25 equivalent.

On January 1, 1989, as part of the new garbage collection contracts, the City began curbside collection of yard waste from all City residences. For a fee of $2 per month, haulers contracting with the City will collect as many as 20 cans, bags, or bundles of grass clippings, leaves, brush, and trees and branches up to 4 inches in diameter. Haulers collect yard waste on the same day as refuse, but at a different time of day. Different drivers collect the yard waste, using rear-loading packer trucks. They haul it to the County-owned Cedar Groves Compost Facility, where it is shredded in a tub grinder and then composted in windrows. The facility is designed to process 30,000 tons annually, but could accommodate more with additional equipment. By the fifth month of this program, the monthly tonnage goal for 1998 had already been exceeded. The program has continued to be very successful. The private haulers provide collection weekly, year-round in the north section of the City. Collection is biweekly, March through October, and monthly for the rest of the year in the south section of the City. In 1989, 31,656 tons of yard waste were collected at curbside.

The Cedar Grove facility charges a tipping fee for yard waste hauled by the City from the transfer stations. This yard waste includes both self-haul and yard waste from the north end of the City. The amount is $5.47 per ton for the first 24,000 tons and $18 per ton for any tonnage above that. Seattle pays the hauler in the north portion of the City $56.36 for collecting the yard waste and delivering it to the City-owned transfer station. The City pays the private hauler in the south end $80 per ton for collection, hauling, and tipping fees for the remainder of the yard waste.

The City has expanded its "Clean Green" program to all open hours at the City-owned transfer stations. Customers pay a reduced fee to dump yard waste at the transfer stations. The yard waste is dumped into two direct-dump trailers placed in slots below floor level. Transfer station employees direct yard waste customers to the "Clean Green" area, assist in unloading, and watch to ensure that no contaminants are dumped with the yard waste.

Source Reduction Activities

The City Utility funds research and development for waste reduction and recycling techniques through its Environmental Allowance Program (EAP), which includes the production and distribution of slide shows, education on proper and non-hazardous disposal of diapers, and waste audits. EAP has also funded the pilot program for curbside collection of mixed plastics, an apartment building pilot recycling project, a small business recycling pilot program, and a paint recycling project.

The Solid Waste Utility co-sponsors several household hazardous waste collections during the year, and operates a full-time household hazardous waste drop-off site, which opened in November 1988, at one of the transfer stations.

Amount and Breakdown of Materials Recovered

Material	Total (Tons, 1987)
Mixed Paper	50,727
Corrugated Cardboard	52,304
Glass	14,473
Ferrous Metal	5,844
Aluminum	1,950
Motor Oil	11,985
Total Recovered	**137,283**

Materials listed in the following chart were collected as follows: 40,732 tons of residential recyclables through the curbside recycling program; 31,656 tons of residential yard waste through the curbside yard waste collection; 38,453 tons of recyclables through various private drop-off centers (1988); 4,405 tons of recyclables through City-owned drop-off centers; 11,248 tons of yard waste through City-owned drop-off centers; and 117,324 tons of recyclables through private commercial recycling activities (1988). Tonnages collected privately from businesses and drop-off sites are not yet available for 1989.

Material	Commercial (Tons, 1988)	Residential (Tons, 1989)	Self-Haul (Tons, 1989)	Total (Tons, 1989)
Newspaper	4,900	41,597	73	46,570
Corrugated Cardboard	51,345	0	227	51,572
Other Paper	48,400	20,477 *	166	69,043
Glass	2,595	13,450	66	16,111
PET Plastic	7	93	122 †	222
HDPE Plastic	97	20	0	117
LDPE Plastic	97	0	0	97
Other Plastic	92	0	0	92
Aluminum	101	1,675	3,581 §	5,357 §
Ferrous Metals	0	1,689	—	1,689
Motor Oil	9,600	0	136	9,736
Appliances	90	184	0	274
Mattresses	0	0	34	34
Subtotal Recycled	**117,324**	**79,185**	**4,405**	**200,914**
Yard Waste	0	31,656	11,248	42,904
Subtotal Composted	**0**	**31,656**	**11,248**	**42,904**
Total Recovered	**117,324**	**110,841**	**15,653**	**243,818**

*Includes corrugated cardboard, high-grade paper, and mixed paper
†Includes PET, HDPE, and other plastic
§ Includes Ferrous metals

The following table gives a breakdown of the recyclable materials collected at curbside from the north and south sections of the City.

Material	North Section (Tons, 1989)	South Section (Tons, 1989)
Newspaper	7,524.8	7,590.8
Mixed Paper	9,118.7	6,030.9
Glass	5,296.5	3,374.9
Aluminum	320.1	113.1
Tin	678	601.9
PET	13.3	75.6

Publicity and Education

The implementation of such a comprehensive program has required an aggressive promotional campaign. Two mailings were sent out city-wide when the new residential recycling program first began. Customers were asked to sign up in order to receive recycling services and were then provided with recycling containers. The City, which manages the promotion of the program, has made a constant effort to advertise. Booths are staffed at street fairs and festivals, and signs are placed on city buses. The City Utility regularly produces media events.

The Utility continually places articles in the newspapers, has an automated phone service with over 100 recorded messages regarding recycling, and circulates an information packet on recycling. The packet stresses selective shopping to avoid plastics and disposable materials, composting of yard waste and food waste, and the donation and resale of household items. The City occasionally inserts selective shopping tips in garbage bills. The two contractors work in conjunction with the Utility in its effort to promote the curbside recycling program.

The City Utility conducted a massive media campaign when it implemented garbage rate structures that entitle residents who generate the least amount of trash to pay the lowest garbage rate.

The City will conduct a $105,000 pilot education and recycling program for ten elementary schools in 1989-90. The Utility will offer technical assistance and financial support, including cash awards to selected schools to recycle and compost materials generated at the school. It will also retain a consultant who will provide schools with posters and classroom educational materials and assistance.

The Utility's promotion budget for 1989 for the curbside recycling and yard waste collection programs was $213,900.

Economics

Costs Cover:

The City's 1989 contract for curbside recycling collection services, and transfer station tons recovered — 88,041 tons in 1989 (40,732 tons recycled and 31,656 tons composted through curbside collection, plus 4,405 tons recycled and 11,248 tons composted through transfer station self-haul). Capital costs are incurred by private companies under contract with the City.

Operating and Maintenance Costs (1989)

	Recycling	Composting	Total
Collection & Processing For Curbside Recycling	$ 2,098,820 *	$ 2,637,531 *	$ 4,736,351
Transfer Station Processing	$ 30,835 †	$ 202,477	$ 233,312
Administration			
Education/Publicity	$ 82,900	$ 131,000	$ 213,900
Total	**$ 2,212,555**	**$ 2,971,008**	**$ 5,183,563**

*Collection costs given above represent contract fees with private haulers and include both collection and processing costs.
†Based on 4,405 tons of recyclables multiplied by $7.00 per ton.

The City pays Recycle America, which handles collection services in the north section of the City, $48.15 per ton with a minimum payment of $2.8 million over a 5-year contract. Recycle America absorbs total market risk. Recycle Seattle is paid $47.75 per ton; its contract includes an agreement with the City to share market risks.

Materials Revenues:

$50,000 in 1989 from the sale of transfer station recyclables. Other revenues are retained by the private haulers.

Source of Funding:

Seattle's residential solid waste is managed through the City Solid Waste Utility and financed through an enterprise fund. Garbage rates are the source of revenue for the recycling program.

Full-time Employees:

11

Contacts

Jennifer Bagby
Solid Waste Utility
710 Second Avenue #505
Seattle, WA 98104
(206) 684-7640

Steve Spence
General Manager
Rabanco Recycling
P.O. Box 24745
Seattle, WA 98124
(206) 382-1775

Marilyn Skerbeck
Recycling Specialist
Recycle America
7901 1st Avenue South
Seattle, WA 98108
(206) 763-2437

Jim Jenson
Seattle Tilth (Master Composter Program)
4649 Sunnyside Avenue North
Seattle, WA 98103
(206) 633-0224

References

Seattle Solid Waste Utility, *Final Environmental Impact Statement: Waste Reduction, Recycling, and Disposal Alternatives,* Seattle, Washington, July 1988.

Seattle Solid Waste Utility, *On The Road To Recovery: Seattle's Integrated Solid Waste Management Plan,* Seattle, Washington, August 1989.

Skumatz, Lisa, *Volume-Based Rates in Solid Waste: Seattle's Experience,* Seattle Solid Waste Utility, Seattle, Washington, February 1989.

CHERRY HILL, NEW JERSEY

Demographics

Jurisdiction: Township of Cherry Hill

Population: 73,723 in 1989 (based on an annual percentage growth of 0.78 between 1985 and 1989)

Total Households: 24,000 (18,810 single-family residences, 3,200 condominiums and townhouse units, and 1,990 high-rise units)

Total Businesses: 1,009

Area: 24 square miles

Other: Cherry Hill is the second largest municipality in Camden County (total County population is half a million) and has experienced the greatest retail and residential development in the County during the past two decades. There are more than 70 industrial businesses and one major industrial park, the Cherry Hill Industrial Center, in the Township. The County as a whole is a commercial, industrial, and residential hub. Located on a large bend of the Delaware River opposite the City of Philadelphia, Camden County is the focal point of southern New Jersey's industry and trade.

Solid Waste Generation and Collection

(Annual Tonnages for 1989)

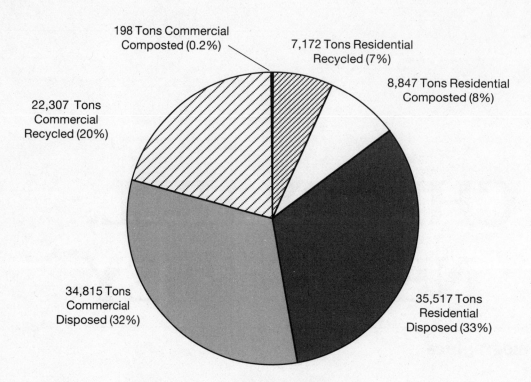

198 Tons Commercial Composted (0.2%)

7,172 Tons Residential Recycled (7%)

8,847 Tons Residential Composted (8%)

22,307 Tons Commercial Recycled (20%)

34,815 Tons Commercial Disposed (32%)

35,517 Tons Residential Disposed (33%)

Total Waste Generated:	108,856 tons in 1989 (including bulky waste recycled, excluding bulky waste disposed)
Residential Waste Generated:	51,536 tons in 1989 (including some commercial waste recovered by private hauler with municipal contract along its residential collection routes, and including residential bulky waste recovered)
Commercial Waste Generated:	57,320 tons in 1989[1] (34,815 tons estimated disposed plus 22,505 tons estimated recovered by private haulers based on 1988 data plus bulky waste recycled [construction debris and tires]; bulky waste disposed is not included in this estimate)
Bulky Waste Generated:	19,740 tons recycled in 1989 (including construction debris, tires, and appliances recycled; excluding tonnage of bulky waste disposed)

---

[1] Commercial waste is largely hauled by private haulers, and tonnages are not available. Tonnage of commercial waste generated has been estimated by using a per capita waste disposal figure of 0.954 tons per year to calculate total residential and commercial waste disposed. (This per capita figure for Cherry Hill was developed by the consulting firm O'Brien-Kreitzberg & Associates, Inc.) Tonnage of residential waste disposed, which is known, is subtracted from this total, leaving commercial waste disposed. Total commercial waste generated is then calculated by adding this estimated 1989 tonnage of commercial waste disposed to the sum of 1988 tonnage of commercial waste recovered by private haulers and 1989 construction debris and tires recovered.

% By Weight of Total Waste Recovered:	35 percent in 1989 (27 percent recycling and 8 percent composting)
% By Weight of Residential Waste Recovered:	31 percent in 1989 (14 percent recycling and 17 percent composting)
% By Weight of Commercial Waste Recovered:	39 percent estimated in 1989 (39 percent recycling and 0.4 percent composting)
Landfill Tipping Fee:	$54.84 per ton at the Pennsauken Landfill
Collection of Refuse:	Cherry Hill contracts out with O'Connor Corporation for refuse collection from residents living in single-family homes and 190 businesses. Residential refuse is disposed at the Pennsauken Landfill in Pennsauken, New Jersey. In 1989, the Township incurred $1,884,000 in contract fees for collection of 35,517 tons of residential refuse (excluding tipping fees).
	Businesses that do not receive municipal service and condominiums must secure their own refuse collection contracts. Private haulers are not required to dispose refuse at the Pennsauken Landfill or to report tonnages disposed to Cherry Hill.
Future Solid Waste Management Plans:	Cherry Hill plans to expand its yard waste collection program in January 1991 to include collection of grass clippings and a pilot program for chipping of brush en route.
	The Township is also looking at ways to collect recyclable materials from its 3,200 condominium and townhouse units.

Materials Recovery

The Department of Public Works has been collecting leaves and brush for composting every fall since 1975.

In November 1984, Camden County amended its Solid Waste Management Plan by incorporating the Camden County Municipal Recycling Plan. The revised plan requires that each municipality institute collection programs for the recycling of newspaper, aluminum cans, and used oil. In addition, the Plan mandates that all whole trees, tree trunks, stumps, leaves, and branches be disposed at facilities approved by the New Jersey Department of Environmental Protection, or mulched for use as a ground cover.

In compliance with the County ordinance, Cherry Hill began a curbside collection program in April 1985. O'Connor Corporation, a subsidiary of Waste Management, Inc., collected newspapers, glass, aluminum cans, and other metal cans. Participation was voluntary. In October 1986, Cherry Hill adopted its own mandatory recycling ordinance. It was at this time that the Township purchased 6-gallon buckets and distributed them to all single-family homes. The local ordinance mandates that residents separate newspaper, glass, aluminum cans, other metal cans, and used motor oil. Glass, aluminum cans, and other metal cans are commingled in the 6-gallon container, while newspapers must be bundled with twine or stored in a kraft paper bag. Motor oil must be brought to a municipally approved station.

The ordinance was revised in March 1987 to include magazines and corrugated cardboard. These materials are bundled with the newspaper. In 1989, the DPW also began collecting appliances from residents on an on-call basis. Recycling of appliances is not mandatory.

O'Connor collects recyclable materials in two white packer trucks. One truck is used for wastepaper, the other for commingled materials. The DPW collects white goods in an old packer truck purchased when the Township still collected its own refuse.

The Township estimates that the recycling program saved $1,800,567 in 1989 tipping fees.

Curbside Collection

Start-up Date:	April 1985 (mandatory as of October 1986)
Private/Public:	Private under municipal contract for collection of residential newspaper, magazines, corrugated cardboard, glass, aluminum and other metal cans. DPW collects white goods, leaves, and brush.
Materials Collected:	Newspaper, corrugated cardboard, magazines, glass, aluminum and other metal cans, appliances, tires, scrap metal, leaves, and brush
Pick-up Frequency:	Weekly collection of wastepaper and commingled items. White goods are collected on an on-call basis. Leaves and brush are collected once a month from November 1 until December 31.
Pick-up Same Day as Refuse:	Yes
Material Set-out Method:	Newspaper, magazines, and corrugated cardboard are bundled together with twine or placed in a kraft paper bag. Glass, aluminum, and ferrous cans are commingled in a 6-gallon bucket provided by the Township. White goods are placed at the curbside, with all doors removed. Leaves are raked loose to the curbside, and brush is cut into pieces smaller than 4 feet in length.
Mandatory:	Yes (except for white goods, tires, and scrap metal)
Service Provider:	O'Connor Corporation, a subsidiary of Waste Management, Inc., and the DPW
Collection Vehicles:	O'Connor uses two privately owned packer trucks: one for commingled and the other for wastepaper. The DPW collects leaves and white goods in its own dump trucks. Brush is collected in pick-up trucks.
Households Served:	18,810 single-family residences

Participation Rate:	92 percent of households served (based on weekly set-out rates)
Businesses Served:	190
Economic Incentives:	Fines
Enforcement:	A series of warning stickers are issued. After two warnings have been issued, residents receive a fine of $50. The second offense carries a $75 fine, and a third offense results in a $100 fine. A resident who still does not comply after the third offense is taken to court. One resident was served a summons in 1989 for non-compliance. The Township also reserves the right not to collect refuse from residents if there are recyclable materials included.

Commercial Materials Recovery Activities

Cherry Hill's October 1987 recycling ordinance mandates that businesses recycle corrugated cardboard and high-grade paper. While 190 businesses located in residential districts are serviced by O'Connor Corporation under the Township's contract, all other businesses are required to contract with private haulers for collection of recyclable materials.   O'Connor Corporation collects corrugated cardboard, high-grade paper, glass, aluminum cans, and other metal cans. No breakdown into commercial and residential tonnages is available from O'Connor.

Businesses that recycle privately are required to submit tonnage reports to the Recycling Coordinator by July 1 of the following year. In 1989, businesses privately recycled food waste, high-grade paper, paperboard, corrugated cardboard, construction debris, wood waste, and tires. Private haulers are not required to dispose of refuse at the Pennsauken Landfill.

When Cherry Hill contracts with private companies to repair the roads, the contract stipulates that the torn asphalt be pulverized and used as a bottom layer on the same street. This process, called Pulverization Stabilization Layover, resulted in 19,413 tons of asphalt being recycled in 1989.

The mid-summer deadline for reporting materials recycled, and the inadequacy of commercial refuse disposal records, have made it impossible for the Township to know at this time the tonnage of materials generated by its commercial sector in 1989. The recovery rate estimated for 1989 assumes tonnage recovered by private haulers is the same as in 1988. According to Ron Hepkin, the Recycling Coordinator, this assumption is a conservative one.

Materials Processing

Haulers are responsible for locating processors for all materials they collect. The contract with O'Connor also stipulates that the hauler absorbs all fees, and receives all revenues, for materials collected. O'Connor delivers commingled glass, and aluminum and other metal cans to the Camden County Recycling Facility (CCRF), an 80 ton-per-day regional processing facility established by the County in order to enable its towns to comply with the county-wide mandatory recycling ordinance. The $700,000 cost of building and equipping the facility was covered by a $200,000 grant from the New Jersey Office of Recycling, $90,000 allocated from the County general funds, and a bond issue of about $400,000. No tipping fees are charged. CCRF was designed and built by Resource Recycling Systems, Inc., which also manages and operates the facility for the County.

The Township pays $90 per ton for the processing of white goods.

Composting Activities

Leaves and brush are collected monthly from November 1 until December 31. Residents must rake their leaves and brush to the curbside. The brush must not be longer than 4 feet. In 1989, Cherry Hill reported collecting 8,847 tons of uncompacted yard waste materials.[2]

The Department of Public Works began collecting leaves and brush for composting from residents in the fall of 1975. Prior to 1987, the Township used all vacuum units, but found this method overly time-consuming. In 1987, the Township revised its collection method by using front-end loaders to load yard waste materials into dump trucks. In 1988, the DPW added snow plows to two of the dump trucks used for collection. Three workers per crew rake leaves to the center of the road while the plow feeds the leaves and brush into a front-end loader, which dumps the leaves into the dump truck. A similar method is used for collecting brush, except that brush is dumped into pick-up trucks. According to Ron Hepkin, this method is the quickest that the DPW has found, allowing it to service 260 miles in 6 weeks.

The DPW has also established several temporary storage sites on undeveloped land or parks throughout Cherry Hill. DPW trucks can maximize their collection time by tipping full loads in the same neighborhood that is being serviced rather than having to unload at the compost facility. The leaves and brush are collected at the end of the season and brought to a public composting facility located at the Department of Public Works. In 1989, there were 12 windrows at the

---

[2]Composted yard waste materials are not weighed, but measured in cubic yards. Cherry Hill estimated the weight of 44,236.5 cubic yards of yard waste by using the State conversion factor of 5 cubic yards of uncompacted leaves per ton.

facility, which are turned with two front-end loaders.   The finished material is donated to private farms to be used as a fertilizer.

Andrew Kapp, the Assistant Superintendent of Public Works, teaches students in the Rutgers University Public Works Certification Program about Cherry Hill's composting activities.

According to Ron Hepkin, Cherry Hill is still looking for ways to improve its composting program.   In 1990, the Township began registering all landscapers and offering them free tipping at the compost site.   By 1991, the Township will collect grass clippings from residents, and will begin a pilot project chipping brush at the curbside to determine if a chipping program would be cost-effective.

Amount and Breakdown of Materials Recovered

Material	Commercial (Tons, 1989)	Residential* (Tons, 1989)	Total (Tons, 1989)
High-grade Paper	722.5	0	722.5
Corrugated Cardboard	1,149.5	†	1,149.5
Other Paper	337.1	4,757.8	5,094.9
Commingled§	0	2,119.2	2,119.2
Ferrous Cans	25	††	25
Truck Tires	38.7	0	38.7
Food Waste	503.4	0	503.4
Motor Oil	117.7	7	124.7
Asphalt	19,413	0	19,413
White Goods	0	288	288
Subtotal Recycled	**22,306.9**	**7,172**	**29,478.9**
Leaves and Brush	0	8,847.3	8,847.3
Wood Chips	198.3	0	198.3
Subtotal Composted	**198.3**	**8,847.3**	**9,045.6**
Total Recovered	**22,505.2**	**16,019.3**	**38,524.5**

*Residential tons include some commercial materials collected on residential routes.
†Included with other paper
§Includes glass, aluminum, and other metal cans
††Included with commingled materials

Publicity and Education

Cherry Hill spent $2,000 publicizing its recycling program in 1989. Each household was sent two pamphlets explaining the recycling program.   In addition, the local newspaper occasionally reports on the successes of the composting and recycling programs.

Economics

Costs Cover: Capital and operating and maintenance costs incurred by Cherry Hill cover (1) curbside collection and processing of 6,884 tons of recyclables, excluding white goods, and (2) collection and composting of 8,847 tons of leaves and brush.

Capital Costs: Collection

Item	Cost	Use	Year Incurred
3 Dump Trucks @ $45,000	$ 135,000	Composting	1985
Pick-up Truck @ 12% composting use	$ 12,000	Composting/DPW	1985
4 Vacuums @ $15,000 @ 12% composting use	$ 60,000	Composting/DPW	1985
5 Dump Trucks @ $45,000 @ 12% composting use	$ 225,000	Composting/DPW	1987
2 Vacuums @ $15,000	$ 30,000	Composting	1988
2 Pick-up Trucks @ $12,000 @ 12% composting use	$ 24,000	Composting/DPW	1988

Capital Costs: Processing

Item	Cost	Use	Year Incurred
Chipper	$ 10,000	Composting	1980
Chipper @ 12% composting use	$ 13,500	Composting/DPW	1984
2 Front-end Loaders @ $8,000 each @ 12% composting use	$ 16,000	Composting/DPW	1988
Chipper	$ 17,500	Composting	1989

Operating and Maintenance Costs (1989)

	Recycling	Composting	Total
Collection	$ 300,000 *	$ 99,000	$ 399,000
Processing	—	$ 5,000	$ 5,000
Administration	$ 2,000	$ 0	$ 2,000
Education/Publicity	$ 2,000	$ 0	$ 2,000
Total	**$ 304,000**	**$104,000**	**$ 408,000**

*Contract costs, which include processing costs

Materials Revenues: No revenues due to terms of contract.

Source of Funding: Local taxes and a $60,000 State Tonnage Grant

Part-time Employees: 8

Contact

Ron Hepkin
Recycling Coordinator and
Department of Public Works Director
820 Mercier Street
Cherry Hill, New Jersey 08003
Phone (609) 424-4422

Reference

O'Brien-Kreitzberg & Associates, Inc., *Projected Industrial, Commercial, Residential Trash Tonnage For The Camden Resource Recovery Facility Service Area For The Year 1992*, Pennsauken, New Jersey, August 24, 1988.

UPPER TOWNSHIP, NEW JERSEY

Demographics

Jurisdiction:	Upper Township
Population:	10,870 in the winter and 16,000 in the summer (1989)
Total Households:	3,800
Total Businesses:	260
Area:	63.9 square miles
Other:	A rural residential community in Southern New Jersey, with a large summer population

Solid Waste Generation And Collection

(Annual Tonnages for 1989)

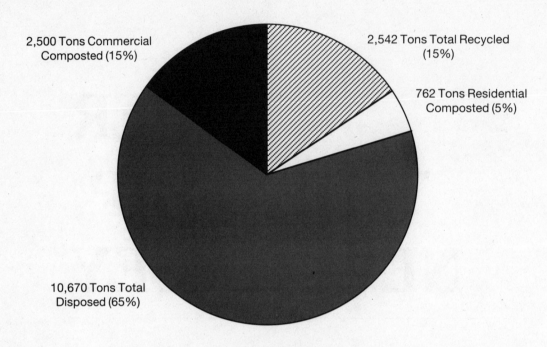

2,500 Tons Commercial Composted (15%)

2,542 Tons Total Recycled (15%)

762 Tons Residential Composted (5%)

10,670 Tons Total Disposed (65%)

Total Waste Generated: 16,474 tons in 1989 (including bulky waste such as tires and white goods, but excluding construction debris)

Residential Waste Generated: Not available: breakdown between residential and commercial waste generation not available due to the Town's simultaneous collection of refuse and recyclables from the residential and commercial sectors.   The drastic population fluctuation in the number of residents and businesses from summer to winter makes it impossible for the Town to estimate the percentage breakdown.

Commercial Waste Generated: Not available

Bulky Waste Generated: 3,302 tons (including tires, appliances, and furniture from residents, excluding construction debris, fencing, and railroad ties)

% By Weight of Total Waste Recovered: 35 percent in 1989 (15 recycling and 20 percent composting)

% By Weight of Residential Waste Recovered: Not available

% By Weight of Commercial Waste Recovered: Not available

Landfill Tipping Fee: $49 per ton

| Collection of Refuse: | The Town collects refuse from households and small businesses. Approximately 90 percent of businesses contract with private haulers for refuse collection services. All collected refuse is taken to the Cape May County Municipal Utilities Authority landfill. |

| Future Solid Waste Management Plans: | None |

Materials Recovery

Upper Township began collecting aluminum and other metal cans and glass in 1984. Participating residents commingled all materials in one container. Originally, workers separated the materials into an Eager Beaver trailer. In 1988, the Township purchased another Eager Beaver compartmentalized trailer. In February 1988, the Township entered into a 5-year agreement with the County for the County to process all glass, aluminum cans, other metal cans, and mixed paper at a Cape May County Municipal Utilities Authority (CMCMUA) facility. In accordance with the terms of the agreement, the Township stopped separating the materials at the curbside. The compartmentalized trailers were no longer efficient, so the Township removed the compartment walls and the individual doors.

In January 1988, Upper Township mandated the recycling of mixed paper (including newspaper, magazines, advertising circulars, high-grade paper, wrapping paper, kraft-paper bags, corrugated cardboard, paperboard such as cereal boxes and shoe boxes, envelopes, and junk mail), glass, metal, aluminum food and beverage containers (including aluminum foil and pie plates), and leaves. In November 1989, the ordinance was revised to include HDPE and PET soda and detergent bottles (but not anti-freeze or oil containers). Residents can place white goods and furniture on the curbside for collection twice a month; however, they must notify the Road Department prior to the day of collection.

The Township Road Department has 3 vehicles on the road 5 days a week to service each household weekly. Upper Township collects commingled materials in two Eager Beaver trailers pulled by pick-up trucks. One 20-cubic-yard packer truck collects mixed paper. White goods are collected in a stake body dump truck.

Residents also have the option of bringing glass, aluminum cans, other metal cans, and mixed paper — but not white goods — to the drop-off center in the yard of the Road Department. The center is open from 7 a.m. until 3:30 p.m. Materials collected there are stored in 40 20-gallon cans that have been purchased for this purpose. The Township does not staff the drop-off center.

Curbside Collection

Start-up Date:

Voluntary program began in 1984, and became mandatory in June 1988.

Private/Public:

Public collection from all residents and 222 businesses. The remaining 38 businesses contract with private haulers.

Materials Collected:

Glass, HDPE and PET soda and detergent containers (not anti-freeze or oil canisters), aluminum and other metal food and beverage containers (including aluminum foil and pie plates), newspaper, high-grade paper, kraft-paper bags, junk mail, magazines, wrapping paper, corrugated cardboard, paperboard (including cereal boxes and shoe boxes, but excluding materials with waxed coatings such as milk containers), appliances, leaves, grass clippings, wood waste, and brush

Pick-up Frequency:

Recyclables and leaves are collected weekly year-round. Brush and grass clippings are collected weekly from spring until November. Appliances are collected twice a month.

Pick-up Same Day as Refuse:

Yes, except for yard waste materials and white goods

Material Set-out Method:

Rinsed glass, plastic, and cans are placed in the same reusable container (metal or plastic can, but no plastic bags); mixed paper products in paper bags, cardboard boxes, or bundled (not in plastic bags); and used motor oil in sealed plastic containers. Leaves and grass clippings are set out at the curbside in plastic bags or trash cans from early spring until November. Brush is bundled and kept separate. During November and December leaves are collected loose. White goods (with all doors removed) are placed at the curb for collection.

Mandatory:

Yes, except for white goods, paperboard, wood waste, brush, and grass clippings

Service Provider:

Road Department

Collection Vehicles:

The Road Department uses four vehicles to collect recyclable materials: two pick-up trucks that pull 15-cubic-yard recycling trailers, one 20-cubic-yard compactor truck for mixed paper, and one stake body dump truck for white goods. Yard waste materials are collected in a 20-cubic-yard compactor truck, but during November and December two dump trucks pulling vacuums collect leaves.

Households Served:

3,800

Participation Rate:

85 percent of the households set materials out each week for recycling, and 60 percent of these correctly separate all materials from the refuse each week.

Businesses Served:

222

Economic Incentives:

None

| Enforcement: | Residents are refused trash removal service if they do not comply with the ordinance. Businesses that violate the ordinance can be fined $250 and/or up to 2 weeks of community service work. A second offense may result in a $500 fine and/or 3 weeks of community service. Although there are violators, to date no fines have been issued or community service required. |

Commercial Materials Recovery Activities

The June 1988 recycling mandate requires all businesses to recycle mixed paper (newspaper, high-grade paper, kraft-paper bags, junk mail, magazines, wrapping paper, corrugated cardboard, and paperboard — including cereal and shoe boxes), glass, and aluminum and other metal food and beverage containers. Owners of gasoline stations or other motor repair facilities are required to recycle used motor oil.

The Township collects glass, aluminum and other metal cans, HDPE and PET plastic soda and detergent containers, and mixed paper (newspaper, high-grade paper, kraft-paper bags, junk mail, magazines, wrapping paper, corrugated cardboard, paperboard — including cereal boxes and shoe boxes) from 222 of the 260 commercial establishments. Upper Township has supplied 460 20-gallon containers to large generators of recyclable materials, such as campgrounds, bars, and restaurants. Businesses that receive municipal collection are not charged for the service, and can have materials collected twice a week, if necessary. The Township does not keep separate records of the tonnages of commercial versus residential materials recovered. Businesses that choose not to receive municipal collection contract with private haulers, but the tonnages collected must be reported to the Recycling Coordinator, according to the New Jersey Statewide Mandatory Source Separation and Recycling Act. In 1989, businesses privately recycled corrugated cardboard (211 tons); mixed paper, including high-grade paper and corrugated cardboard (141 tons); and scrap metals (10 tons). In addition, one business recycled food waste (23 tons).

Materials Processing

Upper Township does not process any of the recyclable materials it collects. The glass, HDPE and PET bottles, aluminum and other metal cans, and mixed paper are delivered to the Cape May County Municipal Utilities Authority facility for processing. There are no tipping fees at the facility.

Empire Returns Corporation (ERC) began construction of the CMCMUA intermediate processing facility in December 1988. The facility started accepting materials in the fall of 1989 before it was on-line. ERC marketed these materials, according to the terms of the County contract, until the facility became fully operational in February 1989. The 33,750-square-foot facility shreds ferrous and bi-metal cans, crushes aluminum cans and glass, bales aluminum foil and plates, sorts and bales plastics according to polymer (PET or HDPE), and sorts and bales mixed paper according to grade (corrugated cardboard, high-grade paper, and low-grade paper) to produce high-quality, marketable materials.

White goods are delivered to local scavenger yards.

Composting Activities

Leaves are the only yard waste material that residents are required to set out for composting. The New Jersey Source Separation and Recycling Act banned leaves from all New Jersey landfills in September 1988, but recovery of grass clippings and brush remains voluntary — although the Road Department collects these materials as well. Leaves are collected weekly throughout the year, while grass clippings and brush are collected from early spring until November. During the spring and summer collection, leaves and grass clippings must be placed on the curbside on Mondays in trash cans or plastic bags. Brush must be kept bundled and separate from the leaves and grass. Leaves are collected loose during the fall and winter.

In the spring and summer, yard waste materials are collected weekly using a 20-cubic-yard compactor and a brush chipper. During the fall and winter collection of leaves and brush, the Road Department uses two vacuums and pick-up trucks to pull them, a brush chipper, and a 20-cubic-yard compactor.

Leaves and grass clippings are taken to the Cape May County Municipal Utilities Authority Compost Facility. There is no fee to tip leaves at the facility. In January 1989, the CMCMUA facility began charging municipalities $30 per ton to chip brush and wood waste. In order to save that tip fee, Upper Township began chipping brush in the Road Department yard. Chipped materials are available to residents at no charge. The wood chips are also used in public parks. In order to discourage illegal dumping of leaves, landscapers are allowed to drop off their yard waste at the County compost facility at no charge. Landscapers composted 2,500 tons of yard waste in 1989.

The Cape May County Municipal Utilities Authority encourages backyard composting of leaves, grass clippings, and food scraps through its monthly newsletter.

Other Recycling Activities

The Cape May County Municipal Utilities Authority placed recycling containers on the boardwalks and beaches in the summer of 1989. It used funds from a New Jersey Department of Environmental Protection recycling program grant to purchase the containers. According to the CMCMUA newsletter, amounts of contamination were "minimal." Tonnages recovered are not included in the Township data.

Amount and Breakdown of Materials Recovered

Material	Commercial (Tons, 1989)	Residential (Tons, 1989)	Total (Tons, 1989)
Mixed Paper*	NA	NA	1,579.3
Corrugated Cardboard†	NA	NA	211.3
Commingled§	NA	NA	627.7
Aluminum	NA	NA	2.0
Non-Ferrous Scrap†	NA	NA	0.8
Ferrous Scrap†	NA	NA	9.5
White Goods	NA	NA	76.2
Food Waste†	NA	NA	23.0
Motor Oil	NA	NA	12.1
Subtotal Recycled	**NA**	**NA**	**2,541.9**
Yard Waste	2,500	762	3,262.0
Subtotal Composted	**2,500**	**762**	**3,262.0**
Total Recovered	**NA**	**NA**	**5,803.9**

*Includes newspaper, magazines, kraft-paper bags, high-grade paper, junk mail, envelopes, corrugated cardboard, and paperboard, as well as 140.8 tons of high-grade paper and corrugated cardboard recycled privately.
†Recycled privately
§Includes HDPE and PET beverage and food containers, aluminum food and beverage containers (including aluminum foil and pie plates), other metal cans, and glass

Publicity and Education

The *Cape May County Recycler* is distributed to all residents. It reports on the recovery rates of the different municipalities, highlights the most successful communities through descriptions of the programs, and informs residents about new County-based programs (such as the recycling containers on the boardwalks). The County prints this monthly newsletter, and no costs are incurred by the Township. In addition, Upper Township mails out fliers to all residents and businesses informing them of collection days and explaining the proper separation of materials for collection.

Economics

Costs Cover: Capital and operating and maintenance costs given below cover (1) the collection of 2,297 tons of recyclables at curbside and at the drop-off center, (2) the collection of 762 tons of yard waste at curbside, and (3) the chipping of discarded tree stumps and brush. All capital costs are estimates due to difficulty locating purchasing records. For the purpose of this study average figures have been used.

Capital Costs: Collection

Item	Cost	Use	Year Incurred
Leaf Vacuum	$10,000 to $15,000	Composting	1975
20-Cubic-Yard Compactor Truck	$65,000 to $70,000	Composting	1980
Pick-up Truck and Eager Beaver Trailer	$23,000 to $25,000	Recycling	1984
Pick-up Truck and Eager Beaver Trailer	$26,000 to $30,000	Recycling	1988
Leaf Vacuum	$15,000 to $25,000	Composting	1987
500 20-Gallon Containers @ $7 each	$3,500	Recycling	1987-1989
20-Cubic-Yard Compactor	$65,000 to $70,000	Recycling	1989

Capital Costs: Processing

Item	Cost	Use	Year Incurred
Chipper @ 10% composting use	$15,000 to $20,000	Composting	1986

Operating and Maintenance Costs (1989)

	Recycling	Composting	Total
Collection	$ 148,000	$ 42,600	$190,600
Processing	$ 0	$ 10,608 *	$ 10,608
Administration	$ 8,400	$ 0	$ 8,400
Education/Publicity	$ 1,000	$ 0	$ 1,000
Total	**$ 157,400**	**$ 53,208**	**$210,608**

*Cost of chipping brush

Materials Revenues: $0

Source of Funding: Local taxes and a State Tonnage Grant

Full-time Employees: 7

Part-time Employees: 3

Contacts

Mary Anne Fieux
Cape May County Municipal Utilities Authority
P.O. Box 610
Cape May Court House, New Jersey 08210
(609) 465-9026

Larry Bond
Recycling Coordinator
Township of Upper Road Department
P.O. Box 205
Tuckahoe, New Jersey 08250
(609) 628-2647

References

Cape May County Recycler, Volume VI, Cape May Court House, New Jersey, December 1988.
Cape May County Recycler, Volume VII, Cape May Court House, New Jersey, November 1989.

BABYLON, NEW YORK

Demographics

Jurisdiction:	Town of Babylon
Population:	213,234 (1989 estimate based on same 2-year population growth from 1987 to 1989 as the 1.84 percent from 1985 to 1987)
Total Households:	53,000 (50,000 single-family and 3,000 multi-unit homes)
Total Businesses:	Approximately 5,800
Area:	51 square miles

Solid Waste Generation and Collection

(Annual Tonnages for 1989)

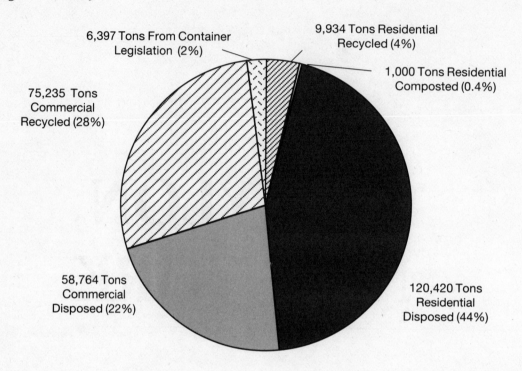

6,397 Tons From Container Legislation (2%)

9,934 Tons Residential Recycled (4%)

1,000 Tons Residential Composted (0.4%)

75,235 Tons Commercial Recycled (28%)

58,764 Tons Commercial Disposed (22%)

120,420 Tons Residential Disposed (44%)

Total Waste Generated:	271,750 tons in 1989 (including bulky waste and tonnage recovered through container legislation)
Residential Waste Generated:	131,354 tons in 1989 (including bulky waste such as tires, scrap metal, and appliances)
Commercial Waste Generated:	133,999 tons in 1989 (including bulky materials such as tires, scrap metal, and construction debris)
Bulky Waste Generated:	72,966 tons in 1989 (including white goods, scrap metal, tires, and construction debris, but excluding 5,200 tons of automobile scrap)
% By Weight of Total Waste Recovered:	34 percent in 1989 (33.7 percent recycling, including deposit containers, and 0.4 percent composting)
% By Weight of Residential Waste Recovered:	8 percent in 1989 (7.6 percent recycling, excluding deposit containers, and 0.8 percent composting)
% By Weight of Commercial Waste Recovered:	56 percent in 1989 (56 percent recycling, excluding deposit containers)
Transfer Station Tipping Fee:	$78 per ton at transfer station

Collection of Refuse:

Prior to 1987, residential refuse was collected by many private haulers. In October 1987, the Town gave the residential refuse and recyclable collection contract to Babylon Source Separation, Inc. (BSSI), an umbrella group of the private haulers that were previously operating in Babylon. Businesses and multi-unit apartments must contract out for refuse collection with one of the 22 licensed haulers. All refuse is tipped at the Town transfer station.

Babylon's $87 million 750 ton-per-day mass burn waste incinerator came on-line in December 1988 and began commercial operation April 5, 1989. The Town guarantees 225,000 tons of waste per year to the plant, although in 1989 the Town only burned 208,120 tons. The incinerator was built and is operated by Ogden-Martin.

Future Solid Waste Management Plans:

The Town is assessing the costs and feasibility of implementing a polystyrene recycling program.

In an attempt to improve markets for recovered materials, Babylon is forming a marketing cooperative with three other towns to sell recovered newspaper and magazines to paper mills in the Northeast and Canada, and is building a materials processing facility. (The Town is currently accepting proposals for the construction of the facility.) The Town is also trying to locate a site for a large-scale composting facility.

The State of New York has set a source reduction goal of 10 percent by 1992, and a recycling goal of 40 percent by 1997.

Materials Recovery

Since 1980, Babylon has collected leaves for composting from part of the Town during the fall season.

Curbside collection of newspaper began in October 1987 when the Town mandated the set out of newspaper for recycling. In October 1988, the Town began a pilot program for curbside collection of glass and metal cans from 2,500 single-family homes and duplexes. The Town recycling law was revised in March 1989 to include glass, aluminum cans, and other metal cans. At the same time, the Town extended collection of recyclables to all single-family homes and duplexes. Recyclable materials (glass, newspaper, aluminum cans, metal cans, and white goods) are collected by BSSI, the same haulers that collect refuse, although the collection days are not the same.

Glass, aluminum cans, and other metal cans must be commingled in a 20-gallon bucket, which residents purchase from the Town for $4. Newspaper and commingled materials are collected on alternating weeks. BSSI will also collect appliances for recycling every week.

Residents also have the option of bringing recyclable materials to the drop-off center on the grounds of the transfer station, a renovated airplane hangar leased by the Town. Open Mondays through Saturdays, the drop-off center accepts HDPE and PET plastic beverage and detergent containers, scrap metal, car batteries, tires, corrugated cardboard, motor oil, appliances, and books, in addition to glass, aluminum and other metal cans, and newspapers. There is a book swap area inside the hangar as well. The drop-off center is not a redemption center for deposit containers. Extra workers are needed at the center on Saturdays to direct residents in the separation of recyclable materials. Babylon has also distributed 11 pairs of igloo-shaped 5-foot-high containers to the hamlets and incorporated villages within the Town. One igloo in each pair is for storage of glass and metal containers, while the other is for plastic bottles (HDPE and PET plastic beverage and detergent containers).

In 1989, as a result of not meeting its tonnage guarantee to the Town's incinerator, Babylon burned half of the 9,142 tons of newspaper collected for recycling.

The schools in Babylon began their own paper recycling program in March 1990. All the schools will be recycling paper by September 1990.

The State of New York implemented a beverage container deposit law in 1983. Institute for Local Self-Reliance staff estimate that 6,397 tons of beverage containers were recovered in Babylon in 1989 through the State's deposit legislation.[1]

Curbside Collection

Start-up Date:

Leaf collection began in 1980. A pilot recycling program began in October 1988 and expanded to the entire Town in March 1989.

Private/Public:

Private haulers with a municipal contract collect recyclable materials. The Highway Department collects leaves.

Materials Collected:

Glass, aluminum and metal cans, newspaper, appliances, and leaves

Pick-up Frequency:

Biweekly collection of newspaper (collected one week) and of glass, aluminum cans, and other metal cans (collected the next). White goods are collected weekly. Leaves are collected weekly during the fall.

Pick-up Same Day as Refuse: No

Material Set-out Method:

Newspapers are placed in kraft paper bags or bound with twine. Aluminum and metal cans, and glass containers, are commingled in a 20-gallon bucket. Leaves may be bagged or raked loose to the curbside. Appliances, with all doors removed, are placed at the curbside.

---

[1] In 1989, the average per capita tonnage of beverage containers recovered in New York State was 0.03 tons. 0.03 tons x 213,234 (the population of Babylon) = 6,397 tons.

Mandatory:	Yes, except for leaves and appliances
Service Provider:	BSSI collects recyclable materials, and the Highway Department collects leaves.
Collection Vehicles:	BSSI uses privately owned packer trucks. The Highway Department uses nine packer trucks with hoppers and nine payloaders during its leaf collection season.
Households Served:	50,000 single-family homes and duplexes
Participation Rate:	63 percent of total households (based on the Town's assessment of the tonnage of materials that would be recovered if participation were 100 percent)
Businesses Served:	None
Economic Incentives:	None
Enforcement:	None

Commercial Materials Recovery Activities

Recycling is not mandatory for businesses, although the commercial sector did recover 75,235 tons in 1989. According to Anne Webster, the Deputy Director for Recycling Programs, a few large businesses are recovering the majority of materials. The materials most frequently recycled are corrugated cardboard and construction debris (75,000 tons in 1989). Businesses also recycled high-grade paper and mixed-grade paper through private haulers.

In addition, 5,200 tons of automobile scrap and 6,110 tons of vinyl scrap (from a local industry) were recovered in 1989. This tonnage is not considered municipal solid waste and is thus excluded from total waste generation and recovery figures.

In January 1990, the Town Code was amended to require licensed haulers to provide data on the tonnage of materials recycled monthly.

Materials Processing

The Town does not process any recyclables. The operators of the Omni Integrated Processing Facility collect glass, aluminum cans, other metal cans, and plastic from the drop-off center, and process these materials at the facility in Westbury, New York, 20 miles from Babylon. Omni charged Babylon $23.66 per ton in 1989 (for a total of $46,019) and $28 per ton in 1990.

Jamaica Ash, also in Westbury, collects and processes newspaper and corrugated cardboard. The Town received $20 per ton for newspaper in 1988, but had to pay $35 per ton in 1989 and $39 per ton in 1990. Tires collected at the drop-off center are picked up by

Metropolitan Tire and Rubber Company, which pulverizes them for use with asphalt. Local scavenger yards collect scrap metal, appliances, and car batteries.

Composting Activities

In order to conserve landfill space, the Town began a yard waste collection program in 1980. Babylon was divided into two districts: "sunny" (that is, with fewer trees) and "shady." Yard materials generated by residents in the shady section are collected by BSSI and disposed with the refuse. Leaves generated by residents in the sunny section are collected by the Highway Department from November 1 through the second week in December, and windrowed at a State-owned composting facility located in Babylon. No tipping fees are paid. According to Edmund Mendello, Supervisor of the Highway Department, it is not cost-effective to recover leaves from the entire Town.

Residents in the sunny section may rake their leaves to the curbside or place them in bags for collection during November and the first part of December. Highway Department employees rake the loose leaves to the center of the road and feed them into hoppers with payloaders. Each house is served twice during the 6-week collection period. The Town uses a total of nine packer trucks with hoppers, and nine payloaders, for leaf collection. Babylon assigns 45 Highway Department employees to leaf collection during the 6-week period.

Amount and Breakdown of Materials Recovered

Material	Commercial (Tons, 1989)	Residential (Tons, 1989)	Total (Tons, 1989)
Newspaper	0	4,571 *	4,571
Corrugated Cardboard	9,000	1,000	10,000
High-Grade Paper	35	0	35
Mixed Paper	200	0	200
Glass†	0	1,880	1,880
PET Containers†	0	0.8	0.8
HDPE Containers†	0	1.2	1.2
Aluminum†	0	63	63
Scrap Metals	0	2,164	2,164
Motor Oil	0	29	29
Concrete	66,000	0	66,000
Tires	0	50	50
Appliances	0	166	166
Batteries	0	9	9
Subtotal Recycled	75,235	9,934	85,169
Leaves	0	1,000	1,000
Subtotal Composted	0	1,000	1,000
Subtotal Recovered	75,235	10,934	86,169
Deposit Containers	NA	NA	6,397
Total Recovered	NA	NA	92,566

*Babylon burned about one half of the 9,142 tons of newspaper collected for recycling.
†Tonnages do not include beverage containers covered under the State's deposit legislation.

Publicity and Education

The Town of Babylon publicizes its recycling program through quarterly newsletters, brochures, mailings, newspaper articles, and announcements on the "Babylon Dateline" program (a community events and news program on the local cable access channel).

The Town designed a series of video presentations on recycling for school children between kindergarten and eighth grade. The children in kindergarten through third grade are shown a "Woodsy the Owl" slide show on recycling. A slide show for the fourth through sixth grades demonstrates the life of a product from the first manufacturing through its use and collection as a recyclable material to processing into a new product. Seventh and eighth graders are shown a video on the Town's recycling program, including proper separation of materials and processing of glass and metal cans at the Omni Integrated Processing Facility.

Economics

The Town of Babylon does not keep records of the capital or operating and maintenance costs it incurs from its curbside collection program, the drop-off program, or its leaf collection program. The Town does not own any processing equipment.

Capital Costs: Collection

Item	Cost	Use	Year Incurred
9 Packer Trucks with Hoppers	NA	Composting	NA
9 Payloaders	NA	Composting	NA
Rakes	NA	Composting	NA

Operating and Maintenance Costs (1989)

	Recycling	Composting	Total
Collection	NA	NA	NA
Processing	NA	NA	NA
Administration	NA	NA	NA
Education/Publicity	$156,496	$0	$156,496
Total	NA	NA	NA

Materials Revenues:	The Town does not earn any revenues for its materials
Source of Funding:	General taxes
Full-time Employees:	2
Part-time Employees:	49 (45 employed for leaf collection, and 4 work at the drop-off center on Saturdays)

Contacts

Anne Webster
Deputy Director for Recycling Programs
Department of Environmental Control
281 Phelps Lane
North Babylon, New York 11703
Phone (516) 422-7640
Fax (515) 422-7686

Barbara Fitzpatrick
Recycling Coordinator
Department of Environmental Control
281 Phelps Lane
North Babylon, New York 11703
Phone (516) 422-7640
Fax (515) 422-7686

Edmund Mendello
Highway Department Supervisor
Highway Department
281 Phelps Lane
North Babylon, New York 11703
Phone (516) 957-3089
Fax (515) 422-7686

Evan Liblit
Commissioner
Department of Environmental Control
281 Phelps Lane
North Babylon, New York 11703
Phone (516) 957-3089
Fax (515) 422-7686

References

Andracchi, Frank, Ogden-Martin, telephone conversation regarding Babylon's incinerator, Babylon, New York, May 25, 1990.

Philips, Joe, New York State Department of Conservation, telephone conversation regarding containers redeemed through deposit legislation, Albany, New York, April 26, 1990.

PARK RIDGE, NEW JERSEY

Demographics

Jurisdiction: Borough of Park Ridge

Population: 8,515 (1980 census). Based on the fact that school enrollment has dropped 50 percent since 1975, and the number of childless couples has increased, Charles Gasior, the Park Ridge Recycling Coordinator, believes that this number is still accurate or even slightly high.

Total Households: 2,500 single residences, 300 condominium/apartment units

Total Businesses: Approximately 75

Area: 2.6 square miles

Solid Waste Generation and Collection

(Annual Tonnages for 1989)

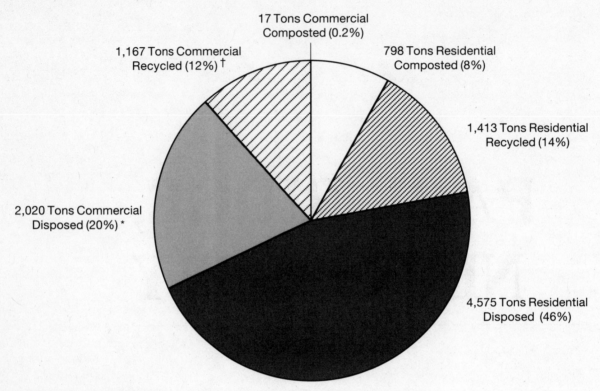

17 Tons Commercial
Composted (0.2%)

1,167 Tons Commercial
Recycled (12%) †

798 Tons Residential
Composted (8%)

1,413 Tons Residential
Recycled (14%)

2,020 Tons Commercial
Disposed (20%) *

4,575 Tons Residential
Disposed (46%)

*These tonnages are based on 1988 data.
†Some of this tonnage is based on 1988 data.

Total Waste Generated:	9,990 tons in 1989 (including 37.5 tons of tree stumps and 438 tons of asphalt; excluding bulky waste tonnage generated from the private sector, which is not available)
Residential Waste Generated:	6,786 tons in 1989 (including multi-family units, four schools, and the Post Office)
Commercial Waste Generated:	Approximately 3,204 tons in 1989 (based on 1988 figures and including 438 tons of asphalt recycled). Complete 1989 data are not available because they are not recorded. Data were available for 1988 only because an engineering company conducted a study based on materials received at the Bergen County landfill. The Recycling Coordinator used the base number from this study to estimate the amount of commercial waste generated in 1988. He believes that the amount changed very little in 1989.
Bulky Waste Generated:	Data not available. (Bulky waste is hauled to a transfer station by DiBella Sanitation, Inc., a private hauler, and no one keeps track of the amount.)
% By Weight of Total Waste Recovered:	34 percent in 1989 (26 percent recycling, 8 percent composting)

% By Weight of Residential Waste Recovered:	33 percent in 1989 (21 percent recycling, 12 percent composting)
% By Weight of Commercial Waste Recovered:	37 percent in 1989 (36 percent recycling, 1 percent composting)
Transfer Station Tipping Fee:	$97.94 per ton in 1989 at the county transfer station. In 1990 transfer station tipping fees increased to $124 per ton for residential waste and $138 per ton for commercial waste.
Collection of Refuse:	DiBella Sanitation Services, Inc., collects residential waste under contract with the Borough. It also collects waste and recyclables from the commercial sector. The Borough collects recyclables from the residential sector (including apartment complexes), and from some institutions such as schools and the Post Office. In 1989, Park Ridge spent $945,000 on refuse disposal ($795,000 in contract fees — approximately $350,000 of which was spent on collection — and $150,000 spent for compactor unit). The refuse collection crew earns $12 per hour.
Future Solid Waste Management Plans:	Thanks to high and steeply rising transfer station tipping fees, the Borough's main solid waste management goal is to maximize recycling, with an emphasis on paper, the largest component of the waste stream. The Borough will target additional materials, such as grass clippings and additional types of paper products, for curbside collection. It will also encourage residents to increase the amount of currently targeted materials they put out for collection. For instance, while mixed paper and corrugated cardboard are currently targeted, some people only put out newspaper. They will be encouraged to put out magazines, high-grade paper, and cardboard as well.

Materials Recovery

Recycling in Park Ridge prior to the current mandatory program consisted mainly of Boy Scout paper drives. In the early 1970s, the Borough got a Department of Environmental Protection (DEP) permit for a trash compactor, which residents could use on Wednesdays and Saturdays. The compactor site was expanded into a complete drop-off center in 1988, with facilities for collecting paper (a 40-foot box trailer), corrugated cardboard, commingled recyclables (aluminum, glass, ferrous cans, PET and HDPE plastic containers), car batteries, waste oil, and scrap metal. The drop-off center began collecting brush and wood waste in 1988 and grass clippings in 1989.

Before implementation of the recycling program, appliances were picked up at curbside (bimonthly, by appointment), as many of them could not be easily transported to the drop-off center. This service has been continued and made part of the current curbside collection program.

Mayor Richard Mancinelli set up a Recycling Advisory Committee on January 1, 1988, to recommend a plan for implementing the provisions of the New Jersey Statewide Mandatory Source Separation and Recycling Act. To supplement the materials being brought to the Borough's Recycling Center, the committee proposed a curbside pick-up program of mixed paper and commingled recyclables, and assisted in the development of a public information program. Although some doubt was expressed about the viability of markets for commingled recyclables, the Committee recommended a 1-year contract with a processor, West Patterson Automobile Recyclers (WPAR), which was just beginning its operations.

Mandatory recycling of residential waste began in April 1988. Within one month, an estimated 22 percent of the Borough's residential waste was being recycled. Good public education and the convenience of the system for residents contributed to the program's immediate success. The Recycling Coordinator believes that Park Ridge's system is particularly "user friendly" because all clean paper (magazines, junk mail, newspaper, and high-grade paper) is recyclable, and need not be sorted by residents. Likewise, no multiple separation of aluminum, glass, tin cans, and PET and HDPE plastics is required.

The Borough is divided into four zones, each having its recyclables picked up on a different schedule. Borough employees pick up paper on one day and commingled recyclables on a different day in each zone. Residents in apartments and condominiums put out recyclables in dumpsters for collection by the Borough. DiBella Sanitation Services hauls the remaining mixed waste.

Initially, paper was collected at curbside once per month, and commingled recyclables were collected twice per month. In 1990, in response to requests from citizens, paper collection was increased to twice per month. This has increased the amount of paper recycled. Between January and May 1989, an average of 148,000 pounds of paper were collected per month. Between January and May 1990, the monthly average increased to 171,000 pounds.

Currently, materials collected at curbside include paper (newspaper, junk mail, magazines, and high-grade), corrugated cardboard, leaves, Christmas trees, white goods, and commingled recyclables (aluminum cans; three colors of glass; ferrous cans; and PET and HDPE plastic beverage, milk, spring water, liquor, and detergent containers). Brush, grass clippings, car batteries, and motor oil can be recycled voluntarily at the drop-off center. Motor oil is stored in a 1,000-gallon tank at the drop-off center.

Residents take scrap metal (appliances, etc.) to the drop-off center unless the materials are too large to fit in a car, in which case they can be set out at the curb for the Borough's biweekly scrap metal collection. (The resident must make an appointment to have scrap picked up at these times.) The Borough sends out a loader which loads scrap metal and appliances into a Borough dump truck.

In order to encourage recycling in general and the use of the drop-off center in particular, the Borough has donated revenues from the sale of materials to organizations (such as the Boy Scouts, the High

School Football Booster Club, and the High School Band) that help staff the drop-off center. In addition, a county-wide incentive program sends a "Reward Van" to visit drop-off centers in the various municipalities and gives a paper bag of groceries to each citizen who recycles. The bag is printed with the words, "Thank you for recycling."

Park Ridge was one of only three of New Jersey's 567 municipalities to receive the first annual *Outstanding Achievement for Recycling* award in 1988 from the New Jersey Department of Environmental Protection. These three municipalities exceeded the state requirement of 25 percent materials recovery within the first year of mandatory recycling.

Charles Gasior, the Recycling Coordinator of Park Ridge, says that a successful recycling program must include what he calls the three "A's" — (1) Aggressive implementation by the town, (2) an Active program coordinator who involves and educates many segments of the population, and (3) an Accommodating attitude on the part of the municipality (i.e., the program should be simple and flexible). Given these three "A"s, a fourth will follow — Acceptance by the community.

Curbside Collection

Start-up Date:	April 1988
Private/Public:	Public
Materials Collected:	Mixed paper (newspaper, junk mail, telephone books, magazines, high-grade paper, and corrugated cardboard), commingled recyclables (aluminum; glass; ferrous cans; HDPE and PET plastic beverage, milk, spring water, liquor, and detergent containers), leaves, Christmas trees, and white goods
Mandatory:	Yes. Residential households must recover all materials listed above.
Pick-up Frequency:	Biweekly for mixed paper and commingled recyclables; twice during a 6-week period in the fall for leaves; biweekly by appointment for white goods
Pick-up Same Day as Refuse:	No
Material Set-out Method:	Paper is bundled; glass, aluminum, ferrous cans, and HDPE and PET containers are commingled and set out in an open container (not provided by the Borough); and leaves are raked into piles on the side of the street.
Service Provider:	Borough of Park Ridge
Collection Vehicles:	A 31-cubic-yard packer truck for most recyclables, (operated by one full-time driver and two part-time laborers), a backup packer truck, a front-end loader with the packer for leaf collection, and a chipper on a dump truck for brush (operated by one full-time driver and two part-time laborers)

Households Served:	2,800
Participation Rate:	Estimated at 90 percent for both curbside collection and the drop-off center (1/2 to 2/3 of the homes in each of the four zones tend to put out recyclables, and many residents use the drop-off center; an estimated 1/3 of total recyclables are collected at the drop-off center). There is close to 100 percent participation in the leaf collection program. The participation rate for the drop-off of grass clippings and brush is not known.
Businesses Served:	5 (four schools and the Post Office)
Economic Incentives:	None
Enforcement:	The main truck driver serves as a compliance officer. He checks for non-compliance and investigates complaints about non-recyclers. However, participation rates have been high, so there has been little need for enforcement.

Commercial Materials Recovery Activities

The Borough's recycling ordinance requires all businesses, commercial properties, and government buildings (including schools) to separate at least one of the following from their waste stream: corrugated cardboard, glass, food wastes, ferrous metals, high-grade office paper, and newspaper. Most commercial establishments recycle cardboard, and meat marketing companies recycle renderings. (Meat renderings are taken to Berkowitz Fats, a company that cooks them down and then reuses them.) All businesses must register yearly with the Borough Recycling Coordinator and report the tonnage they have recycled to the Coordinator semi-annually.

DiBella Sanitation Services is the main hauler of commercial waste and recyclables, although a few local businesses contract with other haulers.

There are four large companies in the Borough (the U.S. headquarters of Sony, the world headquarters of Hertz, the headquarters of the National Utilities Service, and a 300-room Marriott hotel). All are fairly new to the area and thus are just getting started in their recycling activities. Their recycling tends to be separate from the rest of the Borough. Sony, for example, recycled 30 tons of computer paper in 1988. Hertz recycles materials from its copy center and computer room and is planning to expand its recycling efforts; the company contracts through a third party (not DiBella or the Borough) for marketing its recycled materials. The Park Ridge Marriott is the pilot recycling Marriott hotel for the state of New Jersey; it recently bought a glass crusher and a compactor for cardboard. Marriott contracts with DiBella.

The Recycling Coordinator meets with commercial property owners twice a year to discuss ways to implement and improve their recycling efforts, but there is little enforcement of the program.

As part of the Borough's street resurfacing program, any asphalt milled prior to the resurfacing is used for the construction of new road beds.

In addition to the curbside and drop-off programs, Park Ridge developed and implemented the first in-house school recycling program in Bergen County, collecting mixed paper, high-grade paper, aluminum and ferrous cans, glass, and corrugated cardboard from the Park Ridge schools and one parochial school, Our Lady of Mercy. School custodians put clearly labeled recycling boxes in each classroom for the children to put their paper in. Yellow barrels are placed around the school and in the cafeteria for cans and other recyclables. The cafeterias recycle ferrous cans, plastic containers, and glass containers. The schools can target the same materials designated for collection from households. Recyclables are all taken to one dumpster where the Borough picks them up. The Borough's Post Office recycles its mixed paper through a similar system.

Materials Processing

Park Ridge does not have its own materials processing facility or equipment. Since mandatory recycling began, the Borough has delivered all paper and corrugated cardboard to Zozzaro Brothers of Clifton, NJ for processing and marketing. Zozzaro Brothers charges $25 per ton in marketing fees for the handling of paper.

Commingled recyclables are taken to West Patterson Automobile Recycling, Inc. (WPAR), which neither charges a fee nor pays to take the materials. It is about 15 miles from Park Ridge. WPAR is a relatively new, innovative processing facility that accepts commingled recyclables and sorts them via a semi-automated conveyor belt system. The facility handles about 30 tons of materials per day.

Composting Activities

The Borough began its leaf composting program in 1989. Leaf pick-up times are twice per household during a 6-week period in November and December. Residents rake their leaves into the street, keeping them close to the curb. The leaves are then collected with a front-end loader and a packer truck.

The Borough uses a rented truck from DiBella Sanitation Services and a back-up packer truck for leaf collection. This system has proved to be expensive. The Recycling Coordinator calculates that it would be cheaper to buy a used garbage truck for leaf collection, which would soon pay for itself, rather than renting a truck each year. The Borough will explore this option in the future.

The Borough transports its leaves to a compost site about 10 miles away. The site is owned by the Town of Clarkstown, New York, and managed by Organic Recycling, Inc., a private operation. The tipping fee is $10 per cubic yard, and the leaves are composted in windrows. Park Ridge does not have a large enough area for its own compost site.

Residents voluntarily recycle their grass clippings using the grass clipping collection container located at the drop-off center. (Commercial landscapers must discard grass clippings elsewhere; usually they take grass clippings to DiBella to be landfilled.) A company called American Soil leases a 30-cubic-yard collection container to the Borough, and charges a fee for transporting the grass clippings and composting them in the town of Freehold, about 80 or 90 miles away. Finished compost is sold to farmers in that area.

In 1990, the Borough began to pick up brush and tree branches at curbside by appointment. The branches are chipped. Prior to this, residents hauled tree limbs and brush to the drop-off center, where the Borough chipped them with its chipper. In addition, the Borough collected and chipped 15 tons of Christmas trees in 1989. Both residents and the Borough use the wood chips. In 1989 37.5 tons of tree stumps were sent to the American Soil Company to be ground.

Also in 1989, 17 tons of grass and branches from the commercial sector were reported composted. This was a one-time project: a company came in with a large chipper to clear land for a building and reported the tonnages chipped to the town.

Amount and Breakdown of Materials Recovered

Material	Commercial (Tons, 1989)		Residential (Tons, 1989)	Total (Tons, 1989)
Newspaper, Mixed Paper, & Cardboard*	683.3	†	938.8	1,622.1
Commingled Recyclables	0		327.8	327.8
Motor Oil	0		6	6
Asphalt	438		0	438
Scrap Metals (incl. white goods)	0		137.4	137.4
Batteries	0		3	3
Food Waste	45.5	†	0	45.5
Subtotal Recycled	**1,166.8**		**1,413.0**	**2,579.8**
Grass Clippings	0		30	30
Chipped Branches §	16.7		22.8	39.5
Tree Stumps	0		37.5	37.5
Leaves	0		707.7	707.7
Subtotal Composted	**16.7**		**798**	**814.7**
Total Recovered	**1,183.5**		**2,211.0**	**3,394.5**

*The Recycling Coordinator estimates that 75% is newspaper, 20% is corrugated cardboard and phone books, and 5% is high-grade paper.
†Based on 1988 data
§The tonnage of Christmas trees recycled in 1989 is not included because adequate records of the amount were not kept.

Tonnages above include those collected at both curbside and drop-off. The Recycling Coordinator estimates that 1/3 of total recyclables are collected at the drop-off center. DiBella Sanitation Services, which collects from most commercial establishments, gives commercial tonnage figures to the Recycling Coordinator. The tonnages from large corporations that do not contract with DiBella, such as Sony and Hertz, are reported annually to the Recycling Coordinator, and are included above with other commercial tonnages. Tonnages for schools and the Post Office are included with residential tonnages, because their recyclables are collected at the same time as residential recyclables.

Publicity and Education

Initial efforts included a newsletter mailed to all residents, explaining the basics of the new recycling program, and a flyer designed by former Walt Disney artist George Reed illustrating the elements of commingled recyclables. Recycling Coordinator Chuck Gasior described this flyer as "invaluable in teaching the Borough's program to the residents."

The Borough sends out information on recycling throughout the year, in the form of the quarterly "Park Ridge Progress Newsletter," put out by the Park Ridge Mayor and Council. Also, the Recycling Coordinator has given occasional talks at places like Cook College and the Westchester County Recycling Exposition explaining recycling and the Park Ridge program.

Economics

Costs Cover:

The costs given below for capital and for operation and maintenance cover the following: (1) collection of 2,211 tons of recyclable/compostable materials from the Borough's household/institutional curbside collection and drop-off center; (2) transportation and tipping fees for this tonnage at materials processing facilities and composting sites; (3) chipping of 60.3 tons of brush and tree stumps; (4) composting of 30 tons of grass clippings; and (5) collection and milling of 438 tons of asphalt.

Capital Costs: Collection

Item	Cost	Use	Year Incurred
Front-end Loader for Leaves @ 12% of use	$ 25,000	Composting	1980
Back-up Packer Truck @ 12% of use	$ 13,000	Composting	1985
Front-end Loader for Leaves @ 12% of use	$ 75,000	Composting	1986
Fencing for Drop-off Center	$ 3,000	Recycling	1988
31-cu.-yd. Packer Truck	$ 95,000	Recycling	1988
2 28-cu.-yd. Roll-off Containers	$ 5,000	Recycling	1988
1,000 Gallon Tank for Used Motor Oil	Donated	Recycling	1988

Note: The front-end loaders and the back-up packer truck listed above were not purchased solely for leaf collection: they are only used for leaf collection during the 6-week period in the fall. The 12 percent of use is based on the 6-week leaf collection period, which is 12 percent of 52 weeks in a year.

Capital Costs: Processing

Item	Cost	Use	Year Incurred
Chipper for Brush	$10,000	Chipping	1988

Operating and Maintenance Costs (1989)

	Recycling	Composting	Total
Collection	$110,000	$ 68,000	$ 178,000
Processing	$ 58,000	$ 25,000	$ 83,000
Administration	$ 10,000	$ 2,500	$ 12,500
Education/Publicity	$ 3,000	$ 500	$ 3,500
Total	**$181,000**	**$ 96,000**	**$ 277,000**

Note: $20,000 in recycling marketing fees, $15,000 in recycling handling costs, and $25,000 in composting marketing fees are included as processing costs. Also, $18,000 in compost handling costs are included with collection costs.

In 1989, the Borough of Park Ridge paid recycling marketing fees, such as $25 per ton to Zozzaro Brothers for the marketing of mixed paper. Park Ridge also paid Zozzaro $100 per turnaround for the pick-up of paper (45 boxes were collected in 1989, which means that this expense came to $4,500 for the year, plus the usual $25 per ton). WPAR charges no marketing fees for commingled, but they do charge $275 per 30-cubic-yard box picked up from the drop-off center and returned. There were 36 boxes in 1989, which comes out to $9,900 for the year.

Originally, Park Ridge paid the Clarkstown, NY compost site $12,500 for composting its leaves, based on $5 per cubic yard. The town of Clarkstown maintained that since the leaves were so tightly compacted, it was not receiving enough in fees. With the agreement of Park Ridge, the volume of leaves was considered doubled, and the Borough ended up paying $25,000 in compost marketing fees in exchange for a five-year contract with the site.

The Borough paid $18,000 in compost handling fees. Included in this was a truck, rented for leaf collection, which cost $14,000.

The Borough paid $650 per 30-cubic-yard container for rental of containers and transporting of grass clippings to the compost site in Freehold, New Jersey. Three containers of grass clippings were picked up in 1989, at a total cost of $1,950. Also included in handling costs is the $5,200 paid to American Soil Company for the grinding of eight containers of tree trunks.

The Recycling Coordinator thinks that 1989 compost costs were high. This was the first year of this system, however, and other methods will be explored in the future, with the aim of lowering costs.

Materials Revenues:	$500 in 1989 (from scrap metal and batteries)
Avoided Cost in 1989:	$259,602 (1,413 tons residential recycled plus 438 tons of asphalt recycled by the Borough and 798 tons composted — 2,649 tons total — multiplied by the tipping fee of $98 per ton)
Source of Funding:	Local budget
Full-time Employees:	1
Part-time Employees:	3 to 5

Contact

Charles E. Gasior
Borough Administrator/Recycling Coordinator
55 Park Avenue
Park Ridge, NJ 07656
Phone (201) 573-1800
Fax (201) 391-7130

FENNIMORE, WISCONSIN

Demographics

Jurisdiction:	City of Fennimore
Population:	2,430 (1989 estimate)
Total Households:	850 (750 single-residence and 100 multi-unit)
Total Businesses:	96
Area:	2 square miles
Other:	The City of Fennimore is a rural community located 42 miles northeast of Dubuque, Iowa, and 70 miles west of Madison, Wisconsin.

Solid Waste Generation and Collection

(Annual Tonnages for 1989)*

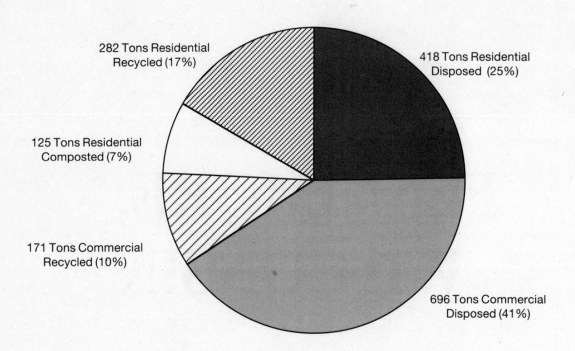

282 Tons Residential
Recycled (17%)

418 Tons Residential
Disposed (25%)

125 Tons Residential
Composted (7%)

171 Tons Commercial
Recycled (10%)

696 Tons Commercial
Disposed (41%)

*All tonnages are projected to 12 months, based on 8 months of data.

Total Waste Generated:	1,692 tons in 1989 (not including bulky waste such as tires, construction debris, and appliances)
Residential Waste Generated:	825 tons in 1989
Commercial Waste Generated:	867 tons in 1989
Bulky Waste Generated:	Not available. (Construction debris generated in the commercial sector is disposed at a private landfill, and bulky waste generated in the residential sector is disposed at a site on a City-owned farm. The amount is not tracked for either.)
% By Weight of Total Waste Recovered:	34 percent in 1989 (27 percent recycling and 7 percent composting)
% By Weight of Residential Waste Recovered:	49 percent in 1989 (34 percent recycling and 15 percent composting)
% By Weight of Commercial Waste Recovered:	20 percent in 1989 (20 percent recycling)

Landfill Tipping Fee: None (the City of Fennimore owned the landfill where all refuse was disposed in 1989)

Collection of Refuse: The City of Fennimore handles all the waste generated in the City. In 1989, the City incurred $32,000 for collection of 1,114 tons of refuse for disposal. Residents are required to purchase special clear plastic bags from local grocery stores to use for refuse.

Future Solid Waste Management Plans: Beginning on March 1, 1990, the City of Fennimore has disposed of all non-recycled waste at the Muscoda incinerator, except for small demolition materials, which are taken to a local landfill. The tipping fee at the Muscoda facility is $32 per ton. The costs of incineration will be considered when the City decides whether or not to sign a long-term contract with the Muscoda facility. The City will begin to take chemicals out of its waste stream and dispose of them separately, and will consider other means of expanding and improving the recycling program. There is also state legislation pending that would mandate the recovery of plastics.

Materials Recovery

The City of Fennimore implemented mandatory recycling on May 1, 1989. During 1988 and the first 4 months of 1989, City Council members visited several recycling programs in Wisconsin and held numerous committee meetings in order to develop the best recycling program for the community. The City needed to reduce its materials disposed as much and as quickly as possible, because the City-owned landfill was scheduled to close in 1990. After it closed, the City expected to have to haul its non-recyclable waste to the Muscoda incinerator, approximately 25 miles north of Fennimore.

The City requires residential, commercial, and industrial establishments to separate their glass containers, tin, aluminum, plastic, newspaper, corrugated cardboard, and mixed paper (junk mail, catalogs, magazines, and paperboard boxes). The City supplies one set of three recycling bins, dark green, lime green, and yellow, to each residence and business. Further, residents must purchase a disposal tag in order to dispose of tires and appliances. The fee for these tags covers the cost to the City for disposal or recycling of these items.

Fennimore was given the *Best Overall Program in a Rural Area* award by the Institute for Local Self-Reliance in its *Record Setting Recycling Contest 1989*.

Curbside Collection

Start-up Date: May 1, 1989

Private/Public: Public

Materials Collected: Glass containers; tin; aluminum; PET and HDPE plastic beverage, detergent, and motor oil containers; newspaper; corrugated cardboard; mixed paper (junk mail, catalogs, magazines, and paperboard boxes); appliances; brush; wood waste; leaves

Pick-up Frequency: Biweekly for recyclables, monthly year-round for brush and wood waste, and by appointment for appliances, twice a year for leaves

Pick-up Same Day as Refuse: No

Material Set-out Method: Materials are separated into a set of three 15-gallon bins, each a different color. Newspaper is placed in one bin, plastic containers in another, and glass and metal in the third. Mixed paper, in a clear plastic bag, and corrugated cardboard are placed next to the bins. Brush is piled at the curb, and leaves are set out loose.

Mandatory: Yes, for all materials except appliances

Service Provider: City of Fennimore

Collection Vehicles: One used beer/pop truck with separate bins in each bay collects residential and commercial recyclables. Three workers operate this truck and sort glass by color and metal cans. A City dump truck with a two person crew collects brush and wood waste.

Households Served: 850

Participation Rate: 100 percent (based on the fact that the program is mandatory, and everyone has participated with little need for enforcement)

Businesses Served: 96

Economic Incentives: None

Enforcement: Residents must use clear plastic bags for non-recyclable waste. If the collection crew finds recyclable materials with refuse, they do not pick up the refuse. Apartment managers are responsible for enforcement at apartment complexes.

Commercial Materials Recovery Activities

The City supplies commercial establishments with recycling bins, the same size as those supplied to residents, and requires that they separate the same materials that residents must separate, including newspaper, mixed paper, corrugated cardboard, glass, plastic containers, aluminum, ferrous cans, and high-grade paper. The City serves all businesses by curbside collection. Corrugated cardboard is picked up three times per week. Other materials are picked up biweekly, on the same schedule as residential recyclables. The small amount of yard waste generated by commercial establishments is collected and composted by the City. One or two commercial establishments required daily refuse pick-up before recycling was implemented; after they began to recycle, they required less frequent refuse pick-up, and their waste collection fees were reduced.

Materials Processing

Materials are taken to the City's Recycle Center to be processed for shipping to market. Corrugated cardboard, mixed paper, plastic, and metals are baled. Newsprint is shredded and baled for use as bedding by local farmers. Glass is crushed. Appliances are given to an individual who salvages as much as he can from them. The City delivers glass and metals to market in Dubuque, Iowa, approximately 42 miles from Fennimore. Midwest Plastic Materials picks up plastic from the Recycle Center, and Paper Processing picks up corrugated cardboard and mixed paper. The City receives revenues for all materials except low-grade mixed paper (junk mail, catalogs, magazines, and paperboard boxes).

Composting Activities

In April 1989, the City stopped collecting grass clippings and garden waste (small materials such as hedge clippings or corn stalks). If residents want to get rid of these materials without home composting, they must haul them to a designated drop-off center at the compost site. This site is located on a portion of what was previously the City's landfill. The City picks up leaves twice a year, once in the spring and once in the fall. Residents must haul their leaves to the compost site at other times. Brush and wood waste (tree branches and stumps) are picked up monthly, year-round. These materials are composted in a pile, which is turned once a week. The City uses composted materials for landscaping projects. Leaves are not put in the compost pile; instead, they are spread on local farms.

Margaret Sprague, the Village Clerk, estimates that only 5 to 10 percent of residents haul their yard waste to the compost site. Many residents have backyard composting areas, and some burn their garden waste.

Amount and Breakdown of Materials Recovered

Materials	Commercial (Tons, 1989)	Residential (Tons, 1989)	Total (Tons, 1989)
Newspaper	4	66	70
Corrugated Cardboard	143	9	152
Mixed Paper	6	108	114
Glass	14	64	78
PET Plastic	0	1	1
HDPE Plastic	0	6	6
Aluminum	0	0.5	0.5
Ferrous Metals	4	27	31
Subtotal Recycled	**171**	**281.5**	**452.5**
Brush and Wood Waste	0	50	50
Leaves	0	75	75
Subtotal Composted	**0**	**125**	**125**
Total Recovered	**171**	**406.5**	**577.5**

Note: The City has extrapolated 8 months of tonnage data to 12 months.

Publicity and Education

The City coordinates the inclusion of flyers with utility bills, writes newspaper articles, makes radio announcements, develops programs for school children, and holds periodic open houses at the Recycle Center.

Economics

Costs Cover: The capital and operating and maintenance costs given below cover 577.5 tons recovered by the City of Fennimore curbside collection program (452.5 tons recycled and 125 tons composted). The City has extrapolated 8 months of operating and maintenance costs to 12 months.

Capital Costs: Collection

Item	Cost	Use	Year Incurred
Collection Truck	$ 8,320	Recycling	1989
1,300 Sets of 3 Bins for Source Separation	$ 25,038	Recycling	1989
Dump Truck @ 10% of use	$ 30,000	Composting	1989
Building/Remodeling	$ 44,000	Recycling	1989

Capital Costs: Processing

Item	Cost	Use	Year Incurred
End Loader @ 1% of use	$ 36,700	Composting	1975
Newsprint Baler	$ 700	Recycling	1988
Forklift	$ 3,400	Recycling	1989
Skidloader	$ 13,950	Recycling	1989
Cardboard Baler	$ 7,500	Recycling	1989
Paper Shredder	$ 9,111	Recycling	1989
Glass Crusher	$ 3,235	Recycling	1989

Operating and Maintenance Costs (1989)

	Recycling	Composting	Total
Collection	$ 11,400	$ 1,000	$ 12,400
Processing	$ 18,500	$ 2,500	$ 21,000
Administration	$ 1,000	0	$ 1,000
Education/Publicity	$ 1,000	0	$ 1,000
Overhead	$ 4,000	0	$ 4,000
Total	**$ 35,900**	**$ 3,500**	**$ 39,400**

Materials Revenues: $6,700 (based on 12-month projection)

Source of Funding: Local budget

Full-time Employees: 1

Part-time Employees: 3

Contact

Margaret A. Sprague
City Clerk
City of Fennimore
860 Lincoln Avenue
Fennimore, Wisconsin 53809
Phone (608) 822-6119
Fax (608) 822-6007

WOODBURY, NEW JERSEY

Demographics

Jurisdiction: City of Woodbury

Population: 10,450 in 1989 (the City Clerk's office estimates that Woodbury's population has remained close to the 1980 population of 10,500)

Total Households: 3,000 to 4,000

Total Businesses: 150 to 200 (estimated by the Community Development Office)

Area: 2.3 square miles

Other: 80 percent single or double homes; 20 percent apartments, government, and commercial buildings. It has been estimated that 70 percent of Woodbury's residents are middle class.

Solid Waste Generation and Collection

(Annual Tonnages for 1989)

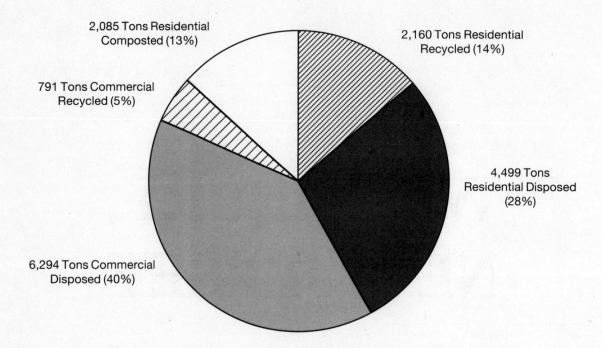

2,085 Tons Residential Composted (13%)

2,160 Tons Residential Recycled (14%)

791 Tons Commercial Recycled (5%)

4,499 Tons Residential Disposed (28%)

6,294 Tons Commercial Disposed (40%)

Total Waste Generated:	15,829 tons in 1989 (including bulky waste such as tires, white goods, and construction debris)
	7,495 tons in 1987[1] (excluding bulky waste and commercial waste collected by private haulers)
Residential Waste Generated:	8,744 tons in 1989 (including some commercial waste collected by the City along its residential collection route)
Commercial Waste Generated:	7,085 tons in 1989[2] (including bulky waste)
Bulky Waste Generated:	2,557 tons in 1989[2] (including tonnage disposed and recovered)
% By Weight of Total Waste Recovered:	32 percent in 1989 (19 percent recycling, 13 percent composting)
% By Weight of Residential Waste Recovered:	49 percent in 1989 (25 percent recycling and 24 percent composting)
	48 percent in 1987

---

[1]As a result of excluding waste disposed by private haulers in 1987 waste generated figures reported in *Beyond 25 Percent: Materials Recovery Comes of Age,* Woodbury's 1987 overall materials recovery level was calculated at 50 percent. This figure more accurately reflects the residential recovery level in 1987, since private haulers serve the commercial sector.

[2]Figures for commercial waste disposed and bulky waste disposed were supplied by the Gloucester County Landfill.

**% By Weight of
Commercial Waste Recovered:**

11 percent recycled in 1989

Landfill Tipping Fee:

$58.72 per ton in 1989
$49.48 per ton in January 1988
$48.14 per ton from July 1987 to January 1988
$47.07 per ton from January 1987 to June 1987
$2 per cubic yard in 1980

Collection of Refuse:

Most of Woodbury's waste is collected by municipal crews. In 1989, materials not recovered were hauled to the Gloucester County landfill 27 miles away. Beginning in 1990, Woodbury has disposed of all refuse at the Gloucester County waste incinerator. The tipping fee is $98 per ton. Most businesses contract with private haulers for waste collection.

**Future Solid Waste
Management Plans:**

Don Sanderson, President of the City Council, envisions contracting for food waste pick-up, adding film plastics to materials collected, and working to achieve a 75 percent reduction in waste disposed. In addition, Woodbury is proposing a County transfer station that would accept source-separated materials from all the municipalities in the County. This facility would be able to access larger markets and generate more revenue than single municipalities can. Revenues above O&M costs would return to the municipalities. Don Sanderson and Ray Jack, Superintendent of Streets and Utilities, believe that this proposal has a good chance of being adopted, especially since the County will not have to come up with capital to fund the facility. A sufficiently large fund has accrued from a surcharge on waste disposed at the landfill.

The City is planning to purchase one or two Eager Beaver recycling trucks in 1990. At 20-25 cubic yards and 6 bins, these will have a considerably larger capacity than the current trailers, which only hold 5 cubic yards and have 3 separate bins for materials.

Materials Recovery

Recycling in Woodbury first began in November 1970, spearheaded by environmentally concerned community organizations. Between 1970 and 1980, 2,500 tons of materials were recycled through curbside collection of glass, aluminum, and waste paper; and a drop-off site open monthly for collection of glass, aluminum, and paper.

A 1980 market study indicated that 60 percent of the City's population supported a mandatory recycling program, and that 45 percent of the waste stream could be recovered. During the same year, New Jersey established a 5-year plan to recover 25 percent of the State's solid waste and encouraged municipalities to formulate their own plans, recommending a landfill surcharge to be used for recycling as a financial incentive.

Following these events, the City of Woodbury proposed a mandatory source-separation recycling program for paper, glass, aluminum, other metal, yard waste, and food waste to begin January 1, 1981. The City Council adopted a mandatory recycling ordinance on December 23, 1980. Although six bids to take food wastes were received from nearby livestock farmers, food waste was excluded from mandatory recycling because many residents expressed objection to kitchen garbage separation.

The law became effective in February 1981, and an official announcement was distributed to all City units receiving trash removal service.

The City of Woodbury originally operated two drop-off centers, both located at major shopping centers, but one was closed recently. The City was collecting sufficient materials at curbside and the curbside program has proven more cost-effective than the drop-off centers. The remaining drop-off center accepts mixed paper (newspaper, magazines, food cartons, wrapping paper, bags, discarded mail, and office paper), glass, aluminum, ferrous metals, and corrugated cardboard. In addition, residents are required by State law to recycle their motor oil. They can take it to the City garage, where it is stored in a 275-gallon home heating fuel tank.

The program has undergone few changes recently, except for the addition in April 1988 of curbside collection of PET and HDPE plastic containers.

Curbside Collection

Start-up Date:
Voluntary recycling since 1974, mandatory recycling since 1980, weekly yard debris curbside collection since 1981, addition of plastic containers in April 1988

Private/Public:
Municipally run

Materials Collected:
Mixed paper (newspaper, magazines, food cartons, wrapping paper, discarded mail, bags, and office paper), glass, aluminum cans, other metals, corrugated cardboard, plastic (PET soda bottles and HDPE milk jugs), appliances, leaves, grass clippings, brush, and wood waste

Pick-up Frequency:
The City collects yard waste and appliances every Wednesday. On Thursday, all other recyclable items are collected from one half of the City, and on Friday they are collected from the other half.

Pick-up Same Day as Refuse: No

Material Set-out Method:
Citizens separate recyclable materials into eight different categories: mixed paper, amber glass, flint glass, green glass, aluminum cans, other metals, corrugated cardboard, and plastics. Grass clippings and leaves must be placed in separate reusable bags or containers. Brush and other wood waste are tied in bundles. Citizens supply their own recycling and yard waste containers; the City does not provide containers.

Mandatory:
Yes, for all materials

Service Provider: The City of Woodbury

Collection Vehicles: Two Eager Beaver "Recycler-4" trailers pulled behind rear-loading Heil compactor trucks are used to collect recyclables. One compactor collects paper and pulls a trailer for the collection of glass that is sorted by color. The other compactor truck collects corrugated cardboard and pulls a trailer for the collection of aluminum and other metals. Each compactor/trailer is operated by one driver with two people collecting materials. Bagged leaves and grass clippings are collected in compactor trucks, except for the months of October through December, when leaves are collected loose at the curb with vacuum machines mounted on dump trucks. Brush is fed through a chipping machine and blown into a compactor truck that pulls the chipper.

Households Served: 3,000 to 4,000 households are served, including apartment buildings up to 4 stories.

Participation Rate: 85 percent (85 percent of the units set out materials every week — yearly average)

Businesses Served: Not available. The City collects recyclables from some businesses along its residential routes, and does not keep track of the number.

Economic Incentives: Fines

Enforcement: If a resident does not recycle, a red warning sticker is attached to his/her trash collection container. Repeat offenders may be fined up to $500. Trash is not collected if residents fail to comply with the mandatory recycling ordinance.

Commercial Materials Recovery Activities

Woodbury's recycling ordinance requires commercial establishments to recycle the same materials that residents recycle. The City collects mixed paper, high-grade paper, glass, aluminum, ferrous cans, corrugated cardboard, and plastic containers from some businesses along its residential route. City crews collect recyclable materials from the same businesses that they collect refuse from. Food waste and corrugated cardboard are privately recycled. Motor oil generated by the commercial sector is recycled through state collection centers (any place that changes oil is considered a state collection center). In addition, Woodbury recycled 550 tons of asphalt in 1989.

Materials Processing

Woodbury does not process any of the materials collected. All recyclable materials are separated at the curbside, so that they can be transferred directly to markets.

Although the Camden County Recycling Facility, which processes mixed bottles and cans, is located near Woodbury, the City has chosen not to deliver materials there because it does not receive revenue for materials brought to the processing center. Woodbury has established reliable markets for the materials collected through the program during its 16 years of operation.

A plastics processor supplies a trailer for the collected plastic. The processor picks up the trailer when it is full and leaves another trailer behind.

Composting Activities

Grass clippings, brush, and leaves are collected every Wednesday throughout the year. During the fall (an 8- to 14-week period, depending on the weather), the City operates a leaf vacuum machine to handle the additional volume of leaves. Yard wastes and leaves are taken to a transfer station. Then the City pays area farmers to till them directly into the soil. Woodbury also collects Christmas trees each year.

Since wood waste takes longer to decompose, the City delivers it to Recycled Wood Products, a company that converts it into mulch.

Woodbury collected 618 tons of leaves and 620 tons of yard debris, and chipped 338 tons of brush and Christmas trees, for a total of 1,576 tons in 1987. The operating cost of these programs totalled $45,887 in 1987, including $17,200 for fall leaf collection, and $28,687 for the weekly yard debris collection and brush chipping programs.

Amount and Breakdown of Materials Recovered

The materials in the following tables include residential and commercial waste recovered by the City's own collection crews and at the drop-off center. Woodbury's high school also contributes to the mixed paper recovery. Also included is commercial waste recycled by business establishments that contract for their own waste collection through private haulers and report their recycled tonnages to the County.

Material	Commercial (Tons, 1987)	Residential* (Tons, 1987)	Total (Tons, 1987)
Corrugated Cardboard	252	181	433
Mixed Paper	0	659	659
Glass	0	373	373
Aluminum	0	11	11
Ferrous Metal	0	616	616
Food Waste	53	0	53
Motor Oil	6	5	11
Automobile Scrap	30	0	30
Subtotal Recycled	**341**	**1,845**	**2,186**
Leaves	0	618	618
Brush Chips	0	338	338
Yard Debris	0	620	620
Subtotal Composted	**0**	**1,576**	**1,576**
Total Recovered	**341**	**3,421**	**3,762**

*Residential tons include some commercial materials collected along the residential route.

Material	Commercial (Tons, 1989)	Residential* (Tons, 1989)	Total (Tons, 1989)
Corrugated Cardboard	211.91	320	531.91
Mixed Paper	0	1,016	1,016
Glass	0	375	375
Aluminum	0	4.6	4.6
Ferrous Cans & Appliances	0	430	430
Food Waste	28.95	0	28.95
Motor Oil	0	5	5
Asphalt	550	0	550
PET Plastic	0	9	9
Subtotal Recycled	**790.86**	**2,159.6**	**2,950.46**
Leaves and Grass Clippings	0	1,676	1,676
Wood Waste	0	408.5	408.5
Subtotal Composted	**0**	**2,084.5**	**2,084.5**
Total Recovered	**790.86**	**4,244.1**	**5,034.96**

*Residential tons include some commercial materials collected along the residential route.

Publicity and Education

Woodbury's education and publicity campaign began with $200 and is now maintained with free advertising on City buses, and through the dedication of City employees. City officials and the Recycling Committee have played a major role in promoting the recycling program by (1) monitoring the separation of recyclable materials and encouraging participation in neighborhoods; (2) rectifying collection problems; (3) conducting on-going education to increase participation with an audio tape and slide presentation titled, "Woodbury, Recycling Pioneers"; (4) preparing and distributing the City schedule of services; (5) giving television and newspaper interviews; (6) speaking to local and surrounding community organizations; (7) arranging to reach new residents through Council member visits and real estate agencies; and (8) publicizing achievements to sustain community interest.

The media report enforcement activities, publicizing the fines issued to people who do not comply with the recycling ordinance, and occasionally featuring the "trashman," who checks residential mixed waste for recyclable materials. The "trashman" often speaks with individuals who have violated the recycling law, explaining the importance of recycling while issuing them a summons.

Woodbury has also developed a recycling curriculum that is used by the local schools. The State used Woodbury's curriculum in developing its own curriculum.

Economics

Costs Cover:

Capital and operating and maintenance costs given below cover (1) City collection of 2,160 tons of recyclables at curbside and drop-off sites, and (2) City collection and composting/chipping of 2,085 tons of yard waste. Operating and maintenance costs are estimated for 1989 based on 1987 cost data.

Capital Costs: Collection

Item	Cost	Use	Year Incurred
Vacuum Machine For Leaves	$ 9,000	Composting	1964 *
Vacuum Machine For Leaves	$ 9,000	Composting	1970
2 Drop-Off Centers	$ 5,000	Recycling	1983-1984
2 Recycling Trailers	$ 15,600	Recycling	1984
2 Garbage Trucks[†]	$ 110,000	Recycling/Composting	1985
2 GMC Diesel Trucks[†]	$ 100,000	Recycling/Composting	1985
Additional Equipment	$ 5,600	Recycling	1985
1 17-Cubic-Yard Dump Truck	$ 55,000	Composting	1988
1 17-Cubic-Yard Dump Truck	$ 55,000	Composting	1988

*The vacuum machines were purchased before the official recovery program began, and the cost has been estimated by the City.
†The trucks are assumed to spend 50 percent of the time on recycling and 50 percent of the time on composting.

Capital Costs: Processing

Item	Cost	Use	Year Incurred
Chipping Machine	$17,000	Composting	1985
Stumping Machine	$19,000	Composting	1985

Operating and Maintenance Costs (1989)*

	Recycling	Composting	Total
Collection	NA	NA	NA
Processing	NA	NA	NA
Administration	NA	NA	NA
Education/Publicity	NA	NA	NA
Total	**$87,896**	**$60,701**	**$148,597**

*O&M costs for 1989 were calculated by ILSR staff based on the assumption that the costs per ton for recycling and composting were the same in 1989 as in 1987. The costs per ton for recycling and composting in 1987 were multiplied by the tons recovered by the City in 1989 as follows:

2,159.6 tons recycled times $40.70 per ton = $87,896

2,084.5 tons composted times $29.12 per ton = $60,701

Operating and maintenance costs for recycling and composting are no longer tracked by the City. The new Superintendent of Streets and Utilities, Raymond Jack, believes that statistics have shown that, if City-run recycling is properly carried out, the costs for refuse collection plus recycling are virtually the same as those for refuse collection without recycling.

In 1987, the following costs were reported by Herbert Hood, then Superintendent of Streets and Utilities: $75,099 for recycling, $17,200 for fall leaf collection, and $28,687 for weekly yard waste collection and brush chipping. Total O&M costs in 1987 were $120,986. These costs covered the tons recovered through the public sector curbside collection of recyclable and compostable materials, drop-off center, and paper recovery at the high school (3,421 tons in 1987).

Materials Revenues: $19,106 in 1989
                               $30,668 in 1987

Source of Funding: General tax revenues, State tonnage grants, and materials revenues

Full-time Employees: 8 City employees work with the materials recovery programs

Contacts

Raymond Jack
Superintendent of Streets and Utilities
City of Woodbury
33 Delaware Street
Woodbury, NJ 08096
(609) 845-1300

Don Sanderson
City Council President
City of Woodbury
435 Morris Street
Woodbury, NJ 08096
(609) 845-0019

Dean McFadden
Gloucester County Landfill
22 North Broad
Woodbury, New Jersey 08096
(609) 848-4002

Reference

Source Separation, The Woodbury Way, City of Woodbury, Woodbury, New Jersey, 1982.

Index

Also Available From Island Press

Ancient Forests of the Pacific Northwest
By Elliott A. Norse

Balancing on the Brink of Extinction: The Endangered Species Act and Lessons for the Future
Edited by Kathryn A. Kohm

Better Trout Habitat: A Guide to Stream Restoration and Management
By Christopher J. Hunter

The Challenge of Global Warming
Edited by Dean Edwin Abrahamson

Costal Alert: Ecosystems, Energy, and Offshore Oil Drilling
By Dwight Holing

The Complete Guide to Environmental Careers
The CEIP Fund

Economics of Protected Areas
By John A. Dixon and Paul B. Sherman

Environmental Agenda for the Future
Edited by Robert Cahn

Environmental Disputes: Community Involvement in Conflict Resolution
By James E. Crowfoot and Julia M. Wondolleck

Fighting Toxics: A Manual for Protecting Your Family, Community, and Workplace
Edited by Gary Cohen and John O'Connor

Forests and Forestry in China: Changing Patterns of Resource Development
By S. D. Richardson

From The Land
Edited and compiled by Nancy P. Pittman

Hazardous Waste from Small Quantity Generators
By Seymour I. Schwartz and Wendy B. Pratt

Holistic Resource Management Workbook
By Allan Savory

In Praise of Nature
Edited and with essays by Stephanie Mills

The Living Ocean: Understanding and Protecting Marine Biodiversity
By Boyce Thorne-Miller and John Catena

Natural Resources for the 21st Century
Edited by R. Neil Sampson and Dwight Hair

The New York Environment Book
By Eric A. Goldstein and Mark A. Izeman

Overtapped Oasis: Reform or Revolution for Western Water
By Marc Reisner and Sara Bates

Permaculture: A Practical Guide for a Sustainable Future
By Bill Mollison

Plastics: America's Packaging Dilemma
By Nancy Wolf and Ellen Feldman

The Poisoned Well: New Strategies for Groundwater Protection
Edited by Eric Jorgensen

Race to Save the Tropics: Ecology and Economics for a Sustainable Future
Edited by Robert Goodland

Recycling and Incineration: Evaluating the Choices
By Richard A. Denison and John Ruston

Reforming The Forest Service
By Randal O'Toole

The Rising Tide: Global Warming and World Sea Levels
By Lynne T. Edgerton

Rush to Burn: Solving America's Garbage Crisis?
From *Newsday*

Saving the Tropical Forests
By Judith Gradwohl and Russell Greenberg

War on Waste: Can America Win Its Battle With Garbage?
By Louis Blumberg and Robert Gottlieb

Western Water Made Simple
From *High Country News*

Wetland Creation and Restoration: The Status of the Science
Edited by Mary E. Kentula and Jon A. Kusler

Wildlife and Habitats in Managed Landscapes
Edited by Jon E. Rodiek and Eric G. Bolen

For a complete catalog of Island Press publications, please write:

Island Press
Box 7
Covelo, CA 95428
or call: 1-800-828-1302

Martha and Hilary
and the Stranger

Danielle Steel
Martha and Hilary
and the Stranger

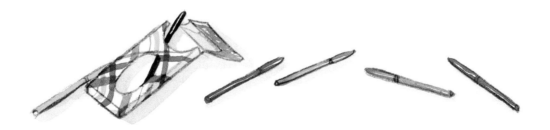

Illustrated by Jacqueline Rogers

Delacorte
Press

Published by
Delacorte Press
Bantam Doubleday Dell Publishing Group, Inc.
666 Fifth Avenue
New York, New York 10103

Library of Congress Cataloging in Publication Data

Steel, Danielle.
   Martha and Hilary and the stranger / Danielle Steel ; illustrated
by Jacqueline Rogers.
      p.   cm.
   Summary: Hilary learns an important lesson in safety: never
accept a ride from a stranger.
   ISBN 0-385-30212-6
   [1. Strangers—Fiction.   2. Safety—Fiction.]   I. Rogers,
Jacqueline, ill.   II. Title.
PZ7.S8143Mai   1991
[E]—dc20   89-77983
                                                 CIP
                                                  AC

Designed by Judith Neuman-Cantor

Manufactured in the United States of America

April 1991

10 9 8 7 6 5 4 3 2

*To Beatrix, my precious first and always
love . . . extraordinary person, how proud and
happy you make me!*

Love, Mommy

This is Martha. Martha is six years old, and she lives in Sausalito, California, with her Mommy and her stepfather, John. Sausalito is a pretty little town right across the Golden Gate Bridge from San Francisco. Her Mommy and Daddy are divorced, which means they aren't married anymore, but they are all good friends. And she spends every Wednesday night, and some weekends, in San Francisco with her Daddy.

Martha loves her Mommy and Daddy very
much, and she is very lucky because she has
an extra person to love her: John, her
stepfather, who is a very kind, loving person.

Sometimes Martha's Daddy even comes to
have dinner with them at their house in
Sausalito, because he and John like each
other a lot. They talk about fishing and
playing tennis and skiing and who is going to
take Martha to the circus.

Except when she spends the night with her Daddy in San Francisco, Martha goes to school in a car pool every day. The car pool she takes is with four little girls who go to her school. Every day the car pool is driven by one of the mothers. On Tuesdays, it's Martha's Mommy's turn to drive, and she picks the girls up at their houses and drives them all to school. After school she picks all five girls up and takes them back to their houses.

Sometimes, one of the Mommies is late in the afternoon, and the girls have to go back inside the school to wait for her. When the teachers go back into school after dismissal, it's safer to wait inside where someone can watch the children. And in cold weather it's warmer.

One day, when Martha's Mommy was late, the girls waited outside school for her to pick them up. They stood with the teachers who were watching them, until the teachers told the girls they would have to go inside and wait in the office because all the other children had been picked up by then. Everyone knew you weren't allowed to wait outside alone without the teachers after dismissal.

Martha and three of the girls did exactly as
they were told, but Hilary dragged her feet.
When Martha walked back into school, she
noticed that Hilary hadn't come with them.
"Where's Hilary?" Martha asked her friends.

"I don't know," Jackie said.

"In the bathroom, I think," Stephanie answered.

But no one was really sure, and no one paid much attention. The girls were playing in the hall, and the teachers had gone upstairs to get their things. And the school secretary was busy answering the phone and putting away some papers.

No one knew where Hilary was, and after a while, Martha forgot about her too. The girls were still waiting for Martha's Mommy, and they were busy playing. Alyson played with the doll she had brought for show-and-tell, Jackie had taken a book out of the library, and Martha showed Stephanie her beautiful new drawing.

After a while, no one even noticed that
Hilary was gone. It was only when Martha's
Mommy came that she looked surprised. She
asked Martha if Hilary had gone home early.

"No. She was here just a minute ago,"
Martha explained. But Hilary wasn't there
anymore. She was gone, and no one could
find her.

Martha looked in the bathroom, and the other girls looked upstairs. The teachers looked for her in all the rooms, and the school secretary ran outside to see if she was there. But all they found was Hilary's lunch box sitting on the sidewalk. It was a pretty blue one with her name on it. Martha knew Hilary had just gotten it as a present from a friend for her birthday.

Everyone was really worried by then, and Martha's Mommy was very serious. "Didn't she know she wasn't supposed to play outside by herself after the teachers went in?" Martha's Mommy sounded upset when she asked. Martha and the girls had tears in their eyes when they nodded. They all knew, and the teachers had told them to go inside, but maybe Hilary had forgotten. She knew she wasn't supposed to play outside by herself. What could have happened?

All the girls knew you should never, never talk to strangers, no matter what kind of stories they told you, or even if they said they needed help, or said they knew your Mommy and Daddy, or that they had lost a puppy. No matter what, never talk to, or go anywhere with, a stranger.

By now everyone was afraid of what might have happened to Hilary. Martha was still hoping that she had just gone for a walk and forgotten her lunch box, but it didn't seem very likely. Hilary had never disappeared before, and they were all beginning to worry that she might be in trouble.

After they had checked all the classrooms and the street one more time, Martha's Mommy and the teachers called the police, and they came very quickly. They spoke to each of the girls, one by one, and asked if they had seen anything or anyone strange around the school. By then Martha and the other girls were crying. They were all afraid of what might have happened to Hilary. What if Hilary never came back or the police never found her? The police asked the teachers to describe what Hilary was wearing that day and what she looked like. The school secretary gave them school photographs of her out of a file in the office.

Martha's Mommy looked like she was going to cry when she called Hilary's Mommy to tell her what had happened. Hilary's Mommy worked at the post office, and she came right away—and she was crying when she got to the school. Both Mommies and all the teachers were very,

very worried because they were all so afraid
of what might have happened. But the
policemen reassured them; they said Hilary
had probably just wandered off and was
somewhere nearby. They drove around the
neighborhood looking for Hilary, while the
Mommies and the girls and the teachers
all waited.

They waited for a long time. Hilary's Mommy was crying while she waited. And then suddenly the doors to the school opened. The policemen stood there with a very frightened, very bedraggled little girl with red hair, the knees of her tights torn, her sweater half off. Hilary's eyes looked huge and her face was streaked with dirt, as though she'd been crying.

Hilary's Mommy rushed toward her and
gave her a big hug, and then asked her what
had happened.

"Where were you?" she asked as she held
her.

"Something very scary happened to
Hilary," one of the police officers explained,

putting a gentle hand on Hilary's shoulder.
"We found her hiding in a basement two
blocks away. She heard us calling her name,
and we told her we were the police and her
friends, and that we'd take her back to
her Mommy."

"I saw their uniforms and the police car from a window where I was hiding, so I knew they really were policemen." Hilary was still breathless and pale, and she looked very frightened. "While I was outside school, after the girls went in, someone came up in a car, and for a minute I thought it was you." She glanced at Martha's Mommy. She looked upset because she knew she wasn't supposed to be out there by herself. "But it wasn't you. It was a lady I didn't know. She said my Mommy had had an accident and couldn't pick me up today. But I knew this wasn't her day to drive anyway. And the lady said she'd take me to her. She opened the car door and tried to pull me into the car. But then I remembered that Mommy always says never to get into a car with someone I don't know, so I just wouldn't. And she looked kind of mad at me when I wouldn't go with her."

Both Mommies looked shocked, and so did the teachers. "So I ran away as fast as I could. And I hid until they came." She looked at the policemen. "And I guess the lady just drove away."

"Why didn't you run back into school?" Hilary's Mommy asked as she held her.

"I don't know. I was too scared. I just wanted to get away from her."

"You should have screamed, Hilary," one of the teachers said, "as loud as you could. You should scream, and run away, just as you did.

"Except it would have been much safer to run back into school. We wouldn't let anyone hurt you."

Hilary nodded. Martha could still see her knees shaking as Hilary's Mommy held her tightly. The teachers talked to the police for a long time.

And the next day, there was a policeman outside school to make sure that no one bothered any of the children. The police had also warned all the schools in Sausalito about the lady who tried to take Hilary.

The policeman stayed for a month, and everyone was very glad he was there, especially Hilary, who had learned some very important lessons. Never stand around outside school alone without a grown-up. Never play outside without a grown-up nearby. *Never go anywhere with a stranger.* Never get in a car with anyone you don't know very well. Ask your Mom and Dad before you go anywhere in a car with anyone, no matter what kind of stories they tell you.

And if someone comes after you, scream as loud as you can, and run away as fast as you can.

Martha was glad Hilary was safe. Hilary was very lucky that nothing worse had happened. Martha and all the children had learned they had to be very, very careful. And everyone was glad that Hilary had been so lucky.

And when Martha talked about it with her Mommy and John, she knew that she would always be careful about strangers too. They had all learned an important lesson.